A TANGLED WEB

MATA HARI
DANCER ◆ COURTESAN ◆ SPY

MARY W. CRAIG

The
History
Press

Cover illustrations. Front: Mata Hari (Courtesy of Bibliothèque nationale de France, colourisation by Klimbim).

First published 2017

This edition published 2018 by
The History Press
The Mill, Brimscombe Port
Stroud, Gloucestershire, GL5 2QG
www.thehistorypress.co.uk

© Mary W. Craig, 2017, 2018

British Library Cataloguing in Publication Data.
A catalogue record for this book is available from the British Library.

ISBN 978 0 7509 8919 0

Typesetting and origination by The History Press
Printed and bound in Great Britain by TJ International Ltd

CONTENTS

ACKNOWLEDGEMENTS

Much has been written about Mata Hari the exotic dancer and Great War spy, and there are many papers about her held at the Archives de Paris; The British Library, London; the Centraal Bureau voor Genealogie, The Hague; the Fries Museum, Leeuwarden; the Nationaal Archief, The Hague; the National Archives, London and the Service Historique de l'Armeé de Terre, Vincennes. My grateful thanks must go to the staff at each of these institutions, who have generously given their time with unfailing professionalism.

Individuals I am indebted to include friends Eleanor Ball and Gordon Mulholland, and the editorial team at The History Press. On a personal note, I would like to thank Dorothy and George for all of their help, support and encouragement with this particular quest.

1

INTRODUCTION

Margaretha Geertruida Zelle was born in the Netherlands in the quiet bourgeoisie town of Leeuwarden in 1876. Her early life was unremarkable and gave no indication that she would become anything other than a respectably married member of Dutch small-town society. Far from following this path, however, Margaretha married young and travelled halfway round the world to the Dutch East Indies, where she discovered the excitement and exoticism of Javanese dance. Her marriage was an unhappy one, marred by emotional and physical violence and finally the death of her young son. She returned to Europe, where she became embroiled in a bitter divorce settlement and ultimately had to give up custody of her daughter. Friendless and with no money, she turned to 'exotic' dancing as a way to make a living – Margaretha became 'Mata Hari'. While this exoticism was all the rage at the time, Mata Hari was neither young nor particularly talented, and a dancing career, precarious for even the most talented, could not financially sustain her in the long-term. Mata Hari turned to the oldest profession in the world and found men who were willing to pay to spend time with her. Thus her story might have ended, but for the outbreak of the Great War.

The Great War was the end of the old order. Who knew what would follow? For a woman like Mata Hari, the Great War was both a threat and an opportunity. Would what followed the war welcome her or would the new order cast her aside? For a woman who was getting older in a new world where she might have few friends, this was a daunting prospect. But what of the opportunities? Whoever won the war would be dominant in Europe; should Mata Hari use her position as an 'international woman' of some renown to help one country over another? In 1915, Mata Hari was recruited first as a German agent and then a French agent, and was finally approached to become a Russian agent. Where did her loyalties lie? For which country would she enter the dangerous world of espionage? Or was Mata Hari more calculating than that? Whatever country won the war, a government that owed Mata Hari for her endeavours as a spy would surely not abandon her. Loyal spy, or calculating mercenary, Mata Hari was arrested by the French in February 1917 and executed by firing squad on 15 October 1917 in Paris.

Mata Hari has a hold on the modern imagination in part because of the times through which she lived. Between the 1870s and 1918, Europe – and its colonial possessions – fell from certainty into chaos, from which there would be no return to the old order. In 1848, the 'year of revolutions', Europe had tottered on the brink of collapse. However, the various nation states had survived and a delicate balance of power was created between these countries. The Great Powers of Russia, Prussia, Austria, France and Great Britain maintained the peace across the continent. Treaties and alliances allowed trade to flourish and peace to be restored. This did not last, and the balance came under increasing pressure as many nation states, in their desire to achieve what they perceived to be their destiny, found themselves to be increasingly in conflict with their neighbours. The formation of the German nation alarmed their neighbour France. The expansionist policies of Russia in the East engendered conflict with Great Britain and the internal issues of nationalism unsettled Austria.

Many in the European nations were aware of but did not fully understand these rising political tensions or how to deal with them, and in their confusion clustered round their old societal certainties. The familiarity of social convention was a comfort in uncertain and confusing times. Moreover, etiquette and decorum, tradition and display became a mask to hide confusion and a method by which to determine friend or foe. The 'done thing' was never questioned and never changed, and was even exported to the European colonies in Asia and Africa.

The Netherlands was, in the 1890s, a wealthy trading country with vast colonies in the Far East. The United Dutch East India Company (*Vereenigde Oostindische Compagnie* – VOC) was a chartered company that had been established in 1602, when the States General of the Netherlands had granted it a twenty-one-year monopoly to carry out trade in Asia. By the end of the eighteenth century, the company was rife with corruption and severely in debt. As a result, in 1799, the government in The Hague revoked the company's charter and took over its debts and possessions. The government had gained control of a company that had possessed quasi-governmental powers, including the ability to negotiate treaties, strike its own coins and establish colonies. As a result, the Netherlands had inherited a vast colony in Asia with a huge financial potential in spices and silks. During the nineteenth century, the colonies in the East provided the Netherlands with a large income, a career path for many within the colonial service and a place amongst the top European trading nations. The eastern colonies of the Netherlands were also a place where those European social certainties were as embedded as in the streets of The Hague or the town of Leeuwarden. Those certainties continued and by the start of the twentieth century, the Netherlands was a prosperous, assured nation, confident in its place in the world and settled in its bourgeois traditions.

The Netherlands was not the only country with colonies. Germany, a country that had only been formed in 1871, viewed colonial acquisitions as a true indication of having achieved nationhood. Initially, Bismarck, the Chancellor, had been wary of colonial acquisitions, viewing them as expensive burdens that the young nation could do without, but in the mid-1880s he changed his mind. In the 1850s and 1860s, several German companies had established trading bases in West Africa, East Africa, the Samoan Islands and New Guinea. These soon developed into German protectorates. Germany's location in the centre of Europe, and thus potentially surrounded by hostile neighbours, drove much of the political call for colonies, despite the drain on the country's finances. A new nation in comparison with the Great Powers in Europe, Germany strove to prove its worth and its 'place in the sun'. Frequently thwarted in its attempts at colonial expansion by Britain and France, hampered by France and Russia on its continental borders and constrained by its ambivalent relations with Austria-Hungary, by the beginning of the twentieth century the drive to be the equal of the Great Powers was uppermost in all aspects of German politics and philosophy. Many Germans sought to reaffirm and elevate the old German customs and traditions. Germanic myths took an ever-increasing place within society, and cultural pride grew in *Das Land der Dichter und Denker* (the country of poets and thinkers). Cultural learning, national pride and a belief in the settled order combined to produce social customs that dictated the lives of most Germans, and, just like their Dutch cousins, this was exported to the colonies.

That German drive was watched cautiously by her neighbour, France. The year 1871 had been a tragic one for France, as she had lost the Franco-Prussian War, seen Germany unified into a single state and then that single state annexe most of Alsace and the Moselle department of Lorraine. The German annexation of those lands was likened to the loss of a child. Military and political recriminations over the loss shook polite French society; a society that was already reeling from the Dreyfus Affair. In 1894, French Army chiefs had wrongly convicted Alfred Dreyfus, a Jewish army officer, of treason. The real culprit, Major Charles Marie Ferdinand Walsin Esterhazy, had been a spy in the pay of the Germans. Esterhazy had used the inherent anti-semitism in the army to implicate Dreyfus and divert suspicion from himself. This was further compounded by the acquittal of Esterhazy and the falsification of further evidence against Dreyfus. The affair dragged on for several years and exposed the levels of anti-semitism and corruption within a brutal military tribunal system. The entire affair was a severe shock to French sensibilities. The French Army held a special place in the nation, and it was difficult for many to accept the truth about the institution. The Dreyfus Affair was not fully resolved until 1906; but the divisions it created continued until the Great War and beyond.

In addition to these divisions and uncertainties, France was also a country in flux. Paris was the pre-eminent capital city of Europe, the home of the *Belle Époche*. Everything that was new and daring came from Paris; or so it seemed. The *Exposition Universelle* of 1889, with its Eiffel Tower and moving pavement, the dancing girls of the *Folies Bergère* and the paintings of the modernists – *Les Fauve* – all showed an exciting face to the world. For the middle and upper middle classes of France, however, this excitement could prove unsettling. The pace of change, the loss of Alsace and Moselle and the corruption in their army combined to disturb the calm existence of normal life. Once again the nation turned to certainties. Gentlemen might visit the *Folies Bergère* of an evening, but most still went home to their wives and families at the end of the night. Calling cards and the certainty of social niceties proved a comforting relief from the outside world.

Britain also had its concerns at the end of the nineteenth century. An island nation with an overseas empire, Britain relied on her navy to protect and connect the various territories of the empire with the mother country. In the first half of the nineteenth century, events in Europe had been considered of less importance to the British government than those of the empire. At the same time, while the colonies brought prosperity to a great number of British households, many more remained in poverty. Workers' demonstrations became more commonplace and trade unions were growing in strength as they sought better working conditions for their members. Fear of revolution – the 'European Disease' – became rife in middle- and upper-class households, which clung to social certainties for security, especially after 1848. By the end of the nineteenth century, tensions started to rise over the situation with Russia vis-a-vis the empire. Russia was exerting increasing pressure in the East. The French had been financing new railways in Russia that could have threatened British colonial trade. To add to these pressures, the situation in Ireland was causing alarm across Britain. The political call for home rule was being joined increasingly by physical violence, and the parliament in Westminster was riven by divisions. In light of the situation, as in other European countries, the upper and middle classes sought sanctuary in the status quo. Men in the civil service, military and colonial service ran the empire, while their wives maintained strict standards of Britishness, whether at home or in the colonies. Trade unionists at home, Russians in the East and the Irish were all defined as 'other'. To be British was the thing; an identity formed of tradition and decorum, an identity that was an anchor in unsettled times.

Russia was another of the Great Powers hiding unrest at home. The glittering court of Tsar Nicholas II and Tsarina Alexandra dazzled visitors but hid the poverty and unrest amongst the Russian population. Court life was all-consuming for the aristocracy, and was aped by the upper middle classes keen to show their sophistication. The formality of court life was mirrored by the etiquette and decorum in the middle classes. However, that ordered social life excluded the vast majority of the Russian people. Many in the cities worked for pitiful wages that did not feed their families. Most of those working on the land were still held in serfdom. Many suffered in silence; some did not. Revolutionaries started to question the status quo. Although seen as something of a threat, most in the middle and upper classes thought the authorities more than a match for the subversive elements. Social galas and balls continued as before. Indeed, the stronger the calls for revolutionary change, the closer the middle and upper classes across the Russian Empire clung to their traditions. The calling cards and social niceties of Moscow were equally those of St Petersburg, Vladivostok and Minsk. Tensions with Britain over territories in Persia, while serious, were seen as part and parcel of being a 'Great Power', but still contributed to a sense of national pride and promotion of Russian values and traditions. Many of these traditions had been adopted from France, all of which gave certainty across the empire.

The other large empire within Europe was the dual monarchy of Austria-Hungary. Ruled over by Franz Josef as Emperor of Austria and King of Hungary, it was a sprawling multi-ethnic entity comprising Germans, Czechs, Slovaks, Slovenes, Ruthenians (Ukrainians),

Hungarians (Magyars), Rumanians, Serbs, Croats, Poles, Silesians and Italians. According to many in Europe, it was slow of purpose and was an empire in decline. And yet for all that, relative to many other countries in Europe, the day-to-day internal life of Austria-Hungary functioned reasonably well. It was also, in comparison to the Russian Empire, less dictatorial, with nothing like the Okhrana, the Russian secret police, spying on those subjects that were unhappy within its borders. That is not to say it did not have problems. The Magyar majority in Hungary resented rule from Vienna. They were also contemptuous of the non-Magyars within Hungary, especially the Slavs. The German majority in Austria did not understand their Hungarian friends, finding their continual complaints – usually about the Hungarian Army – to be tiresome. They were also irritated by those other subjects clamouring for greater autonomy; the Czechs and the Ruthenians. They were most exercised, however, by the Slavs, notably the Serbs. The Serbs in Serbia wanted to expand their territory to include all of 'old Serbia', some of which lay well within the lands of the dual monarchy. In addition, they looked to Russia as the natural mother and protector of all Slavs. Many of the Serbs living in the dual monarchy did likewise, seeing Moscow as their lodestone rather than Vienna. In addition to all this, the dual monarchy had another great problem. The emperor and his successor, Archduke Ferdinand, did not agree on policy, and the emperor found Ferdinand personally difficult. The archduke was uncomfortable in the Viennese court, which shunned his wife due to her non-royal status in the Habsburg dynasty. These political and personal differences exacerbated the dual monarchy's policy development, particularly in relation to Serbia. The process in the dual monarchy followed that of other European nations. Confused and a little afraid of the pressures within the empire, social etiquette became the anchor in troubled times. This was aided by the longevity of Franz Josef's reign. The continuity given to the court and the country by the presence of the 'old man' allowed many to ignore the reality of life and live only for the next ball or hunting season. This was, in turn, used by those politicians aware of the international situation to perpetuate the status quo and maintain order.

The status quo, the sense of order in Austria and Hungary, and across Europe, was most closely threatened by the Balkans, and in particular Serbia. The previous Balkan wars had seen Serbia emerge as the strongest of the nation states, but one which sought to become still stronger. The social norms which bound together the peoples of other European countries also bound the Serbian people, but these were people spread across several lands. Serbs could be found in Serbia, Austria, Bosnia and Albania. The longing of the Serbian people to live together in one Slavic country drove many to dream of a great Serbia, a land where all Serbs lived together. This longing would challenge the authority of Austria, precipitating the Great War and straining the social norms of European society. The early years of the twentieth century saw the 'Balkan problem' become an ever-growing issue within European politics.

For all these political nuances Europe was, and is, a trading continent, with goods and commodities bought and sold across countries and empires. Political tensions rose and fell, but economic interests were paramount as the buying power of the solid middle classes kept trade turning. Trade agreements were made and remade, diplomatic friendships were forged and treaties were signed. By the spring of 1914, Europe was balanced on a spider's web of alliances and pledges. Yet despite the safety that these various economic treaties appeared to offer, all knew that the political tensions, especially in the Balkans, made war, if not inevitable, then at least more than likely. A spider's web, for all its intricacy, can be broken easily.

When the web broke on 28 July 1914, Europe was left picking at the floating strands of agreements and treaties. The previous certainties of European society could not cope with the complex nature of the war, and yet individuals and institutions had little else in which they could seek solace. The war was not conducted as previous European wars had been. There had been huge changes in military hardware, and these changes continued throughout the war. This change was also seen in military intelligence. Previous intelligence-gathering had not altered for centuries, and still relied on overheard conversations, but the new century had also seen the development of the wireless. Radio waves could send a message across the continent in minutes, but these communications were easy to intercept. Codes were developed and broken, and while a suspected spy could be questioned in person, who knew if a coded message was true or misinformation?

Before the outbreak of the Great War, and within Europe's social norms, *La Belle Époque* flourished. Underpinned by the spider's web of treaties and contained within the societal norms of the period, *La Belle Époque* was characterised initially by political optimism, but also by new technology and a great flourishing of the arts. Centred in Paris, the artistic world burst out with art nouveau, impressionism, literary realism and modern dance. Innovative new ground showcasing the primitive was broken by Sergei Diaghilev's *The Firebird* and *The Rite of Spring*. A secondary new strand in dance was Orientalism. This movement attempted to capture the essence of the mysterious East, but often without understanding its underlying philosophy or Eastern culture. Many serious dancers such as Isadora Duncan were sincere in their attempts to interpret and assimilate Oriental styles into their dance. Some others merely used Orientalism as a means by which to perform sexualised dances under the safe veneer of the exotic. The vast majority of audiences, and most dancers, had little actual knowledge of the East. Most of the exotic dances that were performed were little more than entertaining parodies, in which both audience and dancer participated in the charade.

Mata Hari could easily be counted in the second category. A western woman with no true understanding of Eastern culture and no formal dance training, she parodied what she had seen in the East Indies for the amusement of bored Parisians and to earn a living. However, while that is undoubtedly true, Mata Hari's use of Javanese dance as a way to survive was more practical than cynical. Although aware of the charade in which she was a central player, Mata Hari had, when she started dancing, very few options from which to choose. By the time she could no longer earn money by dancing, her options had narrowed even further. A 'loose' woman who danced 'naked' had nowhere to go but into the beds of the men who had watched her dance.

Mata Hari was, like most human beings, a mass of contradictions. She was intelligent, but also impetuous and made poor choices. She was a Netherlander who considered herself an international woman. She was a mother who lost both her children. She was vain and spoilt, but also charming and amusing. She was overly trusting and a poor judge of character. She showed little awareness of the norms of society and their changing complexities, and even less willingness to comply with them. She had no knowledge of politics, and yet embroiled herself in espionage during the greatest war Europe had ever seen.

When viewed from a distance, her life seems to be a catalogue of wrong choices and bad timing, from which she always appeared to bear the brunt of the damage. At 16 she 'fell in love' with the headmaster of her training school, who took full advantage of a teenage crush. She was dragged away in disgrace; he continued teaching with an unblemished reputation until 1925. Her marriage to a colonial officer, whom she barely knew, was a disaster, where she endured emotional and physical abuse; it ended with the death of her son. The divorce gave her custody of her daughter and an allowance from her ex-husband. Her husband reneged on the payments and took their daughter away. Mata Hari then became an artist's model to support herself; her husband used that to blacken her reputation with her family. She turned to exotic dancing, but was 25 by the time she started and had no training. Real dancers shunned her, and her popularity – and she was indeed popular – rested mainly on her apparent nudity and the novelty of Orientalism. Her dancing further distanced her from bourgeois society, and by 1910 she chose to become a high-class prostitute in addition to the dancing, although she would never admit as much.

When the Great War broke out, her poor choices were compounded by her apparent lack of understanding of how society had altered. The Great War changed everything within European society. The countries of Europe, with their colonies and social customs, had been Mata Hari's playground. However, those social customs were, after 1914, the very basis on which Mata Hari was to be judged. The decisions she took, that would have seemed reasonable in 1913, made no sense in 1915. When her fur and jewels were impounded by a theatre manager in Berlin over the non-payment of bills, she decided to spy for the Germans if they would pay her the equivalent sum of the value of her lost furs and jewels. This initial, somewhat ridiculous, decision might have been acceptable just, before the war, but by 1915 merely led her into the labyrinth of wartime espionage from which she was incapable of escaping. Unable to see the danger she was in, Mata Hari blundered on, only to finish up in the condemned cell of the French military authorities and then to execution.

When she was arrested and interrogated by the French, Mata Hari insisted that she did not spy for the Germans. She had, she contended, only taken money from them, which she considered her due for the furs, jewels and money that had been taken from her at the outbreak of the Great War. This may well have been true in theory, but it was not in the Allies' interests to believe her. They needed a spy to blame for the lack of success in the war, and they needed to catch a spy to improve morale. Mata Hari was their spy.

The Germans, after recruiting Mata Hari – one of the most highly visible women in Europe at the time – appeared to have used her for very little actual work; although her high profile certainly drew attention away from other German agents such as Clara Benedix, and it may be that that was the role they had always envisaged for her. The German's authorities certainly appeared to 'help' the French to identify her as a German agent, and may have also 'allowed' British agents to easily find evidence of their payments to her. There are no records existing within the German archives that detail any work that Mata Hari undertook for them.

It is certainly true that Mata Hari made several dubious choices in her life, but given the situations she frequently found herself in, and the society in which she was attempting to operate, the choices that were open to her were limited. If she had 'agreed' to spy for the Germans and then decided, with a theatrical sense of loyalty, to genuinely spy for the French, she might have been lauded as a heroine of the Fourth Republic. But for Mata Hari, espionage was purely a business arrangement; money was always her prime motive. She took money from the Germans and then negotiated a deal with the

French. Given her age, her lack of financial security and the chaos of the times, it was a typically foolish Mata Hari idea. The romantic view of espionage found in spy novels may well have been the foundations of Mata Hari's understanding. The reality was somewhat different, especially in wartime, when spying can and often does result in the death of serving men. There are varying accounts of how many men died due to Mata Hari's work, ranging from 50,000 Frenchmen to none at all. Sensible or not, her decision to accept payment from the Germans led her to be seen as suspect by the French. Her subsequent recruitment by the French was based not on a belief of Mata Hari's patriotism towards France, but that she was a foreign agent who had to be trapped and exposed.

The belief that she was an enemy agent was based, in part, on her sexual behaviour. The double standard of morality that operated in matters of sexuality in the early twentieth century condemned women for having any sort of sexual appetite, while at the same time expecting men to be sexually active. Women such as Mata Hari who were open about their sexual appetites were condemned as depraved. This condemnation was more than just middle-class morality; it was based on the latest scientific and philosophical thinking. Sexual women were seen as depraved criminals; depraved criminals would spy and betray their country. The science of criminology was in its infancy, but certainties about the links between immoral sexual behaviour – especially amongst women – and criminal activity were already firmly fixed in the minds of many within the justice system. Mata Hari's explanation about her recruitment by the Germans merely served to condemn her as a depraved woman. She had been engaged to dance semi-naked at a German theatre, her furs had been bought by her numerous lovers, and then she had either deceived the Germans by taking their money and not spying for them, or had lied to the French by acting as a German agent. Whatever the truth, Mata Hari's behaviour condemned her in the eyes of the French.

Given the pressures of war, the bluff and counter-bluff within the world of espionage and the social attitudes towards women in general, and Mata Hari in particular, it was unlikely that her decision to work for Germany and then France could ever have ended any other way than with her paying the ultimate price.

Mata Hari was a great self mythologiser. She became the exotic legend incarnate. She oozed sex appeal and charisma, and was guaranteed to give a great interview. The newspapers of the day loved her. A Mata Hari story was sure to sell, whether it was true or not. She was a European celebrity who took the pose of the exotic and spun a web of fantasy around that. A non-threatening fantasy figure, she was Indian, Javanese, Malaysian and a dozen inventions in-between. Had the Great War not happened, she would probably have remained a harmless figure on the margins of society, but celebrated in her own way nonetheless. Her great misfortune was to live through a war that was so devastating, so brutal and so terrifying that fantasy could no longer be harmless, but had to be suspicious. The sex appeal of dance became the depravity of the wicked.

2

CHILDHOOD

Margaretha Geertruida Zelle was born in the small town of Leeuwarden in the northern province of Friesland in the Netherlands on 7 August 1876. She was the eldest of the four children of Ardum Zelle and his first wife, Antje van der Meulen. Her brother, Johannes Henderikus, was born in 1878, and the twins, Arie Anne and Cornelius Coenraad, in 1881. Margaretha grew up as her father's favourite and was known to everyone as M'greet. During her early childhood, M'greet enjoyed the lavish attention given to her by her father, and it was this early attention that shaped M'greet the girl, who would become Mata Hari the woman.

Ardum Zelle had been born in Leeuwarden in 1840 into a family of lower-middle-class shopkeepers. Like many of his contemporaries, Zelle was keen from an early age to improve himself. He worked hard at bettering himself, taking care over his appearance, adopting the most expensive and best quality clothing he could. He constantly strove to improve the quality of the goods on offer in the family shop, catering to a better class of customer, and titled himself a 'milliner' or 'purveyor of headgear to gentlemen' rather than a shop assistant. In 1873, he met and married Anna van der Meulen from Franecker. Anna, known as Antje, was exactly what Zelle wanted in a wife; she came from an upper-middle-class family. The Meulens had important connections, which Zelle wasted no time in cultivating. In 1875, King Wilhelm III made a royal visit to Leeuwarden. Zelle managed, through his Meulen connections, to be chosen to be a member of the town's mounted guard of honour. It was a very particular privilege, and one not normally bestowed on an individual with Zelle's background. Zelle ensured this was remembered by commissioning a painting of himself in his guard's uniform mounted on his horse. The painting was displayed in the family home until Zelle decided to donate it to the Fries Museum in the town when it opened in 1881.

As flamboyant and social climbing as Zelle was, Antje was a typical upper-middle-class wife. Little is known of Antje before her marriage, when she seems to have been a dutiful, if somewhat dull, daughter to the Meulens. By the time she married Zelle she was 31 years old and may well have expected to see out her days as the unmarried daughter who stayed at home to take care of the parents as they aged; such was the social convention of the day. Once married to Zelle, she seemed to disappear into the marriage, subsuming her own personality into that of her husband's dutiful wife. She gave Zelle her family connections, four children and a thoroughly respectable home. She was the epitome of upper-middle-class respectability. Dinner parties were held, where she was the perfect hostess; the right combination of sensible housekeeper, supportive wife and lady of quality.

With Antje's connections and Zelle's ambition, the business flourished, and in 1883 the family moved into a large brick house on Grote Krestraat. The children attended private school and the family lived the comfortable life of the successful merchant class. Zelle bought M'greet the latest, most expensive toys and had the most fashionable dresses made for his beloved daughter. Ridiculous and lavish gifts were bought and publicly displayed. On one occasion, M'greet was photographed outside the house sitting in a small trap pulled by a goat. However, Zelle was no real businessman. Despite the success of his by then large and relatively prosperous haberdashery shop, he longed for the life of a 'real' merchant without understanding what that entailed. He started investing in the speculative oil industry, a business that offered huge profits but also carried great risks. Barely understanding how such an industry operated, Zelle was both ambitious and foolhardy. He started to borrow funds to speculate on new oil fields, with the promise to repay once the fields started to produce. When the fields were found to be dry of any oil, his creditors started to demand repayments that Zelle could not afford. For a couple of years, Zelle managed to keep his creditors at bay by a combination of promises, borrowing from one creditor to pay another and finally by reneging on paying his debts and family bills. By 1889, the inevitable happened and Zelle found himself in the bankruptcy courts. The family was devastated.

To be declared bankrupt in the late nineteenth century was a source of huge social and emotional shame. For a businessman to become bankrupt was generally thought of as not only a sign of incompetence, but also of a moral failing. Netherlands society was an ordered one, with the father at the head of the house as provider. Zelle had prided himself on being a good provider, buying a solid, large house and sending his children to private school. What sort of husband and father could not provide?

The Netherlands was a trading nation. Trade was based on trust: a man's word was his bond. To borrow money within the business community and be unable to repay was a breach of trust that put one outside the normal moral sphere of one's community. A community that only a few years previously had asked him to be part of the town's guard of honour, now shunned him. Not only that, but the trading nation of the Netherlands held its head up with the best of European society. To fail in business as a Netherlander was to shame your country. Zelle had shamed his family, shamed his community and shamed his country.

The family were forced to dismiss all their servants and leave the house on Grote Krestraat. They moved to a cramped apartment on the Willemskade and the children left their private schools. On 18 February 1889, Zelle was publicly declared bankrupt. Within three days, Antje suffered some form of breakdown. It is not exactly clear what happened on 21 February, but whatever the medical crisis was, Antje never fully recovered. The stress affected everyone in the family. The children crowded together in the small apartment, removed from their schools and their school friends, and heard every argument between Zelle and Antje, as did the neighbours. Unsure as to exactly what was going on, but equally unable to escape the tension, M'greet remained her father's favourite, but the lavish presents and the comfortable lifestyle had gone and worse was to come. By July 1889, the situation had deteriorated to such an extent that Zelle decided to leave the family home to look for work. He moved to The Hague in order to make a fresh start, but found few openings for a man who was a declared bankrupt. In the meantime, Antje and the children survived on a series of handouts from her family. Although this gave them enough to pay their basic living expenses, it was a miserable hand-to-mouth existence, compounded by the humiliation of having to ask for help.

Zelle returned to the family in May 1890. He had been absent for some ten months and had missed all of the children's birthdays. M'greet had turned 13 without her beloved father there to spoil her. He had also missed the miserable Christmas and New Year the family had spent in their cold, damp apartment. Zelle's arrival was not a happy one. He had not returned with a job or any money to speak of, but rather had come back to Leeuwarden in the hope that some of his old acquaintances there would help him get on his feet. However, Zelle's apparent lack of remorse over his bankruptcy alienated those who might have helped him, and little work was forthcoming. Tensions rose and the arguments in Willemskade started again. In the summer, matters came to a head and eventually Zelle left the family for a second and final time, filing for a legal separation.

A legal separation was, if not scandalous, a matter of extreme disapproval in polite nineteenth-century European society. Couples whose marriages had broken down would usually come to an arrangement between themselves while maintaining the usual social conventions. Even those who chose to separate usually did so without the need to involve the public courts. Given that Zelle had already left his wife and children for ten months, it is interesting that he chose to file for a legal separation. It may have been an attempt on his part to distance himself from his wife and children in order to avoid his responsibilities towards them. Whatever the reason, Antje does not seem to have opposed the move and may even have supported it, given the breakdown in the marriage. The separation was granted on 4 September 1890.

The separation was yet another blow to the family's honour: another scandal to be laid at Zelle and Antje's door. It was yet another breach in the social values held so dear across the Netherlands. Although entirely blameless in the case of the bankruptcy and only partly to blame for the breakdown of the marriage, Antje would have been judged by family and community alike for her husband's actions. A woman who made a poor choice in a husband would be considered at fault for the mistake of that poor choice. One transgression was bad enough and might possibly have generated some pity for Antje, but the legal separation was a step too far for even the most sympathetic amongst her friends and neighbours. The social constraints of Leeuwarden could stretch no further. It is possible that the children may have been somewhat spared the worst of the gossip regarding the bankruptcy, partly as it was a matter for adults and also due to sympathy for a family wrecked by a feckless father. The separation of their parents was another matter. The children may well have had to endure the taunts of other children whose fathers, no matter how worthless, were still at least living with their mothers. M'greet, now 14 years old and on the cusp of adulthood, had to contend with the shame of her father's behaviour, the loss of his presence and the diminished family circumstances while attempting to help her mother – who was by that time quite ill – and care for her younger brothers.

Once the separation was granted, Zelle once again left Leeuwarden and went to live in Amsterdam. His contact with his children was minimal, with only the occasional letter written to M'greet to break the silence. Antje's health continued to deteriorate and M'greet was having to take on more of the caring responsibilities for her brothers. At no point did Zelle appear to offer any form of help to his children. By Christmas 1890, the family were still living in the cramped quarters on Willemskade. While they attempted to scrape together some money to pay for the upcoming festivities, Zelle was openly living with a woman in his Amsterdam apartment. He had money to support a new partner, even if he had none for the family in Leeuwarden. The New Year saw matters deteriorate further, with M'greet increasingly in the role of mother. On 10 May 1891, Antje died. The death notice in the paper stated:

> This day it pleaseth the supreme architect of the universe, to take away from this earth, after a grievous suffering from 21 February, 1889, my dearly beloved wife, loving mother of four helpless children, Mrs Anna van der Meulen Zelle, at the age of 49 years. Ardum Zelle Corniliszoon (son of Cornelius).[1]

On first sight, this death notice is a somewhat curious one from a man who had legally separated from his wife, was openly living with another woman to whom he was not married and had more or less abandoned his 'four helpless children' to look after themselves. However, most newspapers at the time had a set format for death notices that would be placed on behalf of grieving relatives. Spouses were always 'dearly beloved', and any illness that had led to the eventual death was usually noted. It is unlikely Zelle would have argued greatly over the word choice, which for those unfamiliar with the family would have seemed perfectly normal. If any comments had been made by anyone in Leeuwarden, Zelle remained safely 140km away in Amsterdam. Whatever the truth behind the death notice, and after all the family had been through in the previous two years, Zelle did not come back to Leeuwarden to care for his 'four helpless children', and neither did he send for them to come and live with him in Amsterdam. From May onwards, M'greet was the adult in the house. Helped partly by the Meulens and the neighbours, she struggled on until her 15th birthday in the August with little contact and no support from her father. The situation could not continue, and eventually in November the family acted. The Meulens agreed to take Johannes to the family home in Franeker, and Zelle to take the twins to live with him in Amsterdam. M'greet was sent to live with her godfather and uncle in the small town of Sneek. Zelle, it seemed, did not want to care for his favourite anymore.

It is not known why Zelle rejected M'greet or if it was ever explained to the young teenager. In the previous two years, M'greet had seen her world turned upside down. She had seen her family name disgraced, watched her mother sicken and die, struggled to care for her brothers and been abandoned by her father. This final rejection may have been for some simple practical reason, but to the 15-year-old girl still grieving from the death of her mother and the turmoil through which she had passed, the emotional hurt must have been intense.

M'greet's uncle and aunt, the Vissers, lived in the quiet little town of Sneek in south-west Friesland. Smaller than Leeuwarden, Sneek was even more bourgeois and staid than its larger neighbour, and the Vissers were a couple fully at ease in their comfortable and predictable middle-class life. M'greet, unfortunately, did not fit in. The teenager had had to move house again, on top of the previous emotional upset, and found herself stifled in the strait-laced home of her childless relatives. The Vissers appear to have been well-meaning, but were unwilling or unable to deal with the needs of an emotionally fragile teenager. M'greet was expected to live in the household, but without disturbing its well-ordered routine in any way. In addition to her emotional needs, M'greet did not 'fit in' physically. In an era where women were judged by their behaviour and appearance, M'greet made a less than positive impression. She was dark-haired and olive-skinned, in distinct contrast to the blonde, pale-skinned idealised notion of beauty in the Netherlands. She was also very tall, being 5ft 9in. In the late nineteenth century, the average woman in the Netherlands was a petite 5ft. The social norm was for women to be dainty, quiet spoken and shy. M'greet was gangly and awkward, and in addition, outspoken and flirtatious.

M'greet did not settle with the Vissers, and as her grandmother Meulen had offered to pay for further education for the children, it was decided that M'greet should consider taking some form of training in order to obtain employment. Old Mrs van der Meulen had set aside some 5,000 florins for the children's education after Antje's death. It is interesting, however, that at no point did anyone in the family suggest that some of the money could be used as a dowry for M'greet. This was, after all, a very traditional family in which women got married and maintained the home while the men worked. And yet the decision was for M'greet to look for work, not marriage. Did her dark looks count against her? Did the family think her un-marriageable due to her father's scandalous behaviour? Whatever the reason, the family decided training was more suitable. Her early school reports indicated that M'greet showed excellent academic ability, and yet although training for a job would be paid for by her grandmother, no one in the Meulen family offered M'greet a position in the family business or helped her to find a position among their many business connections.

Finally, in the spring of 1892, a position was found for M'greet at a training school in Leiden. This school, run by Wybrandus Haanstra, taught young ladies to become kindergarten teachers. It was a strange choice of career for M'greet, who although having cared for her younger siblings during her mother's illness had little maternal feeling and was not overly fond of or interested in small children. It may be that the Vissers, along with the wider family, made the decision to send M'greet to Leiden with little consultation with the girl. Equally, M'greet may have agreed to go to Leiden to get away from the stifling atmosphere in Sneek. Either way, the move to Leiden would prove disastrous for M'greet.

The school was innovative, teaching the latest theories in education and childhood psychological development, and promoted learning through play. For the students, the curriculum was intensive, and most boarded at the school. Haanstra fostered a family atmosphere among the students, encouraging them to work and socialise together and to share any worries or concerns with the staff. Initially, M'greet appears to have settled relatively well into life at the school, and celebrated her 16th birthday in the August of her first year. She progressed reasonably well in her studies and seemed to be making friends, spending the Christmas holiday period of 1882 at the school. Sometime in the spring of 1893, she started to have a sexual relationship with the headmaster, Haanstra: she was 16, he was 51, and she lost her virginity to him. How the relationship developed is unclear. It may have been initiated by Haanstra, or M'greet may have developed a romantic crush on the older man, possibly as a substitute father figure. If M'greet had made the first move, Haanstra did not dissuade her from her feelings for him, despite his position of authority. However it had started, the situation could not stay secret for long, and rumours soon reached Sneek. In the early summer, Visser became worried by the tales being told about the situation at Leiden, and rushed to the school to find out the truth. What he discovered horrified him.

According to M'greet, she and Haanstra had indeed had a sexual relationship, and moreover, M'greet was reluctant to leave Leiden. Visser forcibly removed her, some weeks shy of her 17th birthday, and brought her back to the house in Sneek. With the truth of the rumours now found to be true, her character was judged and quickly found wanting, due in no small part to M'greet's own attitude. Physically dragged away from her first romantic love, and with unresolved feelings over the previous years of chaos, M'greet acted not with contrition but defiance. And it was that which condemned her in everyone's eyes. The fact that she had been reluctant to leave Leiden and had failed to show any sign of shame merely 'proved' her immorality to all. In the court of public opinion at that time, in any sexual scandal the woman was always to blame, no matter the age of the man, and so M'greet had to contend with the shame heaped upon her by her godmother and local gossips.

In M'greet's case, however, this shame was further compounded by the old scandal of her father's bankruptcy and abandonment of the family, which were remembered by many. The Vissers were horrified by M'greet's behaviour, not least for the slur it cast on their own honour for having failed to protect their goddaughter's reputation while in their care. The situation in the Visser household was strained; M'greet resented having been removed from the school in Leiden, and her godparents remained convinced that M'greet had been the instigator of the affair in the first place and was, as a result, a girl of very loose morals. After only a few weeks, the Vissers sent M'greet to her uncle's house in The Hague. She arrived just after she turned 17 and moved in with distant relatives, the Taconis family.

It is interesting that the Meulens did not offer M'greet a home in Franeker after this incident. It may be that this was impractical, having previously taken in her brother, Johannes, but given the family's wealth, that is unlikely. In any event, she was abandoned again by the Meulens and the Vissers. It is also noticeable that at no point during the scandal at Leiden did Zelle appear to help his daughter in any way. It might be thought that Zelle, like the Meulens, was unable to offer a practical home to his daughter due to his continued straitened circumstances. However, during M'greet's first year at Leiden, Zelle had met Susanna Catharina ten Hoove, and by February 1893 they were married and had moved into a new house. At the same time, Zelle's beloved M'greet was offered neither home nor emotional support.

Wybrandus Haanstra remained as headmaster at the Leiden school until 1925 with an unblemished record. No action appears to have been taken against him for his behaviour with a teenage student, and there does not seem to have been any change in the numbers of young ladies sent by their families to his training school in the years following M'greet's departure.

3

MARRIAGE AND
MOTHERHOOD

The Hague was the seat of the parliament of the Netherlands, and as such was the most exciting town that M'greet had ever seen. It had fashionable shops, cafes and parks in which to promenade. Moreover, it had several different training schools for young ladies. However, M'greet was now a 'young woman of loose morals' who had left her last training school under a cloud. She was most certainly not the sort of person that anyone would wish to be in charge of children, so a career in a kindergarten was no longer an option. This may not have greatly bothered M'greet, but her family continued to pressure her into undertaking some form of training. The main reason for this was their genuine belief that she was un-marriageable. Her father's bankruptcy, her lack of dowry and – most shamefully – her sexual scandal, in addition to her looks and personality, meant that in the eyes of the Meulens, no man from a good family would entertain her as a potential bride. M'greet had to work.

For the first few months of her time in The Hague, M'greet drifted along the city streets with no real plan in mind as to her future. The Taconis household proved to be somewhat boring, and M'greet appears to have preferred promenading on the streets to sitting with her aunt engaged in needlework or actively seeking training or work. The streets of The Hague had one other attraction: in addition to the shops and cafes, it was full of officers from the colonial service.

The Dutch colonial service was a vast organisation which provided the Netherlands with all the riches of the East, Dutch families with employment for their sons and an entire culture of exotic excitement that pervaded all sections of society. Newspaper articles and novels told of the mysterious East; early photographs showed images of strange temples and idols, and even the spices and fruits of the East Indies trade were a world away from the usual diet of Northern Europe. The presence of officers in The Hague, with their neatly pressed uniforms and tanned skin, sitting in the street cafes talking of exotic locations and using strange foreign words, added to the glamour. The reality was, of course, something entirely different.

The Dutch colonies were large and unwieldy, spread across several islands. The land was difficult to work and the climate unforgiving for many Europeans. The average lifespan of an officer in the colonial service was around twenty years. To support the colonial presence in the Dutch East Indies in the late nineteenth century, around 1,785 soldiers had to be sent out annually to maintain levels at 13,000.[1] The local population in the islands varied from grudgingly accepting the Dutch presence through silent resentment to actively trying to drive out the foreigners. The men of the colonial service worked hard in poor conditions, away from friends and family, with the constant fear of uprising while seeing many of their colleagues dying of tropical disease, alcoholism or in combat. It was a life that hardened those who survived.

In August 1872, Rudolf John MacLeod, born in March 1856, entered the military academy at Kampen in the Dutch province of Overijssel. MacLeod was descended from a Norman MacLeod from the Isle of Skye in Scotland, who had been an adventurer and had left his home country at the beginning of the seventeenth century to fight as a mercenary for the Dutch during the Thirty Years' War. At the end of the war, the Scottish mercenaries who had fought for the Dutch had been formed into a regular unit within the Royal Dutch Army, the Dutch Scots Brigade. Norman MacLeod had married a local girl and settled into his adopted homeland. The MacLeod family provided the Dutch Army with men for several generations down to Rudolf MacLeod. Many of MacLeod's male relatives had been distinguished military officers, and his father, John van Brieen MacLeod, who had married the Baroness Dina Louise Sweerts van Landas, had been an infantry captain. No other career could be envisaged for young MacLeod and, despite being only 16 years old when he enlisted, he showed exceptional promise and was promoted, first to brevet corporal and then full corporal within his first year in the academy.

MacLeod graduated from Kampen with the rank of second lieutenant in July 1877. Eager to start his military career, he accepted a posting to Padang in the East Indies and sailed on 3 November 1877 on the packet ship *Conrad*. His initial posting introduced him to the realities of the colonial service and of controlling the men under him, the majority of whom were older and with many years of service. His command included a mixture of native troops and recruited Europeans, mostly Dutch. By the 1870s, the Netherlands did not have a standing army as such and the recruits who made up the bulk of the ordinary soldiers were those who were desperate. Many joined out of economic necessity: some were running away from unwanted marriages or potential gaol sentences, and others had merely signed up for the price of some more beer. Shipped halfway across the world, they made good, bad or indifferent soldiers, as in any European army of its day. However, the danger, climate, foreign food and lack of home comforts made many of them malcontent and many more brutal in their treatment of the locals. Any young officer arriving for the first time had to quickly take control of his men. MacLeod was barely 21 years old when he arrived in the Indies, and within a matter of a few weeks he was sent into action as part of the Aceh War.

The war had started in 1873 and, unbeknown to Dutch officers like MacLeod, would last until 1914. Aceh, an area in the island of Sumatra, was an autonomous protectorate of the Ottoman Empire and had been run by several regional rajas. The region's main crop was pepper, and by the 1820s the growing European and American demand for pepper increased tension between the local rajas and the European colonial powers, especially the Dutch, who controlled large areas of the island in the south. Sultan Alauddin Ibrahim Mansur Syah was the de facto ruler of the Aceh Sultanate from 1838. Politically very shrewd, Syah strengthened and developed the Sultanate of Aceh by bringing the regional rajas under his control, and extended his domain across the south and east of the island.

Following the opening of the Suez Canal in 1869, which changed global shipping routes, the 1871 Anglo-Dutch Treaty of Sumatra ended British territorial claims to Sumatra. This gave the Dutch colonial supremacy across maritime South-east Asia. Although the Dutch could have maintained diplomatic relations with the Sultanate, their territorial ambitions in Sumatra were to have total control in order to exploit the island's natural resources, especially black pepper and oil. The Dutch were also keen to prevent any other rival European colonial powers from regaining territory by the back door of a friendly native power. The Sultanate had to be neutralised.

In 1873, negotiations took place between representatives of the American Consul and the Aceh Sultanate over a potential bilateral treaty. The Dutch saw this as a violation of the 1871 Anglo-Dutch Treaty, and used this as an opportunity to annex Aceh militarily. Initially unsuccessful, the Dutch eventually overran the Sultanate, declaring the war was over in 1874. However, a guerrilla war started in the hills of Aceh and lasted for seven long bloody years. By 1882, the Dutch had more or less established themselves as the colonial power, but in 1883 the war restarted. Sporadic violence continued at varying levels until 1914, sometimes breaking out into open warfare but more often remaining as guerrilla actions. As in similar long-term open conflicts, the fighting was vicious, with few, if any, of the niceties of war observed. The constant violence and threat of violence also led to mutual distrust between the Dutch and the Sumatrans, both groups developing a siege mentality, with all the attendant nervous paranoia that entailed.

When Rudolf MacLeod left Padang, he was sent to Samalanga. As a young officer, he was in the forefront of the fighting and would continue to be so for seven years. He received the Aceh Expeditionary

Cross for his military service between 1877 and 1880, and by the end of 1881 was promoted to the rank of first lieutenant. Early in 1882, he was posted to an area surrounding the Kota Raja. The objective was to eliminate a native stronghold. The task was hard, unpleasant and ultimately only partly successful. In 1884, MacLeod finally received some respite from the Aceh War, being posted firstly to Java and then to Borneo. Between 1884 and 1889, he was stationed in Banjermassan in Borneo, where he undertook the general duties of a colonial army officer. MacLeod was an excellent soldier in the field, but does not appear to have been suited to the role of policeman in a peaceful colonial province. In 1889, after only five years in Borneo, he received no less than four new postings in one year. In May 1890, he requested and received a two-year leave of absence to allow him to return home to the Netherlands. This leave was cancelled by MacLeod himself in June 1890. He was sent to two further postings before finally returning to more active service in Aceh at the end of 1890. MacLeod thrived on the violence of the ongoing conflict, and in 1892 was promoted to captain and received the Officer's Cross for patriotic service.

On 9 January 1894, MacLeod was granted a two-year leave of absence due to illness. This was generous, as it included continued employment and a promise of promotion during his leave. After a period of convalescence, MacLeod boarded the SS *Prinses Marie* on 27 June, bound for The Hague, where he arrived on 14 August. It is not known exactly what illness MacLeod had, although there are any number of diseases that could have necessitated his leave of absence. One of the most likely illnesses for a colonial soldier of that era was syphilis, which, if the case for him, would have consequences not only for MacLeod but for the young M'greet Zelle. In addition, he had the beginnings of rheumatism and diabetes, neither of which prevented him from drinking heavily.

When MacLeod arrived back in the Netherlands, he was somewhat recovered from the initial bout of illness. Over the next few months, took time to think about his career. He was 38 years old, and although an excellent field soldier, he knew that fighting was a young man's game, especially in the climate of the East Indies. Sooner or later he would be looking to move into a more senior colonial position, and for that he might need a wife. Discussing his various options for the future with his colleagues, he started to plan the rest of his career.

During his convalescence, he had become friendly with J.T.Z. de Balbian Vester, a journalist on the *Nieuws van de Dag* (*News of the Day*). Their friendship had developed as de Balbian Vester was covering the fighting that had broken out on the island of Lombok and had actively sought out soldiers such as MacLeod to gain what information he could. By the spring of 1895, MacLeod and de Balbian Vester were firm friends. After one conversation with MacLeod about the structure of Dutch society in the East Indies and the role of colonial wives in advancing military careers, de Balbian Vester placed an advert in the *Nieuws van de Dag* newspaper, a not uncommon method of finding a bride for colonial soldiers:

MARRIAGE

Captain in the East Indies currently on leave seeks to return to the East Indies as a married man. Seeking to meet a cultured young lady of pleasant appearance and gentle character. Any fortune requisite. He will gladly meet with parents or guardians to reach his goal.[2]

MacLeod received sixteen replies to the advert in the fortnight after it appeared. One came from M'greet. She had written and enclosed a photograph of herself. MacLeod wrote back and suggested a meeting. It is not known if MacLeod wrote to any of the other women who answered his advert. It is also unclear what M'greet's motives were in answering the advert, or what her uncle thought of this, if he knew. Whatever the reasons, the two started a correspondence. MacLeod's health remained poor and unpredictable, so no early meeting could take place between MacLeod and M'greet. Ignoring the proper social conventions, M'greet wrote to MacLeod and offered to visit him. She wrote, 'I know well it is not *"comme il faut"* but we find ourselves in a special case, no?'[3]

They met on 24 March 1895 at the Rijksmuseum in Amsterdam. The meeting was a great success and there was an instant attraction between them. M'greet addressed MacLeod as 'my dearest Johnnie' and signed her letters as 'your future little wife'. For his part, MacLeod called her Griet. On 30 March, they became formally engaged.

This whirlwind engagement was the stuff of romantic fantasy, and may well have appealed to the 18-year-old M'greet. However, there were several practicalities that had to be dealt with before any wedding could take place. M'greet had to be approved by the MacLeod family. Norman MacLeod, uncle to Rudolf and head of the family, found M'greet to be perfectly acceptable, calling her 'young but good-looking'.[4] It is not clear if he knew about her father's bankruptcy or the scandal of her behaviour at the kindergarten training school, but she had been approved. Next, MacLeod had to meet her father. As M'greet was underage, his permission was necessary. Zelle duly approved of MacLeod and the wedding was set for 11 July 1895.

As a serving office, MacLeod also had to obtain permission to marry from his superior officer. The military authorities had to approve of a bride before a marriage could take place. Alternatively, they could approve a marriage in general but not approve of a prospective bride if the individual was considered unsuitable as an officer's wife. There is no note anywhere of MacLeod having sought the requisite permission. As he was an officer home on leave, he should have filed for permission with the Ministry of Colonial Affairs in The Hague. That he did not do so raises some interesting points. As a serving officer who came from a military family, the rules would have been familiar to him. His uncle Norman, a retired vice-admiral of the Dutch navy, would have been equally aware of the need for any serviceman to seek permission to marry. Did MacLeod fail to seek permission because he simply forgot, or because he was worried that it might not have been granted? His uncle may have been unaware of M'greet's family background, but the army would have checked. A girl with a reputation of 'loose morals' and a bankrupt father with continuing money worries was hardly suitable for life as a colonial officer's wife. As the army fought the locals in the East Indies to maintain Dutch control, so their wives were expected to maintain Dutch standards of behaviour and etiquette in the European community. M'greet and her family had been unable to maintain Dutch standards while in the Netherlands. If MacLeod did fail to seek permission because he was worried that M'greet might prove unsuitable, he might also have omitted to reveal M'greet's background to his uncle. This would explain Norman MacLeod's only criticism of M'greet being that she was 'young'.

There was another possible reason and it was one that rested not on M'greet's conduct but on his own. His leave to the Netherlands had been granted due to illness. The records are frustratingly missing and incomplete for this part of MacLeod's service, but it is most likely that he had syphilis, in which case he would not have been allowed to marry. Applying for permission would have been pointless, as it would not have been given. This would have dire consequences at a later date.

Whatever MacLeod's reasons, there were consequences. As a serving officer, he had chosen not to follow army regulations and was laying himself open to a stiff reprimand, or at the very least a black mark against his career. In addition, by not applying for permission, the army had no responsibility for M'greet. This then became something of a financial burden. MacLeod would have to bear the cost of M'greet's travel to and from the East Indies. He was also not eligible for the higher rate of pay and larger living quarters given to married officers. When M'greet and MacLeod were first engaged, they seem, from their frequent and passionate letters, to have genuinely loved each other, and so the issue of a potential reprimand and less money may not have mattered. In the long term, however, the issues of M'greet's reputation and MacLeod's army career and finances would prove to be of great significance in the marriage.

They were married on 11 July 1895 in a civil wedding at the City Hall in Amsterdam. M'greet was not yet 19 years old; MacLeod was 39. M'greet wore a yellow silk gown and MacLeod was in full dress uniform. On the surface, the marriage gave Rudolf the wife he thought he needed for his career; it gave M'greet entry back into the Dutch upper middle class and the financial security she had not known since her early childhood. Both assumptions would very quickly prove to be wrong.

The couple honeymooned in the German spa town of Wiesbaden. On their return to the Netherlands, they moved into the home of MacLeod's sister Louise. Within a matter of weeks, the marriage was strained. Louise's house was not large, and as a result no one had any privacy. In addition, Louise did not completely approve of her young sister-in-law. To add to these tensions, finances were tight. MacLeod was on reduced pay from the army due to his illness, and the young couple's outgoings were considerable. MacLeod had a great deal of debt; he had been living above his means while home on leave, and in addition was repaying several outstanding loans he had in the East Indies. This was common within the military, and most young officers borrowed heavily and spent on drink, prostitutes or gambling. However, most young officers were single, and when money was short simply tightened their belts for a time. MacLeod, however, was a newly married man with a young wife who had no experience of housekeeping and expensive tastes. M'greet had expected that the MacLeod family was a wealthy one, which it was, and that Rudolf had a share of that wealth, which he did not, and she had spent accordingly. The MacLeods needed money.

Between May and October 1895, the Hotel and Travel Exposition was taking place in Amsterdam. MacLeod and M'greet visited, along with several thousand others. During their visit, they became acquainted with the chairman of the executive organising committee, De heer Calisch. The friendship that developed was an unusual one, as the MacLeods and Calisch seemed to have little in common. However, at some point in 1895 or 1896, Calisch lent MacLeod 3,000 guilders; the equivalent of six months' salary for MacLeod. It was a substantial sum for Calisch to lend, but offered MacLeod the ability to pay the most persistent of his creditors and give him something of a breathing space until he returned to active service and his full salary. It may also have been necessary to pay for M'greet's travel to the East Indies when MacLeod was recalled. MacLeod signed the promissory note, but Calisch was never repaid. According to a later account written by Ardum Zelle, MacLeod had asked M'greet to 'be nice' to Calisch to prevent any demand for repayment. While this allegation may have been manufactured by Zelle in order to sell the book he was writing about his daughter, given the desperate nature of MacLeod's finances and his subsequent behaviour towards M'greet, it is not entirely outside the realms of possibility that it was true.

This may also point to the reason why Calisch lent MacLeod the money in the first place. MacLeod was a man whose military career is well documented, and one element in his many successes was his ability to manipulate the weaknesses of others, an ability he carried into his civilian life. He was the sort of man who went out drinking and gambling or visiting brothels with other men. But he would also use his knowledge of who had been where to his own advantage if needs be. A drinking buddy might well find himself being asked for a loan by MacLeod, on a friendly basis of course, but with the clear inference that disapproving wives and fathers might be told of the previous night's entertainment if the money was not forthcoming. Calisch, who was a respectable married man and a reasonably wealthy one, might have thought a 3,000-guilder loan was preferable to explaining to his wife and board of directors his night-time activities.

MacLeod was a man who had been living the life of a soldier for over twenty years. He saw no reason to change his behaviour, despite his marriage. Just two weeks after their return from Wiesbaden, MacLeod approached his friend de Balbian Verter and asked him to visit their home to keep M'greet company one evening; MacLeod had a date with two young women. It is not known how quickly M'greet became aware of MacLeod's womanising, but within a matter of weeks she was complaining about him leaving her alone while he went out with his army friends drinking, gambling and meeting prostitutes.

The improvement in MacLeod's health that he had enjoyed before his marriage did not last. After his return from Wiesbaden – possibly due to his continued drinking, smoking and irregular hours – his health deteriorated. On 16 March 1896, MacLeod's leave was extended as his health was still considered too poor for active service. While this gave MacLeod more time to recuperate, it left him still drawing only half pay and the loan from Calisch would not last forever. He and M'greet had moved out of his sister's house to a small apartment on Jacob van Lennepkade. While this reduced some of the tension in the household, it increased the strain on their already difficult financial situation.

By the summer, that strain was further increased when M'greet became pregnant. MacLeod's leave was due to finish in September, when he had expected to be posted back to the East Indies. However, the journey to the East Indies was considered dangerous for women, and one that pregnant women were strongly dissuaded from undertaking. In September, MacLeod's leave was extended for a further six months. Despite his continuing half pay and the increased expense of new clothes for M'greet and furnishing a nursery for the coming baby, MacLeod does not appear to have curbed his expenditure, and may even have taken out several small loans from various money lenders.

On 30 January 1897, their son was born. The boy was christened Norman John, named for MacLeod's uncle and paternal grandfather. MacLeod doted on the boy. In February, uncle Norman MacLeod arranged for his nephew, M'greet and the baby to be presented at court to her highness Queen Regent Emma, the mother of Queen Wilhelmina. Despite the birth and the honour of being presented at court, the household was reaching crisis point. MacLeod was increasingly absent from the home on Jacob Lennepkade, while M'greet coped with a new baby and creditors at the doors. Finally, MacLeod got word of his posting back to the East Indies. On 1 May, MacLeod, M'greet and Norman boarded the SS *Prinses Amalia* and sailed for the East Indies.

4

AN EAST INDIES ADVENTURE

On 7 June 1897, the SS *Prinses Amalia* docked at Tanjung Priok near Batavia (modern Jakarta). M'greet had been unwell during the long voyage and complained of various symptoms. She is reported to have stated, 'Morally I suffered enormous complaints.'[1] Her use of this phrase is somewhat curious. Similar language was frequently used among European women to indicate sexually transmitted diseases. If the disease which had necessitated MacLeod's leave had been syphilis, it is likely that by this time in their marriage M'greet would have contracted it. If M'greet had been suffering from an ordinary bout of seasickness or other recognisable illness, it is unlikely to have had some moral dimension. Equally, it could have been named and subsequently treated by the ship's doctor.

Whatever the nature of the moral 'complaints', the family stayed barely a week in port before MacLeod received his posting to the 8th Battalion based at Ambarawa near Semarang in central Java. The MacLeods boarded the SS *Speelman* to travel the 478km to where they disembarked. MacLeod then organised horses and an oxcart for their belongings to travel the final 50km to the fort at Ambarawa. The family quickly settled into their somewhat cramped quarters and MacLeod began his duties training new recruits.

Ambarawa was not a good posting, and MacLeod was, by this time, a soldier with several years' colonial experience and expecting an imminent promotion. As an officer of such rank and experience, and given the continued pressures the army was under, it was strange for him to be underused. However, during his long leave, MacLeod had also become married without the requisite military permission. His superiors were faced with a *fait accompli* when MacLeod arrived in Batavia, but they were not without options with which to punish his dereliction of military duty. MacLeod was an excellent soldier and was in effect just the sort to train raw recruits. However, the work was not to his liking as it kept him from active service, and Ambarawa was something of a backwater which prevented him from socialising with the sort of senior military officers and colonial staff who might help his career. While the army was unlikely to want an officer of MacLeod's standing to be kept in Ambarawa for long, his posting did act as a humiliating punishment while the recruits received some of the best training available from an experienced senior officer. Meanwhile, M'greet began her life as a colonial wife.

The life of colonial European women in the late nineteenth century was a mixture of hard work and boredom, underpinned by the absolute necessity of maintaining European standards in all matters. This was not just a matter of polite social niceties. The belief across all European countries was one of their superiority to the local native population, and that superiority had to be maintained at all costs. However, in order to subdue the local population and maintain order, European men had to undertake duties in a manner that would have been unthinkable in Europe. Brutality was a matter of course, and was both justified and accepted as part of the burden of empire. The ends, the imposition of 'superior European civilisation', justified the means, the brutal suppression of 'inferior' native societies. As the native populations were inferior, so civilisation could only be imposed by force; their very inferiority rendered the natives incapable of learning in any other way. This violence was then balanced by the rigorous maintenance of the civilised European standards in all other matters. Seemingly trivial matters such as one's dress or manner of greeting took on a highly increased level of importance. Such decorum was maintained by colonial wives. The importance of the role of colonial women was, in part, the reason why the Dutch military 'vetted' potential wives. A woman of weak character or, worse still, 'loose morals' could not be expected to undertake such work successfully, and might easily 'let the side down'. The social facade that hid the brutality of empire was necessary to maintain the fiction of bringing civilisation to the natives, but was equally as important in providing the men of the colonial service with a psychological haven from the realities of their actions. It was just such an onerous role that the 20-year-old M'greet would be expected to fulfil.

One of M'greet's initial tasks at Ambarawa was to employ a *babu* to take over the care of baby Norman. Native servants were seen as a mark of social standing among the Dutch community, and even the lowliest army private or clerk within the colonial service would have had at least one servant, usually a woman, who acted as cook, cleaner and concubine combined. The *babu* who was employed to care for Norman would be expected to remain with the family for the length of their stay in the East Indies. These women would be given the sole care of the child, except in matters of schooling, and could be with a family for sixteen years or more. Despite the length and intensity of the relationship between the *babus* and the children in their care, they were afforded little respect. Their wages were minimal and working conditions often hard, caring for a European child night and day with little or no time off. At the end of their service, they would frequently be dismissed with no understanding or recognition of the relationship they had built up with the child in their care. As far as the family was concerned, they were considered to be disposable, with few if any Europeans even bothering to learn their name. Most were simply called after the child in their care; in this case '*babu* Norman'.

Their time at Ambarawa was an opportunity for M'greet to assimilate into colonial society. It was here that the two seemingly unrelated elements in the MacLeods' lives – M'greet's appearance and the lack of military permission for their marriage – became connected and introduced another source of friction in the marriage. Dutch colonial life in the East Indies was intensely and openly racist. The superiority of Europeans over the local native population was such an ingrained belief that it was not even commented upon. However, the Dutch East Indies was home to people from across the world, each of whom had their place in the racial hierarchy. One such group was the children of mixed marriages. The authorities were well aware of the existence of these children, and under the Dutch civil code of 1896 they were legally recognised as 'European' if they had one European parent. As Europeans, these mixed-race children were allowed to marry other Europeans. They were, nonetheless, despised by both Europeans and locals. It was against this background that M'greet arrived in the East Indies.

It is not known if MacLeod had explained colonial life to M'greet before she arrived in Ambarawa. As a soldier with his number of years of service in the East Indies, he could not have been unaware of the significance of these social elements. He had been sufficiently aware of the benefits of marriage to his career that he had answered M'greet's initial letter to the advert placed in *Nieuws van de Dag*. Had he warned her in advance of the potential gossip her appearance might have generated, especially when combined with the lapse in duty of gaining permission to marry in the first place? Would a whisper have circulated about her possibly being of mixed race? In the tight-knit Dutch community, reputation was all, and to start one's colonial life with even a hint of gossip was a distinct disadvantage.

MacLeod had received several replies to his advert, so why had he chosen M'greet? Here was a young woman who had no money, a bad family reputation and a poor personal reputation. If MacLeod was marrying to help his career, M'greet seems a strange choice. A demure blonde from a good family with a reputation for strict housekeeping and good morals was what MacLeod should have sought. The answer may well lie in two particular strands of MacLeod's personality. He had been in the service for over seventeen years and had been in the military since he was 16. Most of his early, and thus formative, sexual experiences would have been with prostitutes, and during his time in the East Indies with local native prostitutes who would have been olive-skinned and dark-haired. His initial attraction to M'greet may well have been due to the familiarity of her dark colouring to MacLeod's usual sexual partners. In addition, M'greet's early letters to MacLeod indicate that their relationship had been sexual even before their marriage, and that it was an intensely physical one. She wrote, 'You ask me if I'm longing to do crazy things? Well Johnie, rather ten times than only one. Go on, you know that in several weeks I shall be your wife. What luck that we both have the same ardent temperament.'[2]

These letters are, for their day, unbelievably frank, and the sexuality of the young M'greet would again remind MacLeod of his previous sexual encounters. A chaste, well brought up blonde Netherlander would never have written to MacLeod in such a manner. In addition to meeting his sexual needs, M'greet's background gave MacLeod the ability to manipulate and control. Did he deliberately choose a girl with a poor reputation to give himself a psychological advantage over his wife? Without the support of a good family and money with which to run away, M'greet was very much under MacLeod's control. This supposition may seem somewhat fanciful. However, given MacLeod's treatment of M'greet from the start of their time in the East Indies until several years after their eventual divorce, there seems little doubt that control and manipulation were extremely important to the soldier.

Whatever MacLeod's motivation in marrying M'greet, once back in the East Indies he continued the behaviour that he had started in the Netherlands so soon after their wedding, with excessive drinking and gambling, and occupying his evenings with the local girls. M'greet was frequently left alone. She seems to have made few friends among the other Dutch wives.

On 29 December 1897, MacLeod finally received his promotion to major and a new posting. He was to be in charge of the 1st Reserve Battalion at Fort Van Den Bosch at Tumpang just outside Malang.

This was a definite improvement in their social status, and may have indicated that the army had more or less forgiven MacLeod's marriage, although the black mark against his name was never fully erased. M'greet was pleased at the move. Malang was a much larger town, with a greater European population, and she had, after her initial difficulties, started to learn the intricacies of colonial life. In addition, she was pregnant again and Malang offered much more of the home comforts she would need.

The move to Malang seems to have been a time of relative harmony in the MacLeods' relationship. They had a better house, more money – as MacLeod had been given a pay rise – higher social status and M'greet was pregnant. In addition, at this time MacLeod seems to have acquired a *nyais* (concubine). This was a socially accepted practice among colonial society, and it was considered less distasteful and less insulting to a wife if a man kept a single concubine rather than visit the local prostitutes. MacLeod was also becoming a good father to young Norman. By the time of the boy's 1st birthday, MacLeod was settling into the life of a senior colonial. M'greet also seems to have been happier at this time. As the wife of the commander of the battalion, she held a high social standing in Malang, which may have compensated for any rumours that had followed her from Ambarawa, although she still failed to make any friends among the other colonial wives. MacLeod's change in behaviour presumably also contributed to her improved mood. In addition, M'greet seems to have discovered an interest in horse riding, a common pastime for wives. She proved to be an exceptional horsewoman, and this passion for horses would stay with her for the rest of her life. Alongside these European pursuits, however, M'greet took a particular interest in one local tradition.

Far removed from the formality of European society with its rules and protocol, the lives of the local people seemed an almost blissful existence. Of course M'greet did not see, or possibly did not want to see, the poverty, the prejudice, the ever-present oppression of the locals. She saw the flowers, she saw the smiling polite servants and she saw the dancing. The Dutch East Indies included people from different ethnic, cultural and religious backgrounds, all of whom contributed to the local forms of dancing. Most of the dances M'greet saw would have contained local folk elements, traces of courtly rituals and possibly sacred rites. These dances were characterised by controlled, deliberate, refined movements. The dancers were usually composed and serene, but could also be elemental and sensual. M'greet was entranced. The local dancers were as far removed from European society, and MacLeod, as could be imagined.

M'greet quickly discovered that the *babu*, the housemaids and the laundry maids all danced. Moreover, they danced at the back of the house, at the foot of the garden, in the local villages and in the jungle. Watching the maid dance in the garden, it was a short step to following her into a small jungle clearing and watching her dance in front of the ruins of an old temple. M'greet had found an escape from the boredom and arguments of her marriage. It was an escape that no other European in the area appeared to bother with, and it became her secret release from the stresses of her marriage and colonial life.

The phenomenon of a European aping local customs is as old as colonial exploration. The locals in the Dutch East Indies were used to their culture and customs being 'discovered' by Europeans, whether they be anthropologists from European universities, writers in search of the exotic or the bored wives of colonial officers. Their reaction to M'greet's interest in their dancing is not known. Neither is her level of actual engagement. M'greet had little opportunity to do much more than observe, ask the most basic of questions and possibly participate a little. She was, after all, the wife of a serving army officer with a young child. Whatever M'greet's level of understanding, her visits to watch and possibly engage in dancing eased the pressures between her and MacLeod.

On 2 May 1898, M'greet gave birth to a daughter, Jeanne Louise MacLeod. The little girl was named after MacLeod's sister back in Amsterdam, but soon became known as 'Non', a derivation of the local word 'nonna' (little miss). Another *babu* was employed and M'greet recovered quickly from the birth. That September she starred in a local play, *The Crusaders*, staged by the Dutch to celebrate Queen

Wilhelmina's coming of age. The evening would prove to be the high point of the year, and indeed of the MacLeod marriage, as things rapidly deteriorated from then on. After the play, M'greet took the children to the hill country, Gunung Semeru, for a short break away from the oppressive heat that was developing in advance of the rainy season. She spent three weeks on the cool slopes before returning to Malang. The weather had broken, the rainy season had set in and MacLeod had lost his previous relatively good humour. It is not known what triggered the change in his mood, but within a matter of days of M'greet's return he was accusing her of adultery, a charge she later admitted was true.[3] He was again drinking to excess, and although perfectly capable of undertaking his role as battalion commander, at home the alcohol led to increasingly bitter arguments. By the end of the year, M'greet was desperately unhappy and wrote to her father, 'I have no more beautiful illusions about the Indies because if you really look at it, it is not a nice country. It has without doubt many good things but also many nasty ones. If I could, I would come back tomorrow.'[4]

The ill-feeling between MacLeod and M'greet grew. Arguments were daily events and were becoming more intense. Money continued to be tight, despite MacLeod's increased salary. He was spending heavily on drink and gambling, as well as on his *nyais*. M'greet had the usual household expenses associated with two small children, but in addition had been increasing her spending on expensive clothing, jewellery and perfumes. This was common among European wives, partly as a release from the boredom of their existence and also as a way of showing one's social status. To be dressed in the latest European fashions was to state one's superiority over others, but buying and importing were costly. M'greet had a great love of luxury and had never really learned to manage a household budget.

MacLeod was frequently away from home, either on regimental business or visiting his *nyais*, leaving M'greet alone and bored. At the same time, he continued to accuse her of being unfaithful. By the beginning of 1899, the couple were barely speaking and their arguments were bordering on violence. M'greet took to wandering off to visit old temple ruins and watching, and frequently participating in, native dances. She increasingly left her house and walked to the temples to dance alone. She even started to adopt Malay dress. This, although no doubt merely a release for M'greet, gave rise to a degree of gossip. A European with a curiosity for native customs was one thing, but one did not adopt those customs. In addition, the wearing of local dress and jewellery accentuated M'greet's skin colour, adding fuel to the rumours about her racial background. These rumours angered MacLeod, who took to berating his young wife. She then retreated further from proper colonial conduct, and the cycle began again.

In March 1899, MacLeod received a new posting. He was to be sent to Medan as a garrison commander. Although this was a step up for his career, it was a move that was fraught with difficulties. Medan was a small settlement with few Europeans and even fewer European women. It was in Deli, a rural area with extreme racial tensions. The local native and European populations barely tolerated each other when necessary, but generally hated each other. People of mixed race were not tolerated; while pitied or disliked in Malang, they were loathed in Deli. M'greet, with her tendency to occasionally dress like a Malay, would be despised. The few Europeans in the East Indies would know as soon as they met and spoke with M'greet that she was fully Dutch, but even if they explained that to the local natives – and why would they – it would scarcely be believed.

The problems in Deli were long-standing. The European planters of the area continually battled with a difficult climate and terrain to produce crops, the price of which varied from year to year. A bad harvest could ruin an individual. In order to try to offset bad years, many planters paid their staff pitifully low wages. This was a direct consequence of a system put in place in the 1830s by the Dutch governor of the Indies, Johannes van der Bosch. Most of the islanders grew subsistence crops on their land, while the Europeans grew cash crops such as coffee, tea, tobacco and rubber. Bosch ordered the islanders to pay their taxes by working for a set period of time cultivating the cash crops. As this meant, in reality, that planters had workers who sometimes sometimes worked for nothing, there was no incentive to pay a reasonable wage for the rest of the year. Unscrupulous planters would lengthen the unpaid working day of illiterate islanders who had little time or energy left to cultivate their own crops. Subsequently, islanders found it marginally less exhausting to work for planters at low wages than on their own land, which they often gave up to planters in lieu of taxes owed. The loss of land and continual impoverishment of the islanders fostered resentment that frequently broke into violence. These outbreaks were then savagely countered by MacLeod and his troops. His job was dangerous, brutal and unforgiving. In order to restore a semblance of order in the area, he conducted an almost continuously violent guerrilla action. Leading rebellious locals were subject to summary field executions, while followers were savagely beaten before being forced to march home as an example to other villagers. It was exactly the sort of military service that tried the patience of even the most experienced and level-headed of army officers.

But there were other difficulties. M'greet was even more isolated in Medan than she had been in Ambarawa. There were fewer Europeans to socialise with, few shops and the buying of her European clothes, one of her few pleasures, would take longer and be even more expensive. The move to Medan was costly. MacLeod left first to take over his command and establish a house for the family. M'greet was left with closing up the house in Malang, which included selling most of the household items. New would be bought in Medan. This was cheaper and less inconvenient than transportation to the new house. However, between closing the house in Malang and getting passage on a ship to Medan, M'greet and the children needed somewhere to stay. MacLeod decided they should stay with Mr Van Rheede, the governor comptroller of the province, and his wife. This was arranged in a somewhat strange manner, with MacLeod asking Rheede, who was not a close friend, if his wife and children could stay for a week. The request was made only a matter of hours before M'greet and the children, accompanied by their *babus*, arrived.[5] Whatever the Rheedes thought of the manner of the request, M'greet and the children were made welcome until they heard from MacLeod regarding their passage to Medan.

On 17 March, MacLeod boarded the SS *Carpentier* and headed off to Medan. He wrote to M'greet eleven days later in strangely affectionate terms, sending his best regards to the Rheedes but without giving any details of when he was arranging for her and the children to join him. By 1 April, MacLeod had still not sent for M'greet, and matters were becoming embarrassing; she had run out of money and was desperately in need of new clothes for herself and the children. The situation was such that Mrs Van Rheedes wrote to her sister in Medan to ask her to approach MacLeod on M'greet's behalf and urge him to send some money.[6]

What followed was a bizarre correspondence from MacLeod to M'greet. He wrote to her on 11 April, stating, 'wire me if you need money'. He followed that on 24 April, saying, 'I will send you more [money] quickly when you ask for it.' On 2 May he wrote, 'The money is at your disposal, but you have only to ask.'[7] These letters also contained veiled accusations of infidelity on M'greet's part, entire paragraphs where MacLeod called her 'stupid' and 'puerile', and lengthy sections where he labelled her an unfit mother, writing at length about her shortcomings. It was 18 May before he finally sent her any cash.

MacLeod's letters, with their seemingly endless offers of money and the long delay before he arranged for his family's passage to join him, point to some sort of difficulty. The offers of money seem, on the surface, to be genuine, but were they? Why was he telling M'greet to ask for money via a wire, i.e. by open telegraph? This would have laid her open to ridicule. The surest way of finding gossip in the tight-knit European community was through the telegraph service, and M'greet would have been quickly mocked when her request for money from her husband became known. The matter of money was repeatedly mentioned, and yet the simple remedy of arranging for M'greet and the children to join MacLeod in Medan was not forthcoming. The charade was, presumably, a continuation of their daily arguments, but was such a correspondence necessary?

If M'greet was as stupid and puerile as MacLeod made out, was he writing because he was genuinely concerned about her mothering skills? If so, again, why not arrange for her and the children to join him as quickly as possible? Even if she was the incompetent mother that MacLeod implied, she had two *babus* caring for the children. Equally, M'greet's alleged infidelity was surely most easily curbed if she was in the same house as her husband.

Some unknown factor was preventing MacLeod from sending for M'greet and the children, and, knowing his history, it was most likely a shortage of money. The letters to M'greet gave the outside world the impression that his finances were in order. If he had money troubles again, and was either being chased by money lenders or seeking another loan, the lie would either buy him some time from his creditors or give more confidence to prospective new lenders. MacLeod, at this point, had a family, household staff and a *nyais* to maintain. He had a social standing to keep up which necessitated a certain amount of socialising, and all that cost money. This was on top of his heavy drinking and gambling and the expense of having moved between three different postings within twenty-one months.

The rest of the letters, the insults and the accusations – justified or not – show the state of the marriage. MacLeod was also trying to cope with a demanding job.

M'greet, unhappy and lonely, with few friends, sought solace in spending money on pretty dresses, flirting with other officers when the opportunity arose and dressing and dancing like a local. It could not last.

5

TRAGEDY

In June 1899, tragedy struck. When M'greet finally arrived in Medan, MacLeod was concerned about the health of Norman and Non. He felt the children looked unwell and arranged for them to be examined by the garrison doctor. Illness and disease were of great concern to colonials in the East Indies: the mortality rate for young children was high, despite the presence of European doctors. All of the usual childhood illnesses such as measles or scarlet fever were compounded by the climatic conditions; outbreaks of cholera and typhus were also common, as were tropical diseases such as malaria and dengue fever.

Whatever the children were suffering from, the doctor prescribed a special diet for Norman and medicines for both children. Within a week, the children seemed to improve. Despite this, the tension between MacLeod and M'greet had not changed, and in early June, MacLeod wrote to his sister about the deterioration:

> how am I to disentangle myself from such a floozy while keeping the children? … each day I give thanks to God that I have hastened their return. This vain and egotistical creature would have killed them, by not thinking of them … If I could deliver myself of this bitch I would be happy.[1]

This letter is an interesting one in its exposure of MacLeod's apparent concern for his children. However, as MacLeod had delayed the arrival of his children to Medan for over two months, he had hardly 'hastened their return'. Was this line written to assuage his own guilt? On 27 June, both children became seriously ill. They had a high fever and were being violently sick, vomiting black bile containing blood clots. Norman appeared to be more ill than Non, but despite this MacLeod took the boy out in his carriage for a short ride, perhaps hoping that some fresh air would benefit the child. Within an hour, the boy died and MacLeod brought him home. Non remained seriously ill.

The following day, at 5 p.m., Norman John MacLeod was buried; he was just 2 years and 4 months old. The burial was quick, as was the custom in the tropics, but the garrison doctor was concerned about the cause of death and wanted to perform an autopsy. He suspected poisoning. The garrison pharmacist examined some of Norman's vomit, but was not sure as to the cause of death. MacLeod categorically refused permission for an autopsy.[2] As MacLeod doted on his son, it is curious that he did not wish to determine the cause of death, especially as the garrison doctor had suspected poisoning.

On 4 July, MacLeod wrote to his sister Louise about his grief. The letter ends on a strange note: 'If I were dead myself and my wife had to continue his education, it would be all and badly turn out; also God alone knows if it is not for the best this way.'[3]

Why would the death of his son be 'for the best'? Was M'greet such a bad mother? Just what had killed little Norman? Had he been poisoned?

It is possible that the children suffered from and were being treated for syphilis. MacLeod had most likely had syphilis when he had met M'greet. He had been treated and the symptoms had gone into remission. Upon their marriage, MacLeod had passed the syphilis to M'greet and this was subsequently passed *in utero* to both children. The treatment for syphilis at that time was mercury. This had terrible side effects – including severe mouth ulcers, loss of teeth, neuropathies and kidney failure – and many patients died of mercurial poisoning rather than from the disease itself. If the patient survived, treatment would typically go on for years, with the disease occasionally going into remission before frequently flaring up again.

Although syphilis was recognised as a venereal disease, its exact means of transmission and the implications for marriage remained constrained under European notions around sexuality and decency. While MacLeod could have easily approached the army doctor for treatment for himself, for M'greet the implied slur on her character could well have ostracised her in the close-knit colonial society. There would still be a suspicion that she had contracted the disease due to promiscuity, especially as MacLeod was continually accusing her of infidelity.

For the children to have syphilis could only mean that it had been passed onto them by her. Not only, therefore, would M'greet be thought of as promiscuous, but she would also be labelled a bad mother. Treatment with mercury could have been given to the children discreetly to avoid a scandal affecting MacLeod's standing in the community. This, however, was problematic for two reasons.

Firstly, who would administer the mercury to the children? Medicines were usually given to children by the *babus*, or in the case of a more serious illness, by a qualified nurse. A European nurse might well gossip about the matter, while an illiterate and subservient *babu* merely told to give two or three drops of a medicine could not talk about what she did not know. However, the use of an illiterate local, while protecting reputations, ran the risk of the *babu* easily giving an incorrect dose, either accidentally, without realising the risk, or maliciously.

Secondly, mercury as a poison is extremely potent and its effects on small children can be extremely dangerous unless the dosage is calculated precisely. Even if the doctor had correctly calculated the dosages for Norman and Non, small children can, and frequently do, react badly to medicines. Although mercury can usually be tolerated in very small doses, there is no real safe level of exposure. This is especially true in children, as their bodies are still developing. The liver and kidneys which naturally filter out body toxins do not fully mature until an individual reaches their late teens or early twenties; the organs are obviously extremely immature in small children, leaving them particularly vulnerable. Norman and Non were so very young that, by 27 June, no matter how meticulously the doctor had calculated the dose and how carefully the *babus* had administered the medicines, the children would probably have absorbed so much mercury since the treatment began that an adverse reaction was likely.

MacLeod would have been aware of the dangers of mercury. His remark that it was 'for the best' may also indicate an understanding that untreated long-term syphilis can cause dementia and blindness. In addition, as MacLeod himself knew, long-term treatment with mercury was extremely unpleasant. Knowing what his son potentially faced, MacLeod may well have considered Norman's death as 'for the best'.

It has been suggested by some that the children were deliberately poisoned by their *babu* as revenge for MacLeod's brutal treatment of a local who was a friend or possibly lover of one of the *babus*. While this is not outside the realms of possibility, there are several reasons why this theory may be discounted. Firstly, it relied on the *babu* poisoning the children, whom she loved and cared for, rather than MacLeod himself. Secondly, it relied on both Norman and Non's *babus* being involved in the plot, given the intimacy of their duties and living quarters. It also required at least one of them to find or purchase poison in a town in which they had only been resident for a couple of weeks, and to have had the time to do so while carrying out their household duties.

The murder of a white person by a native with the use of poison was a common motif in the literature of the day. However, most murders in the East Indies were either a case of white colonials killing natives, fights between men in bars or the domestic murder of wives by husbands. Between 1894 and 1899, fifteen Europeans and thirteen natives were treated for poisoning, almost all by accident. None of them was a child.[4] Murder by poison remained largely in the mind of the romantic novelist.

A murder and attempted murder by a native on a Dutch family, especially of children, would have resulted in a full-scale official inquiry. If the *babu* had been suspected in any way, she would have been instantly arrested. If the *babu* had attempted to harm the children, any mercury found in Norman's body would point to poisoning by a native and MacLeod's syphilis would have remained unknown, with his reputation intact. So if deliberate poisoning was suspected, MacLeod had nothing to fear from an autopsy, and yet despite Norman being his 'beloved son', he refused to allow the autopsy to be performed.

There was no official investigation into Norman's death and there was no newspaper speculation. The death notice simply read, 'Our darling NORMAN JOHN MACLEOD passed away this night. R. MACLEOD M.G. MACLEOD-ZELLE'.

Death from an unknown childhood illness was a convenient if somewhat obvious excuse for Norman's death; child mortality rates in the East Indies were around 50 per cent at the time. The medical records could then be discreetly filed away rather than expose MacLeod's syphilis, as well as M'greet's syphilis and possible adultery and bad motherhood. Two other pieces of supporting evidence exist for the theory that Norman's death was due to mercury poisoning. Firstly, there is the letter written by M'greet to her father at the end of her marriage, where she clearly states that MacLeod had syphilis when he married her.[5] Although this letter was written after the marriage had broken down, and could simply have been an accusation by an angry ex-wife, it would explain MacLeod's failure to seek permission to marry in the first place, knowing it would be denied. M'greet alludes to this in the letter to her father when she writes of the regimental doctors stating that MacLeod was not fit to be married.[6] The second piece of evidence for the syphilis theory comes from Norman's sister. Non died in 1919, at the age of only 21, from a cerebral haemorrhage, an unusual cause of death for a young woman.[7] Unexpected cerebral haemorrhage is a common symptom of congenital syphilis.

Whatever the cause, on 27 July M'greet wrote to her father, 'my lovely little Norman has died and I am not in a state to write about it'.[8]

Curiously, M'greet also wrote that on 29 December the couple were intending to ask for an army pension and were then planning to come back to the Netherlands. This letter was written just days after MacLeod was given another new posting. On 24 July, he was informed that he was being posted to Banjoe Biroe near Semarang.[9] Banjoe Biroe was a small fishing settlement and was not an area in need of a senior officer of MacLeod's rank. The posting was, in effect, a demotion, but what could have triggered this sudden change in his standing in the colonial service? There is no evidence of any lack of duty or disapproval of MacLeod's conduct as the garrison commander in the previous months. No complaints were lodged against him. Were there rumours about the cause of Norman's death? Had the refusal to allow an autopsy triggered the interest of his senior officers? MacLeod's medical condition would have been known to his superiors, as syphilis was a common enough event among the service. However, as with most aspects of European social convention, appearance was all, while reality was hypocritically ignored. Officers were known to take *nyais*, as long as it was done discreetly and their wives remained faithful. A man might have syphilis and be treated by the garrison doctor, but no public acknowledgement of the disease was allowed. To infect one's own wife and child, however, would have been scandalous. Was MacLeod's new posting a way of the colonial service removing a potential embarrassment?

Whatever the reason for the posting, within three days of being notified, MacLeod decided to leave the service as soon as he was able. By the following December, he knew he would be able to apply for a pension and quit the service. In September 1899, MacLeod, M'greet and Non left for Batavia on the SS *Riebeck* at the start of their journey to Banjoe Biroe.

Norman's had devastated the couple, and the marriage broke down completely. Each blamed the other for the death of the child. From their arrival at Banjoe Biroe, the arguments, which had previously been heated, frequently descended into violence. M'greet wrote to her father that MacLeod was frequently 'looking for a brawl' or hitting her with his 'cat-o-nine-tail'. She writes of her desire for a divorce and of her hopes to return to the Netherlands and possibly to study drama.[10] The letter was written early in December 1899. As M'greet knew that she and MacLeod were only some three weeks from being able to apply for a pension to allow them to return home, the letter does not seem to be an exaggerated plea for sympathy but more a reflection of the reality of her situation. While MacLeod descended into using violence against M'greet, this was not uncommon at the time. Although husbands were expected to show restraint, wives were also expected to behave in such a manner as to not 'provoke the violence' in the first place. Given the personalities of MacLeod and M'greet, it is likely that neither showed much control. With the grief, loss and guilt they both must have felt over Norman's death, goading each other into physical arguments may have been commonplace. In the same letter that contained M'greet's complaints against MacLeod, she writes of her irritation at her lack of good clothes and of the young lieutenants around her who were so amorous.[11]

For every letter of complaint that M'greet wrote to her family, so MacLeod wrote to his, detailing M'greet's faults at great length: she was 'scum' and he was desperate to keep Non away from M'greet's 'filthy influence'.[12] Interestingly, MacLeod claimed that he offered M'greet a divorce but she refused, stating she did not want to lose out on her widow's pension. The letters continued, with complaints of violence and jealousy from M'greet and accusations of adultery and lack of care of Non from MacLeod. Although he stated he had offered a divorce, MacLeod also wrote that he was so jealous of the attention she received from other officers he wanted to kill her.

By the beginning of 1900, both parties loathed each other. M'greet accused MacLeod of having ruined her life by burying her in the East Indies, her own impetuous decision to marry within three months of their meeting and excitement at the initial posting having been conveniently forgotten. He accused her of having ruined his career with her promiscuous behaviour, ignoring his own drinking, gambling, debts and violent behaviour.

In March 1900, M'greet became ill with typhoid. She quickly recovered, but two letters written about this period give a further insight into the state of the marriage. MacLeod wrote to his cousin to complain about having to pay for milk for M'greet and of the fact that he had to take care of Non, despite the presence of the child's *babu*.[13] The doctor who treated M'greet, Dr Roelfsema, wrote that her behaviour was 'absolutely correct, notwithstanding the many rude insults she had to endure in public from her husband'.[14]

The marriage stumbled on. He was still a serving officer and could not escape until his discharge came through; she had no money and was equally trapped. They could only try to wait it out. Finally, on 2 October 1900, MacLeod received his discharge from the service. This was not quite the escape that both had hoped it would be. Early in November, MacLeod was notified that his pension would be 2,800 guilders per annum; his salary had been 9,600. Money, which had been contentious throughout their marriage, now became even more acute. Previously, MacLeod had barely been able to support himself, his gambling habit, his *nyais* and his family on 9,600 guilders in the East Indies, where the cost of living was relatively cheap. He now had to survive on an income under 30 per cent of what he was used to, and without the help of the reduced service accommodation in which they had lived. If he wished to return home to the Netherlands, he then had the additional costs of paying his family's passage and the increased cost of living in Europe. He had several debts in the East Indies which remained outstanding, as did the debt to De heer Calisch, and possibly others, back in the Netherlands.

Immediately upon leaving the service, MacLeod moved the family to the small village of Sindanglaja. The village was an inexpensive one for a variety of reasons, not least of which was its remoteness from other areas and Europeans. The expense of entertaining and socialising was thus removed, giving the family a degree of breathing space. While this suited MacLeod financially and gave him time to think about his future, the isolation frustrated M'greet and she started writing a series of letters to her father and, interestingly, her mother-in-law, complaining about how unhappy she was.

Before long, the arguments and violence were renewed. MacLeod was anxiously trying to sort his finances; M'greet was unhappy and wanted to go home to the Netherlands. Dr Roelfsema noted the ever-increasing level of bitterness between the two.[15] Not only that, he noted that MacLeod was opening and reading M'greet's outgoing letters.[16]

On 27 May 1901, M'greet wrote to her father, complaining of MacLeod's continued ill-treatment of her and pleading for help. This letter went further than before in its complaints and stated that she genuinely thought her life to be in danger. Violence had become an almost daily event, far in excess of anything that was tolerated even in the homes of army officers. M'greet wrote to her father again in July; despairing of her situation, she stated, 'If I stay here another year, I think I will be dead or mad.'[17]

The letters continued. On 3 August, she wrote another letter to her father. It was in this letter that she revealed MacLeod's medical restriction on marriage. She also revealed that she had booked her passage to the Netherlands, but needed MacLeod's permission to leave and to take Non with her. Adamant that she would not leave her child behind, she remained trapped. Moreover, she wrote that MacLeod 'has an enormous amount of debt that is really scandalous, debts from many years, still from Aceh and before that.'[18]

While caution must, of course, be exercised in the interpretation of any of M'greet's letters, it is curious to note that she claimed she had her passage. Had MacLeod booked this for her? Was he happy for her to leave, so long as she left her daughter behind? Or had she somehow managed to acquire the money to buy her own passage but not yet that for Non? The confusion over her passage to the Netherlands lends an air of authenticity to the letter. The issue of MacLeod's debts was, as Ardum's had previously been, both a practical matter of money and a social matter of honour. MacLeod's debts would have been, hypocritically, tolerated by the army so long as they remained unknown to the general public. When he became a civilian member of the expat community, they became a matter of shame and scandal. M'greet had chosen a husband who could not provide for his family, as her mother had done before her.

Her father had responded instantly to M'greet's letter of 27 May, although there was, of course, a delay before his reply arrived by ship from the Netherlands. On 28 June, he wrote to M'greet to inform her of his actions in writing to the Honourable Officer of Justice of Batavia in order to secure her safety. Zelle wrote to the Officer of Justice outlining his fears for M'greet's safety and asking the Officer to find a lawyer for M'greet to allow her to initiate divorce proceedings. He concluded, 'At the same time I also beg you to take the necessary steps to avoid any ill-treatment by Major MacLeod so my daughter will be protected against future abuse.'[19]

Zelle wrote to M'greet, advising her to seek a legal separation, taking care to ensure she obtained her full rights as to a portion of MacLeod's pension. He concluded that letter by stating:

> So dear M'greet, angel of my life, have courage, be wise and pious; always be careful that your life is irreproachable and then everything will go well; at the same time, be very wary and prudent; take care about everything so that no one can do wrong to you or your child. Then come as soon as possible back to your father.[20]

It is notable that both letters were sent to the Honourable Officer of Justice. Zelle states in his letter to the Officer that were he to send M'greet's letter directly to her, then MacLeod would destroy it or ill-treat his daughter as a consequence.[21] She had obviously discovered that MacLeod was reading her letters and had managed somehow to write to her father letting him know this.

What is even more notable is the letters' content. Zelle was instructing his daughter to get a '*separation subsidair*', a legal separation which would have protected her interests and ensured she received financial support from MacLeod for herself and Non. While separation and divorce were not unknown among the Dutch community in the early twentieth century, it was still the social taboo it had been in the nineteenth century and was thus a huge step for M'greet to take. The law demanded a high level of proof of ill-treatment or immoral behaviour, and most courts still favoured the husband over the wife.

There was no guarantee that during any legal proceedings MacLeod would not challenge M'greet on her alleged infidelity. Accusation and counter-accusation would be played out in open court, and whatever the outcome and whoever 'won' the case, both parties would be publicly humiliated and their reputations damaged. Just as in previous centuries, most women in the Netherlands, and indeed across Europe, preferred to come to an understanding with their husbands whereby the couple lived separate lives while publicly remaining together. However, being in the East Indies with nowhere to go and with little money between them, it is hardly possible that such an arrangement could have been an option. Given the depths to which the marriage had sunk, it is unlikely that either party would have allowed the other an easy option. There was also no guarantee that given MacLeod's constant accusations of M'greet's infidelity, that she would have received custody of Non in any legal separation. It may be that which stopped her from following the legal route.

While she received a degree of protection from the Officer of Justice, MacLeod moderated his behaviour towards her. However, during this time his true feelings were revealed in a further letter to his sister, in which he wrote, 'to ruin my reputation and to serve for her some years in prison no, not so bad'.[22]

This may, of course, merely be the words of an angry man venting his frustration at the ongoing situation and possible humiliation at the intrusion of the Officer of Justice into his private life. Interestingly, however, Zelle replied to M'greet's August letter and stated that, 'I have spoken to the sister of MacLeod and she knows of everything ... The first day of August was to be, with her connivance, the day that you have to die?'[23]

The situation does appear to have calmed sufficiently after the intervention of the Officer of Justice for MacLeod and M'greet to start talking about their various options. Over the following months, they started to make plans for their return to the Netherlands. He stated that due to their financial situation, they would have to live with his sister Louise. Although M'greet did not wish to stay with Louise, she had little other option; it was, at least, a return home. The plans for their return allowed them to at least tolerate each other until they finally started on their journey home. On 19 March 1902, they boarded the SS *Koningin Wilhelmina* bound for Amsterdam.

On their arrival, the MacLeods moved in with Louise and her family. However, despite MacLeod's previous insistence that they had to stay there for financial reasons, they moved out just two weeks later and took an apartment at 188 Van Breestraat. They had barely settled into their new home when several of MacLeod's creditors, including De heer Calisch, started to visit the apartment to demand repayment of the money owed to them. Despite MacLeod's reduced pension and continued expenses, he had not stopped drinking or gambling; he could not repay his debts. Several creditors initiated legal action against him. The couple spent a miserable summer dodging creditors and legal officers while fighting with each other.

On 26 August, MacLeod took Non out with him on a short walk to the post office. Non had been ill the day before and Macleod said that some fresh air would be good for the little girl. By the early evening they had not returned, and M'greet contacted the police and reported them missing. MacLeod had left M'greet – and his creditors and their legal action – and had taken Non with him to the town of Velp to live with some friends. M'greet journeyed to Arnhem to stay with MacLeod's cousin, Madame A. Goodvriend, née Baroness de Sweerts Landas. M'greet had managed to strike up something of a friendship with Madame Goodvriend while still in the East Indies. Madame Goodvriend seemed well aware of MacLeod's behaviour and was sympathetic to M'greet.

On the morning of 27 August, M'greet filed for divorce. The papers were lodged at the court of Amsterdam by her lawyer, De heer Edward Philips. The papers list fourteen grievances against MacLeod. These include:

> she was beaten almost daily and spat at in the face … he gave her a beating
> with a walking stick so that the maidservant had to come between them …
> he ran after her with his slipper to beat her so that one of the servants had to

come between them … [he] took their only child of only 4 years old … named Louise Jeanne, with him to Velp.[24]

M'greet filed for the divorce on the condition that she received custody of Non and a monthly maintenance payment of 100 guilders from MacLeod.

On 28 August, Zelle met with MacLeod. What was said at the meeting is not known, although Zelle later claimed that MacLeod had asked him for 2,000 guilders or he would ruin M'greet's reputation.[25] Zelle did not have 2,000 guilders, and MacLeod did not contest the legal action. On 29 August 1902, Rudolf MacLeod and Margaretha Geertruida MacLeod née Zelle were given a legal separation, with all of M'greet's terms and conditions agreed upon. The final divorce was to be granted in 1906.

On the same day, despite being legally responsible for M'greet and Non's financial support, MacLeod placed a public notice in two local newspapers:

WARNING.

Do not furnish credit or merchandise to Mme. MacLeod, née Zelle, because the undersigned has resigned all responsibility for her. (R. MacLeod).[26]

This was prominently featured in the *Nieuws van de Dag* and *De Arnhem Täglich* (*The Arnhem Daily*). At the same time, MacLeod wrote to as many friends, acquaintances and relatives as he had in order to blacken M'greet's name. He also wrote to some friends back in the East Indies, telling them that she had left him but that he vowed to always care for her and Non.[27] On 2 September, M'greet and Non moved to a small boarding house in Worth-Rheden near Arnhem and M'greet started to look for work. She wrote to her father about her shame at MacLeod's notice in the papers:

[M]y situation has been made impossible by that advertisement. I dare not put my name anywhere. It ran in big letters also in the *Arnhem Daily*; shame, shame! ... it might be more judicious to go to Brussels or Wiesbaden to live. All of the Netherlands knows my name and he has insulted me so! ... I have placed a newspaper advertisement to do housekeeping for a lady who lives on her own.[28]

The original settlement of the courts had been that MacLeod should pay M'greet 100 guilders every month. On 10 September, MacLeod convinced the courts of his inability to pay such a sum, and it was reduced to fifty guilders. In addition, the court ruled that his pension could not be garnished in order to pay M'greet. The money had to come from elsewhere. The fifty guilders due for the month of September was not paid. When M'greet was notified of the court ruling, she wrote to her father on 12 September, 'The court awarded me and my child 1,200 guilders a year, and now he does not want to pay ... If nobody helps me, I must return [to MacLeod] out of poverty. I cannot go back to let him beat me and treat me in such an unworthy manner.'[29]

Zelle sent M'greet twenty-five guilders, but it was merely a stopgap and a more permanent solution had to be found. Then on 13 October, MacLeod wrote to Zelle asking to see him. The meeting was brief; MacLeod was adamant that he would not pay what he owed because he had no money. Although no progress was made with the money, Zelle suggested that Non could be sent to live with friends of MacLeod in Velp. Although not ideal, the child would at least have a secure home with Captain van Mourik and his family. She would receive proper food, clothing and schooling, and both MacLeod and M'greet could visit to see her. Initially nothing came of this suggestion, as shortly after the meeting MacLeod wrote to M'greet through Mourik and offered a reconciliation. It was, however, an offer based on a threat.

When the court had granted M'greet custody, MacLeod had been furious. He had not changed his opinion that his wife was a bad moral influence on his daughter. Despite his pleas of poverty, he had hired two private detectives to watch M'greet and report back to him on her behaviour. The detectives duly followed her and reported back to MacLeod that she had been entertaining gentlemen callers in *maisons de rendezvous*. These were houses where ladies and gentlemen could meet for discreet sexual liaisons, and although not strictly illegal, were considered totally scandalous. M'greet was a breath away from working as a full-time prostitute.

When MacLeod wrote to her suggesting a reconciliation, he made it clear that he knew all about her activities. M'greet was not stupid. Despite the hypocrisy of the fact that MacLeod was, by that time, in a sexual relationship with another woman, M'greet knew that if her behaviour became known she would be branded an unfit mother, and would lose custody of Non and any financial support from MacLeod. She had no choice. In order to keep her daughter, she had to return to her husband. In November 1902, the MacLeod family moved into a small apartment on the Ruyterkade in Amsterdam.

What happened behind the closed doors on the Ruyterkade is not known, but within weeks – days possibly – the relationship had broken down. This time, however, MacLeod held all the cards. He had proof of his wife's activities as a 'prostitute', with which he could take Non away from her in an instant. M'greet, after having been granted a legal separation by the courts on the grounds of MacLeod's violent behaviour, had voluntarily returned to her husband. Her few friends and family, after all her pleas for help, cooled in their opinion of her. Whatever went on in the MacLeod home, M'greet agreed to leave and, apparently, never see Non again.

In early 1903, she arrived in Paris and changed her name to Lady Gresha MacLeod.

6

THE DANCER EMERGES

The problem that M'greet had was how to furnish herself with an income. She was 27 years old with no money, no training and no family support to speak of. She was from a middle-class background but with an upper-class outlook, a woman who had been used to having servants in the East. This rendered her incapable of contemplating, much less undertaking, working-class jobs such as in a laundry or in service. The middle-class professions required training, of which she had none, and most barred women from their ranks. Her only option was to work in the arts, but this too required training and a modicum of talent. Her options were limited. For the first few weeks she was in Paris she tried to become an artist's model. However, she had no contacts, no understanding of the art world and how it functioned, and was competing in a crowded market against other women who were attempting the same, many younger and prettier.

Her modelling endeavours were unsuccessful, and she was forced to get by as a prostitute. Unfortunately, MacLeod heard what M'greet was up to and threatened to have her arrested and possibly even sent to a state institute for 'incorrigibles'.[1] At that time it was perfectly possible for a husband to have a wife institutionalised as criminally insane. M'greet had a husband, a child and a home, but had left all that to prostitute herself in Paris; what sane woman would do that? The average bourgeois doctor and judge would have had her institutionalised without question. She had left MacLeod and he had Non, whom M'greet had, allegedly, agreed never to see again. So why was MacLeod bothered about what she was doing? It cannot be known for certain, but it is likely that her use of the title 'Lady MacLeod' angered him. MacLeod was proud of his Scottish ancestry; he was proud of his name and would fight to retain its honour.

In addition, there is no evidence that he was anything other than a loving father to Non. A mother, unfortunately mad but locked away, was a tragedy for his daughter, but would not severely harm her chances of a good marriage in later years. A mother running round Paris earning her money as a prostitute was a disgrace, and a source of shame and scandal that could be attached to Non. It is possible that the potential scandal that could have followed Non into her adult life drove MacLeod to make his threats to M'greet.

MacLeod need not have worried, however, as M'greet was finding matters to be less than favourable in Paris. Prostitution is not an easy profession, and again M'greet was competing against younger, prettier girls whose French was flawless and whose bodies had not borne two children. After several miserable months in Paris, she wrote to one of MacLeod's uncles begging for help. General Edward MacLeod was another of the retired military men in the MacLeod family. He lived a relatively quiet life in Nijmegen in the province of Gelderland. A generous and honourable man, he was unaware of how M'greet was living in Paris and, unwilling to see a lady in distress, opened his home to her. M'greet moved in with General MacLeod and his wife in the early autumn of 1903.

It is noticeable that M'greet did not write to Madame Goodvriend. One of the problems M'greet constantly faced was that any sympathy she gained from the MacLeod family was always short-lived. Initially shocked by M'greet's tales of MacLeod's behaviour, the family would rally round and offer help. MacLeod would then appear, tell his version of events, and his family always sided with him. The only point in her favour was that the MacLeod family was large and rarely spoke to each other. This lack of contact between them meant that there were several relatives upon whom she could call for help before she exhausted the family's sympathy.

Her stay with the general, therefore, would not last forever. M'greet's initial begging letter and her conversations on arrival in Nijmegen, describing MacLeod's treatment of her, scandalised the good general. After she had been in residence for a few months, General MacLeod, having heard all of M'greet's accusations, wrote to his nephew to upbraid him. MacLeod promptly wrote back to his uncle with his version of events, adding for good measure how she had been disgracing the family name. M'greet was politely but firmly told to leave as soon as she was able. She sat out the worst of the winter in Nijmegen, knowing she had to leave and determined to try her luck again in France. In the spring of 1904, she moved once more to Paris.

This second attempt was more successful than the first, as she managed to secure a job as a rider in Ernst Molier's equestrian circus. The *Cirque Molier* had been established by Molier in 1880 as an extension to his riding school in the Rue Bénouville. It featured trick riding displays by skilled riders, but also had a special novelty section given over to amateur riders to show off their riding prowess. M'greet was an excellent horsewoman, and impressed Molier gaining regular employment. The horse-riding act gave her some breathing space with which to contemplate her future. After a few conversations with Molier about her experiences in the East Indies, he advised her to look for dancing work. Horse-riding was not overly lucrative, except for the top professional riders. However, Orientalism was all the rage in Paris, indeed across Europe, and M'greet's knowledge of Eastern dance gave her a considerable advantage over many others. Molier, who had several high-class contacts, agreed to introduce M'greet to some of these to further a possible career.

While Molier was correct that Orientalism was a fad that would last for some time, it is unlikely that he was aware of M'greet's limited knowledge and skill in Eastern dance. M'greet was not daunted by this and capitalised on the public's interest but lack of knowledge of the Orient. M'greet may not have been the youngest or the most talented dancer in Paris, but she had lived in the East Indies for some time and could use that knowledge to great advantage. She presented the world with the image of 'sacred' Eastern dance. Playing to every European stereotype about the Indies and the Orient, she created an illusion that masked her inabilities as a dancer.

Molier had been true to his word and introduced M'greet to Madame Kiréevsky. A society hostess in Paris, Kiréevsky was a patron of the arts, which included the new, the exciting and the avant-garde. Lady MacLeod and her sacred Indies dancing fitted the bill exactly. She was booked to perform at a private performance at Kiréevsky's elegant Parisian salon. M'greet was an unknown in the Parisian scene at that time, and took advantage of her obscurity to spin several different tales about who she was and where she came from. She allowed people to presume she was Javanese, or, at the very least, of Eastern descent. Her husband – who was, according to M'greet, conveniently dead – had been a Scottish soldier. It was an excellent subterfuge which added to the mystery of her dance.

Her first performance at Kiréevsky's salon was witnessed by Francis Keyzner, Paris correspondent for London society magazine *The King*. Keyzner's review of M'greet's performance, which appeared in *The King* on 4 February 1905, introduced the world to Mata Hari, the exotic dancer, although she was at that time still using the name Lady MacLeod. Keyner's review was extremely influential and set the tone for almost all of the subsequent press M'greet would receive, up to and including her execution. He wrote:

> Vague rumours had reached me of a woman from the Far East, a native of Java, wife of an officer, who had come to Europe laden with perfumes and jewels, to introduce some of the richness of the Oriental colour and life into the satiated society of European cities, of veils encircling and discarded, of the development of passion as the fruits of the soil, of a burst of fresh, free life,

of Nature in all its strength untrammelled by civilisation ... Her olive skin
blended with the curious jewels in the dead gold setting. A casque of worked
gold upon her dark hair — an authentic Eastern head-dress; a breast plate of
similar workmanship beneath the arms. Above a transparent white robe, a quant
clasp held a scarf around the hips, the ends falling to the feet in front. She was
enshrouded in various veils of delicate hues, symbolising beauty, youth, love,
chastity, voluptuousness and passion ... Lady MacLeod is Venus.[2]

M'greet's performance caused an instant sensation across Paris;
everyone was talking about the mysterious dancer from the East.
One of those who heard about the latest Paris sensation was Émile
Étienne Guimet, the millionaire industrialist from Lyon. Guimet
had travelled extensively across the East Indies, and in 1876 was
commissioned by the Minister of Public Instruction to study
the religions of the Far East. On his return to France in 1879,
Guimet had opened a small museum in Lyon where he could
display those objects he had acquired during his travels. The extent
and importance of his collection was such that the museum was
transferred to state control, although Guimet retained his position
as director, and it was rehoused in Paris in 1889 in the Place d'Iéna
as the *Musée National des Arts Asiatiques* (*Musée Guimet*). Guimet
realised the impact Lady MacLeod would have if she performed in
the museum.

He does not appear to have seen her dance before he booked
her to perform on 13 March 1905, so it is unclear if he knew how
unauthentic her dancing was. One change before the performance,
possibly to enhance her authenticity, was a new name. Lady
MacLeod was dropped and she decided to become Mata Hari. The
name change was certainly a shrewd move, blurring the lines even
more about her origins. Mata Hari is a Malay phrase meaning 'sun'
or 'eye of the day'. It was a name that M'greet had talked about
using back in 1897 or 1898, when she had first thought of a dancing
career. In Padang in Sumatra, one of the local Masonic lodges was
called Lodge Mata Hari, and it may be that was where M'greet
first saw the name, or she may have heard it used by some of the

locals during her time in the East Indies. Wherever it was found, it was an infinitely better stage name than Lady MacLeod. It had the added bonus of having no connection to her estranged husband. He could no longer threaten legal action over the scandalous use of the family name.

When M'greet started working as a female rider and then as an exotic dancer, MacLeod appears to have stopped taking an interest in her. It may be that dancing, although often thought of as only one step removed from prostitution, was not actual prostitution, and as such did not slander the family name. Or it may be that exotic dancing, in other words dancing naked in public was so scandalous that MacLeod wanted to distance himself from M'greet as far as possible. He was no doubt grateful for the name change to Mata Hari. In either event, his active interest in M'greet faded and it seemed as if the couple would no longer have any need for contact, except in the case of Non. However, MacLeod's interest had not entirely gone, and he was to keep a distant, if watchful, eye out for the activities of his estranged wife for some time. These activities would prove useful to MacLeod in the couple's final divorce hearing in 1906.

On 13 March 1905, however, M'greet was apparently free of her husband's influence and becoming the sensation of the year. Guimet decided to capitalise as much as possible on the fashionable interest in the Orient. He decided to use the library of the *Musée National des Arts Asiatiques* for M'greet's performance. The room was packed with heavily scented flowers, and vines were wound round columns. A bronze of a dancing *Shiva* from the eleventh century was placed centrally at the back wall, surrounded by candles. A small orchestra played music with Javanese and Indian overtones. The stage was set, and Guimet stepped into the centre of the room to introduce Mata Hari.

Guimet had taken time to select his audience for the night. How much of the evening was about launching Mata Hari onto the world stage, how much was about promoting 'his' museum and indeed how much was about promoting Guimet, is unclear. The audience chosen to attend was certainly not one entirely devoted to dance, nor indeed merely attending in order to see the latest Paris novelty. Six hundred noted individuals were invited to witness Mata Hari's performance. These included artists, musicians, writers, intellectuals, officers, ministers, diplomats, bankers and industrialists. These were the sorts of individuals who were used to the formality of ballet and were aware of the new movements in Expressionist dance. They also knew about, although they might not publicly admit to having ever seen, the can-can dancers at the Moulin Rouge, but Mata Hari was something new again. Her dancing was not the elegant formality of ballet, and yet it was elegant. Her movements were not the embodied emotions of Expressionism, and yet they were highly emotional. She did not perform the wild openly sexual dancing of the Moulin Rouge, and yet she was sexual. Audiences were left transfixed with what they saw.

Much of her performance relied on her appearance. She accentuated her dark looks with multiple layers of translucent veils, which were shed during the dance to reveal an, apparently, almost nude figure wreathed in a gold and jewelled headdress and breastplate. M'greet actually never danced naked, but wore a body stocking and breastplate. The scandal of apparent nudity drew in the audience, and the authorities. While Mata Hari retained the illusion of naked flesh, she relieved the minds of her audience by claiming a spirituality and sacredness for her dances that negated any charges of indecency.

The dance on 13 March set the tone for the rest of M'greet's dancing career. Using the techniques she had learnt in the East Indies of body movement and arm gestures, she incorporated them into a dance of her own devising. She used all of the stereotypes of 'Oriental' exoticism; lust, passion, Eastern religion, sacred practices. She mimicked the movements of the dancing *Shiva*, mysterious and a little frightening.

The reviews were overwhelmingly positive. *Parisian Life* wrote of her as 'Mata Hari, the Indian dancer, voluptuous and tragic, who dances naked in the latest salons'.[3] *Le Gaulois* stated she was 'feline, extremely feminine, majestically tragic, the thousand curves and movements of her body trembling in a thousand rhythms'.[4] Lepage of Éclair wrote that Mata Hari was, 'slender and supple like the sacred serpents balanced erect by snake charmers'.[5] Henri Ferrare wrote in *La Press*, 'she coils around her waist an opaque and gleaming belt, throws around her hips transparent material marked with the emblem of the divine bird'.[6]

Whatever the qualifications of the reviewers on the matter of dance, it is obvious that all of them had been entranced by Mata Hari's performance. The audience in the *Musée National des Arts Asiatiques* were equally enthralled, and their gossip ensured that within days all Paris was talking about Mata Hari.

Paris at the beginning of the twentieth century was the leading city of Europe for sensation and the latest fashion. *La Belle Époque* was at its height when Mata Hari appeared on the scene. Chic society embraced every new novelty. At the turn of the century, *L'Exposition universelle* took place at the *Champ de Mars* and attracted fifty million visitors. The world's largest Ferris wheel, *Le Grande Roue de Paris*, towered 100 metres above the city, carrying 1,600 passengers into the sky in forty cars, and on the ground the world's first escalator was on display. Modern art was blossoming, and art nouveau startled and amazed all who viewed it. The works of Gauguin – with their Tahitian colours and exotic, sensual moods – had been influencing much in Parisian society for several years, increasing interest in the exotic.

Mata Hari, the exotic dancer, arrived at just the right time. True students of dance, although possibly ignorant of the realities of Indonesian dance, nevertheless quickly became aware of M'greet's lack of artistic technique. Those who were knowledgeable about the East Indies and their culture also soon saw through the illusion. However, for the casual sensation-seeker, Mata Hari struck just the right note. Her dancing was just 'Eastern' enough to be interesting, without being so authentic as to be impenetrable. Her nudity was not the salacious titillation of the can-can but the primitive nakedness of sacred ritual. Her audience may well have realised that much of what they saw was an illusion, but it was an illusion that entranced and entertained.

Mata Hari enhanced the fantasy at every turn, inventing herself as the daughter of an Oriental potentate and the child of a temple dancer. Both audience and performer entered into the fantasy, neither taking the fairy tale too seriously.

So in the spring of 1905, Margaretha Geertruida Zelle, the 28-year-old estranged wife of an ex-army officer and mother of two children, became Mata Hari, a professional dancer. Her success was instant. She danced in elegant salons and in theatres. Baron Henri de Rothschild invited her to dance in his salon and found her charming. She danced in the salon of Gaston du Menier, who thought her enchanting. The infamous Natalie Barney booked Mata Hari to appear at her scandalous lesbian parties as Lady Godiva riding a white horse. Photographs of her in exotic costumes were bought and sold across Europe. Newspapers and society magazines vied to produce the latest reviews of her dancing. In all this, M'greet made the most of her celebrity. She promenaded along the Bois de Boulogne wearing the latest fashion; she shopped in Les Galeries Lafayette. She dined in the most fashionable restaurants in town, to see and be seen.

Her career was certainly building. By the late spring of 1906, M'greet and lawyer Edouard Clunet were lovers, although as far as M'greet was concerned, this does not appear to have been an exclusive relationship. Clunet was considerably older and had lived in Paris for many years. He was extremely well connected and desperate to impress his young lover. Clunet introduced her to everyone he could think of to enhance her career, the most important being his close friend Gabriel Astruc. Businessman, manager, theatrical agent and impresario, Astruc was struck by M'greet's unique position as an exotic dancer in high society. Astruc's client list included the dancer Vaslav Nijinsky, the composer Igor Stravinsky, opera singer Feodor Chaliapin and Diaghilev's *Ballets Russes*. Astruc was at the cutting edge of Parisian theatre, promoting daring avant-garde artists and performances that audiences loved, critics raved over and the authorities worried about. The exotic dancer Mata Hari would be his next sensation. Astruc recognised that the blend of sensual and sexual dance with, allegedly, sacred elements gave audiences the right level of frisson while remaining just within the code of morality that governed theatre performances. Here was a dancer just as nude, or apparently even more so, than the can-can girls of the *Folies Bergère*, but retaining her respectability and deliciously wrapped up in the mysteries of the East.

Astruc took over as M'greet's manager and agent, and booked her into the Olympia Theatre on the Boulevard des Capucines in Paris for a performance of *Le Rêve*, commencing on 20 August. *L'Olympia*, as it was known, was a high-class theatre and the starting date of 20 August was a shrewd move on Astruc's part. August was traditionally the month when Parisians left the city to seek cooler climes elsewhere. Most shows began their 'autumn runs' in late August, allowing performers to start with what would be smaller than usual audiences. Once the crowds had returned in early September, performances would have settled in and early nerves or scenery malfunctions would have been resolved. The early start also allowed shows that were somewhat *risqué* to hide from the authorities, as the civil servants responsible for the moral codes in public performances were still enjoying their summer break away from the city. If an objection was then raised about the dubious nature of the performance, most theatre managers would plead a *fait accompli*, the moral damage having already been done at the August performances.

There were other advantages to the August start for M'greet. Established performers rarely opened before September in Paris, so Mata Hari would have little, or no, competition from other professional dancers such as Isadora Duncan or the *Ballets Russes*. With no competition and an initial reputation from her early salon performances, the newspapers would flock to review the latest Mata Hari spectacle, especially as these performances were public and not restricted to the invited guests of a salon. Over the summer, M'greet and Astruc worked on refining her performance, costumes and advance publicity. On 18 August, she gave an advance performance; dance, costumes, music, lighting and props all worked seamlessly. *Le Rêve*, starring Mata Hari, opened at the Olympia Theatre on 20 August.

The performance was a sell-out, and the following week saw a series of ecstatic reviews in the papers. The critic in *La Presse* raved, 'One could simply say that this woman is rhythm, thus to indicate, as closely as possible, the poetry which emanates from this magnificently supple and beautiful body.'[7] The reviewer in *Le Journal* wrote, 'Mata Hari personifies all the poetry of India, its mysticism, its voluptuousness, its languor, its hypnotising charm.'[8]

Although M'greet had received similarly positive comments when she had danced in the spring in private salons, the reviews of her first public engagement brought her to everyone's attention. The crowds adored the performances and the adoration delighted and inspired Mata Hari. Her dancing became more fluid and sensual as her confidence increased. Mata Hari the professional dancer had truly arrived. Her payment for the Olympia shows was 10,000 francs. To put this sum into perspective, the seamstresses who worked in the Olympia and created Mata Hari's flowing Eastern costumes probably earned around 1,000 francs per year, while the bank manager who sat in the stall watching the show would earn around 3,000 francs at the height of his career.[9] By the beginning of September, when most Parisians were returning from the summer vacations, M'greet's performances at *L'Oympia* were a complete sell-out and tickets were fetching a premium among the touts who thronged the Parisian theatre district.

Mata Hari was beside herself with joy, and among all of the purchases her new-found wealth afforded her, the most long-lasting was Anna Lintjens, a lady's maid. Dutch like Mata Hari, Lintjens would stay faithful to her mistress until the very end.

While *Le Rêve* was a sell-out, Astruc used the unanimously positive press to arrange for Mata Hari to appear in Russia. Moscow society loved everything French, and was excited by the news of Mata Hari, the latest sensation from Paris. M'greet was equally excited by the idea of performing on stage in Moscow. On 8 October, she wrote to her father, 'At the moment I have my own carriage and within a month I go to Russia where I can enjoy myself. I am still very beautiful, healthy, and full of life. I don't fall in love with anyone and I like this kind of life … I am happy.'[10] .

However, despite claiming to be happy, M'greet had still left her daughter behind. Her October letter to her father contained a plaintive few lines about Non, 'I know … that [Non] of course has no clothes and will be polluted by a woman like [MacLeod's sister Louise] who doesn't even clean herself but my dear God, I cannot do anything about it!'[11]

For all M'greet's success, she was still unable to wrest Non from MacLeod, all too aware, perhaps, that the success she did have as an exotic dancer counted against her in the eyes of the law, were she to attempt to take her. She may also have been unsure as to how long her success would last and wished to see a greater degree of solidity to her career before embarking on the return of her daughter. There were, of course, financial as well as legal considerations. Despite her payment for the performances of *Le Rêve* and the upcoming Russian performances, October was the month that saw a legal suit for debt lodged against M'greet. A Parisian jeweller had supplied her with items worth 12,000 francs, and the account remained unpaid. Aware, as was all Paris, of her show at *L'Olympia*, the jeweller had finally lost patience with her and filed a suit, demanding immediate payment or the return of the jewellery. Clunet, the lawyer, stepped in and persuaded the jeweller to accept monthly repayments of 2,000 francs to repay the debt.[12]

At the beginning of November, M'greet started on her Moscow performances. At the same time, Astruc negotiated a short, two-week engagement in Madrid, followed by performances in Monte Carlo and Berlin for 1906. On her return to Paris from Russia, she found herself one of the most sought-after women in the capital. Her photograph appeared in newspapers across Europe, her dress style was commented upon and her dancing was praised. The gossip surrounding her nationality and ethnicity continued, fed in part by Astruc, who knew how to use a sense of mystery to enhance publicity, and partly by M'greet as she continued to fashion and refashion herself as Mata Hari. She finished the year by dancing to full houses in Vienna before returning to her beloved Paris.

In February 1906, she danced in the opera *Le roi de Lahore*, by Jules Massenet, in Monte Carlo. *Le roi de Lahore* was one of Massenet's first major successes in 1877. An instant favourite with audiences and critics alike, it quickly established Massenet's musical reputation. M'greet's performance was, obviously, not a leading role. Crucially, however, *Le roi de Lahore* was part of the established theatrical world, and thus gave M'greet and her dancing the seal of respectability. She was now starting to be considered a serious artiste rather than a low-brow, if exciting, novelty.

Massenet saw her performance in Monte Carlo and was entranced. He sent her a small but appreciative note of congratulations. From Monte Carlo, M'greet journeyed to Berlin, followed by Massenet. A meeting of some sort took place between the two. Although the exact details remain unclear, directly on leaving M'greet for business in Paris, Massenet sent her a short note, 'How happy I have been to see you again! Mata, Mata, I am leaving for Paris within a few minutes! Thank you, thank you – and my fervent admiration.'[13]

It cannot be stated with certainty that Massenet was M'greet's lover – he may well have just been a besotted admirer. In any case, M'greet had acquired another lover, Lieutenant Alfred Kiepert of the 11th Westphalian Hussars, the noted cavalry unit of the Royal Prussian Army and German Imperial Army, nicknamed the *Krefelder Tanzhusaren* (Dancing Hussars of Krebs).

Kiepert and M'greet had originally met in Vienna the previous December, and by the February were lovers. During her time in Berlin, Kiepert established M'greet in her own apartment on NachodsStraße in the fashionable west of the city, just south of the Tiergarten. The apartment was close enough to the centre of Berlin's fashionable streets to enable her to enjoy the delights of the city, but also a discreet distance away from Kiepert's wife. Frau Kiepert had never quite resigned herself to her husband's many mistresses, but developed an uneasy tolerance so long as Kiepert kept them well away from her. M'greet was a flamboyant beauty, but she was merely the latest in a long line of conquests and Frau Kiepert knew she would not last.

Within a year, M'greet had gone from near poverty to almost financial security. Able to charge exorbitant fees for her performances, and quite happy to receive gifts of all kinds from adoring male admirers, M'greet was no longer the desperate young woman of 1904. Indeed, if it had not been for her need to maintain a certain social life and buy extravagant outfits, she would have been well off in a very short period of time. By the beginning of 1906, she was earning a considerable amount of money, enjoying the successes of her dancing and had acquired several devoted admirers. Her life had improved immeasurably. Unfortunately, it was at this time that her estranged husband reappeared in her life.

MacLeod had made a life for himself in Velp. After he and M'greet had separated, he met a young lady, Elisabetha Martina Christina van der Mast. MacLeod wanted to marry, so needed a divorce. His lawyer journeyed to Paris to discuss the divorce with M'greet. From the start of Mata Hari's dancing, newspapers had speculated on her origins, and the Dutch press had not been any less interested in the exotic dancer. As early as April 1905, the *Nieuws van de Dag* carried an article speculating that Mata Hari was '*Een Hollandsche danseres*' (a Dutch dancer).[14] An interview in the *Nieuw Rotterdamsche Dagblad* (*New Rotterdam Daily*) in May 1905 revealed Mata Hari to be 'Dutch ... Mrs MacLeod'.[15] When MacLeod decided in 1906 that he wished a divorce, his estranged wife was easily found.

In the spring of 1906, when M'greet was enjoying the first successes of Mata Hari, she was visited by MacLeod's lawyer. MacLeod intended to retain custody of Non and did not want M'greet to fight the case. When first approached by the lawyer, M'greet was undecided as to what she should do. A series of meetings and discussions took place over a matter of weeks while MacLeod's lawyer attempted to persuade her to agree to all of his terms. When M'greet and MacLeod had previously separated, MacLeod had alleged that M'greet had agreed never to see Non again. This seems unlikely, given that when approached regarding the divorce, M'greet refused to give up any legal rights to her daughter. It may be that M'greet had previously left her daughter behind in the care of friends of MacLeod until she had made a home for Non, a common practice in Europe at the time. Just as M'greet was beginning to be in a position where she was able to fetch Non to live with her, MacLeod came looking for a divorce and legal custody of Non. M'greet informed his lawyer that she had decided to fight for her daughter.

At this point, MacLeod's lawyer produced a photograph of M'greet, apparently nude, and threatened to use the image in court. M'greet knew that such a photograph would be viewed as scandalous, and probably result in custody of Non being legally given to her father. With few options open to her, and despite the scandal that would ensue, M'greet decided to fight for custody.

In April 1906, MacLeod lodged a divorce action against M'greet on three grounds:

> [T]hat she had carnal knowledge of other men and by consequence rendered herself a culpable adulteress, which is the motive for divorce; that the defendant who lives actually in Paris produces in the aforesaid city in the cafés, concerts, and the circuses and there executes the so-called brahmanique [*sic*] dances and presents herself almost entirely nude; that she also posed entirely nude as a model for a sculptor and this work of sculpture was offered to public view.[16]

MacLeod petitioned for a divorce with full custody of Non on the grounds of M'greet's adulterous behaviour. His lawyer produced supporting statements from General Edward MacLeod, Vice Admiral Norman MacLeod and Madame Goodvriend, all of whom wrote of M'greet's immoral behaviour. These statements were challenged by Ardum Zelle, who appeared on M'greet's behalf to plead her case. Finally, MacLeod's legal team produced the photographs of M'greet in which she appeared almost nude. On 26 April 1906, the divorce was granted. MacLeod was awarded full legal custody of Non; M'greet was not granted any access rights.[17]

The result was predictable. In the eyes of the court, M'greet had abandoned her husband and child, and cavorted nude or semi-nude in Paris in front of men. While the evidence of MacLeod's witness statements might have been tainted with familial bias, photographs of Mata Hari in very revealing costumes and the extensive newspaper articles about her sexualised dancing could not be ignored. In addition, her status as Lieutenant Kiepert's mistress was an open secret in European society. What is more curious is the action of M'greet. Was she unable or unwilling to attend the court in Amsterdam to fight for Non, and so asked her father to attend on her behalf? Did she have a dancing engagement she felt unable to break by travelling to Amsterdam? Or was she unwilling to face MacLeod and the possibility of unpleasant questions in court? Given her level of fame at that time, it is likely her appearance in the divorce courts would have been reported in the press. Did that have a bearing on her actions? As it was, there was no coverage in the press, except for the mandatory dry little notice of the divorce of Rudolf MacLeod and his wife Margaretha Geertruida née Zelle.

A second point of note in the divorce case was the presence of Zelle on M'greet's behalf. Zelle was a failed businessman with a poor reputation and no experience or knowledge of law, and yet he represented M'greet in the case. By early 1906, M'greet had no lack of male admirers, chief amongst whom was Clunet, the lawyer who had previously helped her. Clunet was completely infatuated with M'greet and would do anything for her. Yet, when fighting for her daughter, M'greet does not appear to have sought his advice. Even if their relationship was not then at a stage where she felt she could ask for his help, M'greet was earning enough money to be able to afford legal representation. So why did she not seek a lawyer to fight for custody of Non? One of the reasons why she claimed she had fled to Paris and started dancing in the first place was to build a home for herself and her daughter. Did M'greet realise that her choice of career would probably prevent her gaining custody of Non, and as such the use of a lawyer was futile? Had she asked her father to fight on her behalf knowing it to be hopeless, but using his presence to let Non know she had not been entirely abandoned by her mother?

There is no evidence that M'greet maintained contact with Non in these early days of her dancing career. No letters to Non appear to exist from that time. If M'greet did write, MacLeod may have destroyed any correspondence sent to the child; equally, when Non grew older, and given her mother's notoriety, she may have destroyed any remaining correspondence. It should be remembered that what may appear to modern eyes to be something of an abandonment of Non for the sake of her career, was not entirely unusual in the early twentieth century. Women trying to create a career on the stage frequently had to leave small children with family members, often for years at a time. Of course, men frequently left their children behind in pursuit of their own careers, and indeed to have taken children with them would in most cases have seemed abnormal. For M'greet, leaving Non in the care of the MacLeod family was a painful but necessary decision she had to make in order to pursue her career, but one she possibly fully intended to reverse as soon as she could.

While Mata Hari danced on stage, she was also beginning to take over the rest of M'greet's life. It was at this point that she started to refer to herself both publicly and privately as Mata Hari, and M'greet slipped quietly into the background. This became evident in the so-called 'war of the tights'. This had been initially sparked in Vienna, where the press reported on the latest dancing sensations. Isadora Duncan, an established dancer with impeccable dance training credentials, Mata Hari, an 'authentic' exotic dancer, and Maud Allan, a Canadian pianist turned exotic dancer, were all on the stages of Europe. All three had, in their own ways, shocked the theatre-going public and the art establishment by dancing nude or semi-nude. The press, scenting a good story, especially given the rumours of ill-feeling between the three women, dubbed the situation the 'war of the tights' and regaled their readers with lurid tales of naked flesh and cat fights. None of the women actually danced nude. In reality, Duncan had danced with bare legs and no corset, but perfectly respectably covered with flowing toga-style costumes. Mata Hari danced wearing a jewelled top bra and body stocking that gave the impression she was nude under her veils, which she readily discarded. Allan danced in costumes similar to Mata Hari's, but also in more flowing robes, depending on the dance. Steering clear of commenting on the professionally trained Duncan, Mata Hari turned her attention to Allan. The Canadian had danced the role of Salomé in the production of *Vision of Salomé* in Vienna. Based loosely on the Oscar Wilde play *Salomé*, Allan's version of the Dance of the Seven Veils became famous and bore comparison with Mata Hari's exotic dance style. Allan was billed as 'The Salomé Dancer', which enraged Mata Hari. Exotica had become all the rage, and several of the dances at places such as the *Folies Bergère* now used 'Eastern' themes in their shows. Mata Hari disparagingly commented that Allan's dancing was more akin to the *Folies Bergère* than to her own sacred interpretation, and condemned Allan as one of those 'ladies who style themselves "Eastern Dancers", [who] have sprung up and honour me with imitation'.[18]

In the same interview, she then expanded on the roots of her own understanding of Eastern dance:

> Born in Java, in the midst of tropical vegetation, I have been taught from my earliest childhood the deep meaning of these dances which constitute a cult, a religion. Only those born and bred there become impregnated with their religious significance, and can impart to them that solemn note to which they can lay claim.[19]

It was a bold lie, and a masterstroke. Not even the professionally trained Isadora Duncan could compete with an apparently authentic Javanese dancer. Although many serious dance critics continued to doubt her ability, they were at a loss, without having seen any actual Javanese dancing themselves, to give a critical assessment, and thus remained silent. At the same time, the public and press adored Mata Hari, with the *Neues Wiener Journal* (*New Vienna Journal*) proclaiming, 'Isadora Duncan is dead! Long live Mata Hari!'[20]

The fake had won the 'war of the tights'.

7

AN INTERNATIONAL
WOMAN

By 1907, Mata Hari could do no wrong in the eyes of her adoring admirers. She appeared on stage in Berlin, Vienna, Prague, Budapest, Rome, Madrid, London, Moscow, Warsaw, Oslo and Copenhagen, but her great love was Paris. Her relationship with Kiepert continued, although not necessarily exclusively, and she was fêted wherever she went. The only disappointment in her life was the lack of contact with Non, but Mata Hari the international woman was a huge success. Then, at the end of 1906, a book appeared about her which exposed details of her background and would have shattered her claims about her Eastern origins; it was written by her father.

Zelle later claimed that he had written the book to counter the attacks on Mata Hari's character put forward by MacLeod at the divorce trial. However, as at the time of the divorce his daughter was the mistress of a married German cavalry officer and was dancing publicly in a costume designed to make her appear nude, most of MacLeod's assertions in the court had been true. In addition, as the connection between Mata Hari and Zelle had not been made in the press, there had been little negative public comment. It is more likely that being short of money, as he frequently was, Zelle had decided to benefit from his daughter's success.

Whatever Zelle's true motives, he wrote an account of Mata Hari's life, based, he claimed, on her own writing when she 'undertook a journey to America'. The book is a curious mixture of fact and fiction, not least of which is the fact that Mata Hari never travelled to America. It portrayed MacLeod as an old-fashioned bully of a husband and, very damaging for Mata Hari, exposed her solidly Dutch roots. Curiously, given Mata Hari's celebrity status, the first publisher that Zelle approached refused the manuscript. Undaunted, Zelle approached the publishing house of C.L.G.Veldt, who accepted the father's book and published *De Roman van Mata Hari, Mevrouw M.G MacLeod Zelle: De Levensgeschiedenis Mijner Dochter en Mijne Grieven tegen Haar Vroegeren Echtgenoot* (*The novel of Mata Hari, Madame M.G MacLeod Zelle: The life history of my daughter and her early grievances against her husband*). The reception to the book was muted. The theatre-going public of the Netherlands in the early 1900s were not great readers, and those who did read the book were confused, as it flatly contradicted Mata Hari's own assertions as to her identity. As the book was written in Dutch, and in addition in the Friesland dialect in places, it had little impact outside the Netherlands, so Mata Hari's origins remained unexamined by most across Europe. One individual who had read the book was G.H. Priem, a Dutch lawyer, who was puzzled by the discrepancies between the facts in Zelle's book and those in the press surrounding Mata Hari's origins.

Early in 1907, Priem approached Mata Hari and asked for an interview, to which she readily agreed. Priem interviewed Mata Hari over a number of days, and eventually wrote the interviews into a book entitled *De naakte Waarheid omtrent Mata Hari* (*The naked truth about Mata Hari*). The interviews combine fact-finding and flattery. Priem started by asking her what she thought of her father's book. Her reaction was revealing.

Priem: 'What do you say about this book?'

Mata Hari: 'I? I do not say anything about it! Do you think that they [her father and his wife] make money out of it?'

Priem: 'I think so.'

Mata Hari: 'Well that is the main point! What do I care what they say about me in Holland! I am happy that I am out of it and I do not wish to go back.'

Priem: 'But why do you ask if I think they make money out of it?'

Mata Hari: 'Well, everything started of course in the first place because of that.'

Priem: 'And your father says he does this for the honour of his daughter.'

She burst out laughing: 'I read it too. Heavenly, heavenly.'[1]

Mata Hari continued:

This beautiful 'novel' is no compliment. With all their good intentions, I am even willing to overlook the financial motive for a moment, they didn't do me a service. They spoilt my whole image; the artistic side [of me] is completely absent. They made a tearful wifey out of me, one that gnashes her teeth, that scolds, that scratches, like a woman from a back street who works with her pins. I am not like that, truly not, I am not like that. I have a tally [of lovers] and there is almost no room for [another] notch, but I am not ashamed of that. I confess this frankly. A woman like me, as I am, is quite unmanageable in a marriage.[2]

This candour continued as Priem probed more deeply into her marriage to MacLeod.

'Look,' she began, 'I shouldn't have married. I was not the kind of girl to marry.'

Priem: 'Many say that. Regret comes after sin.'

Mata Hari:

Exactly! From the time that I was a child I loved men: a strongly built male brought me to a state of ecstasy. I say this *sans gêne*, because a journalist appears to me as a kind of doctor, to whom I can say calmly: so many centimetres above my knee I feel this or that.[3]

Mata Hari proved extremely honest about her own shortcomings within the marriage and admitted that she had been unfaithful to MacLeod:

Now I understand fully, I was in the past not the person that I should have been; a man who marries a woman has the right to expect from that woman what has already been dictated by the law, in the first place: faithfulness. And in every respect I have not been faithful.[4]

After these revelations, Priem pressed Mata Hari about her life in Paris. She replied, 'Certainly, this life suits me. I can satisfy all my caprices; to-night I dine with Count A and tomorrow with Duke B. If I don't have to dance, I make a trip with Marquis C. I avoid serious liaisons.'[5]

Priem concluded his book by condemning Zelle's novel and finding MacLeod more sinned against than sinning. The most startling elements in the book were Mata Hari's revelations of marital infidelity, numerous lovers and an unabashed admission of female sexual desire. This sort of language, and frank openness about sexual matters, was shocking for early twentieth-century European society. Or it would have been had anyone read Priem's book. Unfortunately for the lawyer turned amateur journalist, like Mata Hari's father he wrote in Dutch, a language not widely spoken outside the Netherlands. He also failed to capitalise on the book by taking its revelations to the Parisian press. Mata Hari may have complained that her father's book portrayed her as a 'tearful wifey' and Priem's condemned her as an unfaithful wife, but neither was widely read or even known to exist; and certainly not in Paris. However, for the *beau monde*, Mata Hari's sexual liaisons with Count A, Duke B and Marquis C were already becoming widely known.

What is interesting in Priem's work is his exposure of Mata Hari's completely Dutch ethnicity, and thus the fantasy about her alleged Javanese origins. This revelation came almost without comment in his discussion about her marriage to MacLeod. Priem did not call Mata Hari to account for this. Did he accept the fantasy as a harmless piece of theatricality of no real import? Whatever the reason, Priem's exposure of Mata Hari as a Dutch woman through and through was almost entirely ignored by the outside world, and the fantasy remained in place until well after her death.

While the fantasy continued, her relationship with Lieutenant Kiepert did not. In the early summer of 1907, the lieutenant's family had finally had enough. They issued him with the ultimatum that he had to finish with Mata Hari, because she damaged both his career prospects and the family honour. Mata Hari later reported that, 'His family having given him an order to abandon me under penalty of a judiciary council, he separated from me and gave me 300,000 marks.'[6]

As always where Mata Hari is concerned, her version of the truth is somewhat limited. From the beginning, the love affair between the two had not been exclusive; these affairs seldom were, and military men usually had more than one lover. However, the double standards on the notion of morality that existed for male and female behaviour extended even to when those men and women were breaching the codes of marriage within their own sexual relationships. Men could have multiple lovers; woman could not. Women had to accept their lover's multiple conquests, and indeed be passive recipients and grateful that they had been chosen to join such esteemed company. For Kiepert to have a lover was accepted by the family, if not by his wife, as part and parcel of military life. For Kiepert to have a lover who then took other lovers was a step too far. Mata Hari's multiple sexual liaisons reflected badly on him. Her lack of passivity took her immorality out of the female zone of behaviour and into that of the male.

It may seem, therefore, somewhat curious that Kiepert should reward such an immoral lover with such a large sum of money. Two possible solutions present themselves to this conundrum. Kiepert was an honourable man and was trying to disentangle himself from Mata Hari in order to retain that honour. One mark of an honourable man was that he would give an ex-lover a large sum of money with which to support herself until she found a new protector. Kiepert would therefore have settled just such a sum on Mata Hari. However, the Kieperts, although wealthy, were unlikely to have handed over 300,000 marks, given Mata Hari's behaviour. When Mata Hari made the statement about the money, it was eight years after the event and was while she was undergoing interrogation as a German spy. It may well be that she confused and conflated the figures, deliberately or not, to arrive at the fantastic sum of 300,000 marks.

After Kiepert and she parted, Mata Hari decided to travel to Egypt. She had no pressing dance engagements at that time, and so travelled by train from Berlin to Naples, where she boarded the SS *Schleswig* sailing to Khartoum. René Puaux, the society reporter from *Le Temps*, was also on board and interviewed the great Mata Hari. She spoke of 'going to Egypt for the purpose of discovering new dances'.[7]

Puaux's article hinted at the unravelling of the Eastern fantasy. He wrote she had become, 'Berlinoise and speaks German with an accent that is as un-Oriental as possible.'[8]

After a mere few weeks in Egypt, Mata Hari returned to Paris and took up residence at the Hotel Meurice, where she spoke to the press, telling them of her 'two years' in Egypt and India. She spoke of the new dances she had developed and her manager Astruc arranged for her to give several private performances of the three new dances. While generally enthusiastically received by the audiences, there was little new in the content. She performed her new routines at a benefit show at the Trocadéro, where again she was well received but with little of the initial ecstatic enthusiasm of her earlier performances.

However, the disappointment in the response to her performances was eased by her finding a new lover, Xavier Rousseau. An extremely wealthy stockbroker, Rousseau established her in a country château at Esvres near Tours. The château was owned by the Countess La Taille-Trétinville, and Rousseau gave Mata Hari *carte blanche* to furnish it as she wished. He also provided her with extra staff to help her maid Lintjens run the establishment, and a coach and four horses for Mata Hari to enjoy the surrounding countryside.

She spent most of the rest of the year accompanying Rousseau to the races to watch his horses win, entertaining his stockbroker and banker friends when they were out with their mistresses – not their wives – and providing a convivial home for Rousseau when required. Rousseau's wife and mother were less than enthusiastic when they discovered the identity his latest lover. While his wife kept her distance, his mother was of an older and somewhat more determined nature. Madame Rousseau ordered her carriage and drove out to visit Mata Hari at Esvres to try to convince her to abandon the affair. However, Mata Hari charmed the old lady, to the extent that Madame Rousseau stayed for some time with her son and his lover at the château.[9]

By 1908, Mata Hari's grand passion with Rousseau had settled into that of an established mistress. She was in a position to choose, to an extent, when and where she danced, and although criticism of her dancing remained in the artistic community, her performances were as popular as ever. The problem was, however, that having now made a name for herself, she wanted to be thought of as an artiste. She constantly pushed Astruc to find her 'classical' or 'artistic' roles. She longed to receive the critical reviews lavished on Isadora Duncan, albeit without having spent the years of training that Duncan had undertaken. Mata Hari continued to dance at small salons and in larger theatres in popular roles or in one-woman performances, but more serious roles continued to elude her, despite Astruc's best efforts. In the meantime, she maintained her profile by spending time being seen and photographed at the races and public events.

Finally, in the autumn of 1909, Astruc succeeded in securing a serious role for her. She was to play Cleopatra in the opera *Antar*. The opera was due to open in Monte Carlo in January 1910, with a possible extension of the run to Paris. She was delighted. November and December were taken up with costume fittings and developing the dances. The opera duly opened to favourable but less than ecstatic reviews. Mata Hari's performance was noted, but opera was not taken too seriously by the fun crowd in Monte; the role may have been artistic, but the audience was not. The real test would be the French run.

It was in Paris that Mata Hari's weaknesses were revealed. *Antar* was to be performed at the Odéon under the directorship of André Antoine. She now had to attend rehearsals along with the other dancers. The comparison between the over-30, overweight amateur and the younger, fitter professional dancers was all too obvious, and she knew it. Matters came to a head when she refused to practise in front of the ballet mistress, claiming she was protecting her dances from being plagiarised. Whatever the reason, and despite her fame, Antoine was adamant; all dancers had to practise in front of the ballet madame. Mata Hari refused, so Antoine fired her and she sued for breach of contract. The story made the gossip columns, much to the delight of the public. Edouard Clunet took the case to court on her behalf. Mata Hari sued for 8,000 francs; the 3,000 franc fee she would have been paid had she performed and a further 5,000 francs for damage to her professional reputation. The case was settled in 1912 in her favour. She was awarded the 3,000 francs for her fee, but the payment for damage to her reputation was rejected. The newspapers carried the story. Antoine was philosophical about his loss and paid the 3,000 francs. Mata Hari was furious at the slur on her dancing ability.

Despite her pyrrhic victory over Antoine, Mata Hari had to face facts. She remained an untrained dancer in a world of professionals; her unique element of Orientalism had been copied by dancers across Europe, many more talented than herself; and she was past 30 and out of condition. The theatres, and their audiences, wanted professionalism, novelty, youth and vitality.

In 1911, as part of a fresh start, Mata Hari moved from Evres to Neuilly-sur-Seine. The house at Rue Windsor was furnished just as sumptuously as the château had been. Rousseau showered her with just as many gifts as before. Although the artistic world of the theatre still seemed somewhat elusive, her life of elegant clothes and beautiful horses was secure. Unfortunately, this came to an abrupt end when a bill for some furniture for the house in Rue Windsor was delivered in error to the Rousseau family home. Rousseau's wife, who had received the bill, was outraged, and the subsequent row revealed the parlous state of the family's finances. The stockbroker was broke.

Rousseau was declared bankrupt and, in the confusion over his financial state, claim and counterclaim were made as to whose fault it was. According to Madame Rousseau, her husband was a well-known 'skirt chaser'[10] who had been deliberately targeted and then ruined by Mata Hari and her profligacy. According to Mata Hari, Rousseau had 'squandered'[11] all of her money. Whatever the truth of the matter, Rousseau had creditors he could not pay and clients whose money he had purloined. Lucky to avoid a prison sentence, he was bankrupted and his reputation ruined. Mata Hari packed up her belongings, and she and Anna Lintjens moved into a small but fashionable hotel near the centre of Paris. She informed Astruc that she was available for work. By the summer, he managed to get her a booking for two months at La Scala Milan in the opera *Armide*.

Mata Hari's dancing career was a curious mixture of the serious and the comic. Audiences loved her, but this was as much for her apparent naked theatricality as her dancing ability. Serious dance critics were divided; some thought her a gifted amateur, while most found her a ridiculous poseur. And yet among all the popular performances and private salon shows, she gained some artistic roles where she conducted herself reasonably well. She certainly used the popular trend for Orientalism to her own advantage, as did most popular entertainers of the day. But it was her insistence on the authenticity of her dancing that caused most to call her artistic integrity into question. European colonial appropriation of 'native' culture was recognised, although not necessarily condemned, in the early twentieth century. Mata Hari could have claimed that her dancing was inspired by or was a European interpretation of native dance. Equally, upon her return to Europe, she could have sought at least some basic training in dance. That she did not do so raises some interesting speculation. The initial fantasy about Mata Hari's ethnicity and the authenticity of her dances had gained her an audience and marked her out as unique amongst the dancers of her day. To then admit all was a fantasy and to seek training might have exposed her to ridicule. However, within the artistic community, there was already a strong element of derision in their critique of her abilities. So was there also an element of fear? If Mata Hari had attended formal dance lessons and been found lacking, she would then have been left unable to perform as a professional dancer, but also unable to carry off the fantasy of being a 'genuine', if amateur, Eastern dancer. The fantasy was believed by many who saw her, but was equally known by others to be a mirage and accepted as thus. Many of her fans guessed she was not really a Javanese princess, but participated in the charade. To have publicly exposed her true Dutch roots would have spoiled the fun, and like the fourth wall in a theatre, once the fantasy was broken it could not be repaired. Yet despite all the fantasy, the lack of training and the fact that she was overweight for a dancer and getting older, Mata Hari could still captivate audiences and critics.

In Milan, her performance in *Armide* received glowing reviews. She was offered the part of Venus in the ballet *Bacco e Gambrinus*, also in Milan, starting in early 1912. Although it exposed her to comparison with trained ballerinas, her performance was a solo one and there was no French ballet mistress to comment on her lack of skill or technique. Tullio Serafin, the conductor, thought her 'adorable'.[12] Her performance brought her to the attention of Prince di San Faustino. He invited her to his palace, the Palazzo Barberini on the via delle Quattro Fontane and asked her to pose for him as Salomé. San Faustino commissioned an unknown artist to paint her as Salomé reclining semi-nude on a divan, her fingers lightly caressing the severed head of John the Baptist.

Her fee in Milan was 3,000 francs per month; the annual wage for an ordinary worker was approximately 300 francs, and Mata Hari needed the money. Whatever the truth of the situation with Rousseau, she had spent all of the money that Kiepert had given her and she no longer had a rich lover to support her lifestyle. Dancing roles, artistic or otherwise, were becoming increasingly scarce. She returned to Paris in February and turned to Astruc for help. On 8 February 1912, Mata Hari wrote to him:

> I wonder whether you would know of anyone who would be interested in the protection of artists, like a capitalist who would like to make an investment? I find myself in rather difficult circumstances and need immediately about 30,000 francs to pull me out of this unpleasant situation, and to give me the

tranquility of mind which is so necessary to my art. It would really be a pity to
cut such a future short. As a guarantee for this loan I offer everything I have in
my home, including horses and carriages.[13]

This letter gives rise to some questions. Why, after her successful
performances in Milan, for which she had been well paid, was Mata
Hari in need of 30,000 francs 'immediately'? What were the 'difficult
circumstances'? Why was she willing to put up her furniture, horses
and carriages as loan collateral? And why had she approached her
agent rather than a bank? Then there is the question of what Mata
Hari meant by a protector. Did she mean an old-fashioned patron of
the arts, or was she alluding to something much more erotic? Was she
asking Astruc to find her a new rich lover? Was she so out of touch
with Paris after an absence of only four months that she needed
Astruc to affect an introduction for her? It seems unlikely. In any
case, if Mata Hari's intent was for Astruc to find her a new lover, the
offer of a guarantee for the loan seems somewhat redundant. To add
to the confusion, despite her plea for immediate funds, she continued
to appear in the latest fashions, promenading or riding in her carriage
on the Bois de Boulogne. Were the difficult circumstances and
immediate need for funds merely another instance of her dramatic
exaggeration?

In the spring of 1912, she visited Monte Carlo to meet Diaghilev
and discuss a possible role in his upcoming ballet. It is not entirely
clear what happened at the meeting. The costume designer for the
Ballets Russes, Léon Baker, is said to have examined Mata Hari nude
and found her to be overweight.[14] While there is no doubt that Mata
Hari was overweight, she could have dieted and Baker was more
than capable of creating a costume that could hide any 'flaws' in her
figure. Also, given Diaghilev's total control over his company, if he
had truly wanted Mata Hari to dance in his ballet, then the opinion
of Baker would not have stopped him. It is more likely that Mata
Hari, free spirit that she was, could not have coped with the artistic
interpretation and rigours of discipline necessary to dance with the
Ballets Russes. The charge of being overweight, although a little cruel,

was possibly less hurtful than being told that Diaghilev thought her not capable of dancing.

It was at this point that Mata Hari attempted to re-establish contact with her daughter. Non was now 14 years old. MacLeod had separated from his second wife, Elisabetha van der Masi,[15] and Mata Hari felt that the time was right to mount a legal challenge to his custody. Clunet, her lawyer, was approached to prepare a case based on three points: Non lacked a mother figure in her life, a teenage girl was thought to need a maternal presence, and then there was Mata Hari's changed circumstances. Since she was no longer married to MacLeod, any sexual liaison, although scandalous, was not strictly adulterous under the law, unless the other party was married. In addition, Mata Hari's lack of dancing engagements allowed Clunet to truthfully claim that she was not dancing semi-nude in public. Nevertheless, the case failed before it even started, partly due to Clunet's lack of understanding of the laws with regards to child custody and also due to Mata Hari's reputation. A string of lovers across Europe and the retention of a well-known theatrical agent undermined Clunet's attempts to redraw her character. Unfortunately, Mata Hari refused to give up her attempt to gain custody of Non. In a bizarre episode, Mata Hari's maid Lintjens was sent to the Netherlands to fetch Non back to Paris. Lintjens travelled to the Netherlands and arrived at the girl's school with the intention of persuading, or possibly coercing, Non into travelling to Paris. However, alerted no doubt by the previous legal action, MacLeod was already at the school gates when Lintjens appeared. The maid was instantly dismissed from the scene.[16]

It is not known what Non thought about her parents' situation, especially that of her mother. As a girl growing up in a middle-class home in the Netherlands, Non could not have been unaware of her mother's transformation from M'greet to Mata Hari. She had seen and heard every argument between her parents in the East Indies and at home again in the Netherlands. She had seen her mother leave the family home to go to Paris, only to return and leave again. Non may have experienced some of the rancour involved in the divorce case, even if only in snatched overheard conversations. Every newspaper and periodical in Europe carried a Mata Hari story, and by the time Non was a teenager she could scarcely have failed to be aware of them. The arts pages were alive with descriptions of her 'naked' dances; the gossip columns were full of stories of her various love affairs. In addition, as if that were not enough, picture postcards of Mata Hari in various stages of apparent undress were openly for sale across Europe. For a young girl on the verge of womanhood living in bourgeois Netherlands, all of this must have been confusing and embarrassing. There would, no doubt, have been elements of anger and guilt at her mother's abandonment of her. Children of divorced couples frequently feel themselves to be responsible in some way for the breakdown in the relationship. Non may have felt that she had, in some way, been 'bad', and that was why her mother had left. Given the level of acrimony that existed in the marriage before their separation, it is unlikely that MacLeod, or the rest of the family, would have been shown any degree of discretion when discussing Mata Hari and her failings as a parent.

Whatever Mata Hari's reasons for this escapade, it was a failure, and with few bookings coming from Astruc, she threw herself into a round of private performances. A piece of good fortune came her way with the arrival in Europe of the Indian musician, Ustad Inayat Khan. He had left India in 1910 and travelled to Europe, ostensibly to introduce the West to classical Indian music. He would go on to found the Sufi Order in the West in 1914. He was also heavily involved in the early independence movement in India, which would have a negative bearing on Mata Hari in later years. In 1913, Khan met her after she invited him and his orchestra to play at one of her private parties at the house in Neuilly. The audiences were carefully invited to these events, and photographs of Mata Hari dancing in Indian costume accompanied by the Indian musicians were widely distributed.[17]

Henri Liévin, a stockbroker and one of Mata Hari's lovers at that time, stated that:

She lived then in a small mansion at Neuilly, and when she found herself short of money, she rented it for soirées and dinners. When I say she rented it out, the expression is not quite right. In reality, she gave parties at which certain friends (of the Bank of France, notably) and I paid the expenses.[18]

The society pages were full of the latest incarnation of Mata Hari, and in London *Tatler* published a photograph of her with Khan entitled, 'Lady MacLeod dances in the light of the moon to Her Friends.'[19]

However, despite the publicity generated by dancing with Khan and his musicians, and the prestige that this brought, lucrative artistic performances were becoming even harder to come by. Astruc was struggling to find her good roles. Mata Hari was reduced to dancing in less salubrious venues and in poorer quality productions. One area where she did find work was in comedy dances. Although this paid the bills and kept her in the public eye, it exposed her to a degree of ridicule from audiences and critics. Those who had always thought little of her talents felt vindicated in their earlier criticisms, while others who remembered the exciting early dances were quick to laugh at the by then rather stout, matronly figure who was reduced to dancing as a comedy turn within a show. The great Mata Hari was now dancing at the *Folies Bergère* alongside dancers whom she had previously dismissed as 'ladies who style themselves "Eastern Dancers"'.[20] But worse was to come.

She was reported to be among those ladies who availed themselves of *maisons de rendezvous*.[21] She had not had to do so since the desperate days of 1902. These houses were where women met their lovers for an hour or two. They were generally cheap boarding houses, with a landlady who rented rooms by the hour. Not officially classed as brothels by the Paris police, they were tolerated so long as a degree of discretion was exercised. The women who worked in such places were known to the police, and so long as they were not underage and worked discreetly, they were usually allowed to go about their business unmolested. The *maisons de rendezvous* were rather down-at-heel, squalid places in back streets with little or no glamour attached. Mata Hari's appearance at such places, was a far cry from the fashionable promenades she used to take on the Bois de Boulogne. She was also a world away from the international woman of the château at Esvres. The year ended on a miserable note, with performances in dingy music halls interspersed with visits to the *maisons de rendezvous.*

The next year, 1914, started on a much happier note. Mata Hari had finally acquired a rich lover: Constant Bazet, a bank director. She had also spoken to Astruc about adapting her dances and introducing more Egyptian themes. While Astruc worked to find her some bookings, she decided on a trip to Berlin, where she resumed her affair with Kiepert. The Berlin gossip columns took great glee in speculating on the motives for her return. Had she spent the 'several hundred thousand [marks] she had received from Mr K, as a farewell present'?[22] Mindful of the wrath of the notoriously hot-headed Frau Kiepert, the editor had used the pseudonym Mr K. This gave rise to speculation in some quarters that Mata Hari was in fact the mistress of Crown Prince Wilhelm – heir to the German Emperor – although as she and Kiepert were seen together at the Berlin Tiergarten and walking down Unter den Linden, it was quite obvious that Kiepert was Mr K. Mata Hari spent a pleasant spring in Berlin, and finally received word from Astruc that he had managed to secure her a short two-week engagement at the Berlin Metropol for the end of May, followed by a six-month run starting in September of that year. Not only that, but he had managed to negotiate a payment of 48,000 marks for the September engagement.[23] Mata Hari told Kiepert her good news, noting that she would be away from her beloved Paris until well after the end of the year. He then remarked, 'You will be there [presumably meaning Paris] before then and so will I.'[24]

On 23 May 1914, she appeared on stage at the Berlin Metropol and performed her 'Hindu' dance. A complaint was lodged that the performance was immoral. The law on morality and decency was enforced by the *Sittenpolizei* (morals police). The laws, that had been strengthened by the Kaiser, were based on codes of morality that came from the 1880s. Dancers such as Mata Hari routinely fell foul of such laws. The complaint was not upheld, probably as she continued with the fantasy of the sacred nature of the dance, but it had brought her to the attention of Herr Griebel, one of the chiefs of police in Berlin, who shortly afterwards became one of her lovers.

Mata Hari was starting to enjoy life again. She now had four lovers: Bazet, Kiepert, Griebel and Captain Lieutenant Runtze, commander at Seefliegerhorst, Putzig, which was the base of the *Marineflieger-Abteilung* (Naval Air Arm) of the German Empire, founded on 1 July 1913. She spent a pleasant spring and early summer preparing for her autumn dancing performances and dining with her different lovers. But this summer idyll was broken in July when the politics of the Balkans broke into her world and shattered it forever.

8

THE PATH TO WAR

A great deal has been written about the July crisis of 1914. What must be remembered is that history has the luxury of hindsight not afforded to those living through it. The crisis that arose in the Balkans in the summer of 1914 was merely the latest in a series of crises that had been rising and falling like an angry sea since before the Annexation Crisis of 1908, when Austria-Hungary had annexed Bosnia and Herzegovina. Time and again things had threatened to spill over into a more serious conflict before settling down once more to simmer before the next crisis came. People in Europe, even those apparently unconcerned social butterflies like Mata Hari, were aware that there had to be a 'final reckoning' with the Balkan problem some day, but few except those involved in the machinations of international politics could have foreseen the global conflict that would develop.

At the start of the twentieth century, the Austria-Hungary dual monarchy was entwined in a series of treaties and alliances. Indeed most of the European nations were bound to each other with trade agreements and treaties of various kinds. Although generally allowing trade and diplomacy to function, these treaties ensured that the difficulties faced by the dual monarchy would not be localised to the Balkans.

By 1914, the tension in the area remained unresolved, with the potential to explode at any moment. That moment came on 28 June, when Gavrilo Princip, a Bosnian Serb, assassinated Archduke Franz Ferdinand in Sarajevo. The killing led to a series of diplomatic manoeuvrings which tugged and pulled at those treaties and alliances that lay across Europe. Key among these manoeuvrings was the Austro-Hungarian ultimatum which was delivered to the Serbs. This had been deliberately worded so as to be almost impossible for the Serbs to comply with its terms. This would, it was hoped by the war party in Vienna, be rejected, allowing Austria-Hungary to declare war on Serbia, a conflict that would be localised to the Balkans and allow the Slavic question to be finally resolved.

At the beginning of the July crisis, Germany had given its full support to Austria. In the Annexation Crisis of 1908, this stratagem had dissuaded Russia from involvement on behalf of her Slavic cousins. It was assumed that this would continue to contain the Austro-Serb dispute and prevent its spread. However, on 28 July, Russia ordered a partial mobilisation of troops along her southern and western borders, alarming the Germans, and on 1 August, Germany declared war on Russia.

The slide from peace to war had repercussions across Europe, not least in the change in power politics in many nations. Cabinet politicians across Europe saw their status shift as generals and spymasters came to the fore. Memories of previous conflicts and military tactics were discussed, alongside the effectiveness of intelligence-gathering and the use of spies.

While generals prepared for war and spymasters considered how best to deploy their agents, Mata Hari was in Berlin. At the end of July, she was dining out with her lover, police chief Griebel, when a demonstration broke out:

> We heard the noise of a great disturbance. This demonstration was certainly spontaneous and Griebel, who had not had any warning of it, took me in his car to the place where it was held. I saw an enormous mob that was giving way to a frenetic demonstration in front of the Emperor's palace and shouting

'*Deutschland über alles!*' Several days later war was declared. At the time, the police were treating foreigners like animals. Several times, I was stopped in the street and transported to the station, because they were absolutely convinced I was Russian.[1]

On 1 August, Germany declared war and the international situation deteriorated further. Mata Hari decided to return home to Paris. She was concerned that her home in France might not be safe, because she was not French. She was contracted to appear at the Metropol in September, but attempted to break the contract, arguing that war was an act of God and therefore something for which she could not be sued. The theatre manager, Richard Shultz, disagreed, but failed to initiate legal proceedings against her in the chaos of those first few days. Her costumier was also demanding payment, and when that was not forthcoming seized some of Mata Hari's furs and jewellery in lieu of the debt. Desperate to retrieve her property, but equally keen to leave Berlin for the safety of Paris, Mata Hari turned to the German agent Astruc had employed to handle the Berlin side of her affairs during her time at the Metropol. However, the agent had decided, possibly under the impression that Mata Hari was French, to keep all of the cash that she had lodged with him for safe keeping. The Berlin bank then froze her account under the terms of the emergency regulations put in place by the German government. Unsure how to proceed, Mata Hari filed a legal action against the costumier. She would later lose the case by default as she was not in Berlin to appear when the case was called to court. However, it was becoming obvious that as a long-term French resident, Mata Hari was viewed as an undesirable alien.

She packed her bags and headed for Paris. The emergency restrictions meant it was unlikely she would be able to cross the German–French border directly. On 6 August, therefore, she boarded a train for Switzerland, hoping to gain a connection to Paris from Zurich. She was stopped at the border by the German guards, who demanded to see her papers and to know her destination. Incautiously, she said she was heading for France, but also that she was a Dutch national. Unfortunately, she did not have a passport and was unable to prove her nationality. The guards refused to allow her to pass, and she was forced to return to Berlin, but without being allowed to keep her luggage.

Passports had previously been in force across Europe, but when railways started to cross the continent they had increasingly been seen as inconvenient, expensive and time-consuming. Upper-class travellers resented having to produce their papers to border guards, and smaller countries found the time and expense of having guards checking passports to be counterproductive. By the mid-nineteenth century, many regions merely paid lip service to the idea of border checks and several countries – including France, Italy, Germany, Belgium, Spain, the Netherlands and Switzerland – abolished passports altogether. Passports were reintroduced at the outbreak of war, but were by no means ubiquitous and many individuals continued to travel with minimal papers.

Mata Hari arrived back in Berlin and called Griebel, who refused to give her any assistance. The state of war rendered him unable to offer help to a foreign national, even had he wanted to do so. Mata Hari was left friendless and with little money. She turned to the small Dutch community in Berlin, and after a few days met a Dutch businessman willing to help her. The businessman was leaving Berlin for the Netherlands immediately, but gave her the money to survive for a few days and bought her a ticket home. Although she now had some money, she still needed a passport and was required to travel to Frankfurt, where Dutch nationals without papers were processed after proving their identity. The passport issued in Frankfurt had a few interesting anomalies. The document described Mata Hari as being 1m 80cm tall (she was 1m 78cm) with a big nose, brown eyes and blonde hair (her natural hair colour was dark brown, almost black). Her age was written by hand correctly as 38, and was then subsequently overwritten as 30. It cannot be confirmed, but the change in age may have been made by Mata Hari herself. Having received the passport, she returned to Berlin, where she boarded a train to Amsterdam.

Upon her arrival in Amsterdam, she booked into a room at the Victoria Hotel and reviewed her options. She met with the Dutch businessman and his wife, who had helped her in Berlin, to express her thanks. From there she re-entered Dutch society and very quickly acquired a new lover – a Dutch banker, van der Schelk, who mistook her for a Russian émigré.[2] It is unclear how and why this deception arose, although it is possible that Mata Hari was reinventing herself again. The beginning of the Great War was a confusing time. The romance and adventure of war caught the imagination of many, unaware of the horrors that lay ahead. Neutral Netherlands may have appeared as a perfectly safe little haven for the bourgeoisie-minded in Amsterdam, but for Mata Hari to be Dutch at a time of heightened emotions may have been somewhat tedious. A harmless reinvention as a Russian may have given her just the required air of mystique. The deception could not last, however, and after a month she was recognised, her lover was embarrassed and the affair was over. During that time, Schelk had given Mata Hari the finances with which to re-establish herself and, with his banking connections, had even managed to get some of her money released from the bank in Berlin.

Mata Hari next met with an old lover, Baron Edouard Willem van der Capellan, a colonel in the Dutch cavalry. He was exactly what she wanted in a lover: he was a soldier; he was ten years older than her; he was undemanding; he was married; and he was wealthy. Within a matter of weeks, she was re-established as his mistress and he was looking around for a suitable property for her. In October, she found a house she liked at 16 Nieuwe Uitleg in The Hague, and spent several months overseeing repairs and renovations and ordering new furniture while staying at the Paulez Hotel. In the same month, Non started attending teacher-training college in The Hague, but mother and daughter do not appear to have met during this time. Mata Hari spent the end of 1914 in a whirl of domestic arrangements, sorting out stabling for the horses that had been bought for her, and attending parties and the theatre on the arm of Capellan.

In the New Year, Mata Hari had few dancing engagements but remained a celebrity in the public eye. Astruc had managed to interest a Dutch magazine in interviewing her, and she was photographed for the front cover. The March 1915 edition showed her wearing a hat, white dress and a pearl necklace. The photograph caused a considerable commotion as the dress was extremely low-cut.[3] Not only was it immodest for a woman of her age and class, it was considered bad taste to wear such fashion during the war. Most women in Europe were 'doing their bit' for the war by dressing in a much more sombre fashion.

Mata Hari either failed to notice, or chose to ignore, the changing mood in Europe. In addition to her giving interviews, she recommenced overseeing the house renovations, which went on for some time. The agreement with the contractor was for payments to be made in several instalments over a two-year period. However, as the weeks dragged on well into 1915, Mata Hari changed her mind time and again over what work she wanted done and her relationship with the contractor became increasingly strained. The contractor, having to order and then re-order materials, demanded early payment; Mata Hari demanded completion. After the intervention of her lawyers, the work was finally completed and she moved in on 11 August 1915. Her troubles were not over, however, as the bill from the Victoria Hotel and several costumiers and milliners remained outstanding. Despite the generous allowance from Capellan, Mata Hari spent several weeks fending off demands from creditors and threats of legal action.

In addition, Mata Hari was bored. Riding her horses gave some relief, but there were few young officers to admire her as she cantered through the local parks. The initial glamour and excitement of the war had worn off, and the Netherlands had settled into relatively placid neutrality. Capellan was almost 50 years old and a colonel in a non-combatant army. He was not a dashing heroic figure. Life in the Netherlands was uneasy and dull. There were several shortages, although none too severe to affect the likes of Mata Hari, and the ever-practical Dutch buckled down to the business of surviving a war. Mata Hari was not practical. The newspapers were filled with reports of the war, with long casualty lists and detailed analysis of battles and manoeuvres. She only read the society pages and the gossip columns.

In 1915, she made one of her most stupid mistakes: instead of remaining in the safe Netherlands under the protection of Capellan, she decided to return to Paris. Her only problem was how and when.

9

THE UNDESIRABLE ALIEN

Mata Hari had settled into life at Nieuwe Uitleg when suddenly, in the autumn of 1915, she had an unexpected visitor. Karl Kroemer,[1] the honorary German Consul in Amsterdam, was a career civil servant within the German intelligence services. The outbreak of the war had seen his role change from monitoring the low-level surveillance in a friendly nation to the active recruitment of potential agents for the German state.[2] His clear intention was to recruit her as an agent. It is unclear why she was thought suitable to be a German agent, and whether this had been Kroemer's decision or that of his superiors. However, at the meeting, Mata Hari did not refuse but merely haggled over the salary she might receive. He offered 20,000 francs, which she did not feel was high enough. Kroemer countered that initially this would be payment towards a trial period, and were she to prove successful she would be paid more. Mata Hari agreed and was ecstatic that Kroemer had given her the means to return to Paris. She failed completely to see the danger involved in espionage work, even when Kroemer gave her three bottles of invisible ink and gave her the codename H21, which she was to use in all communications. This codename indicates that Mata Hari's German handler would have been one Captain Hoffman, and as the agents were numbered sequentially, the date of her recruitment can be fixed around the autumn of 1915.[3]

Hoffman and Kroemer both came under the direction of Major Walter Nicolai, head of Department IIIB of the German General Staff in charge of espionage and counter-espionage. Nicolai ordered her to Cologne for six weeks of training under the instruction of Major Roepell. This was normal procedure for all new agents. Mata Hari denied ever having attended any training, and no records exist to prove or otherwise. Her reports were to be sent to the *Kriegsnachrichtenstelle West* (War News Post West) in Düsseldorf under Roepell, as well as to the Agent Mission in the German Embassy in Madrid under Major Arnold Kalle.

Mata Hari consistently claimed she never had any intention of spying for the Germans. When questioned, she maintained that when her furs, jewellery and money had been seized at the outbreak of war, her feelings had turned against Germany. Kroemer's offer of 20,000 francs was, as far as Mata Hari was concerned, repayment for all these losses. She stated, 'I bowed Kroemer out the door, but I assure you that I never wrote him anything during my time in Paris. I add that once I was on the canal between Amsterdam and the sea, I threw away my three bottles [of invisible ink] after emptying them.'[4]

This version of events was repeated in various forms throughout her questioning by the French intelligence services.

Despite the 20,000 francs payment from Kroemer and the fact she was now 39 years old, Mata Hari continued to appear on stage, albeit in short pieces and in solo dances to avoid the embarrassment of being alongside younger, better-trained dancers. In December 2015, Astruc managed to secure her a place in a production being put on by the French opera at the *Koninklijke Schouwburg* (Theatre Royal) on Korte Voorhout in the centre of The Hague. Her performance consisted of one solo, fully clothed, dance. The reviews were kind, if not overly enthusiastic in their praise. The opera then moved to Arnhem, where again the reviews were polite.

After this renewal of her dancing and the relatively good reviews, she finally started to plan her return to Paris in late December.

Travel from the Netherlands to France via Belgium was impossible, so the only route was by sea via the British port of Folkestone. She sailed on the Dieppe boat-train, and on arrival at Folkestone on 4 December she was questioned by the British police under the Aliens Act 1914. Police constable Bickers found her to be unsatisfactory, and reported the matter to his superiors, Sergeant Warrell and Superintendent Quinn. Although she had done nothing untoward, something in her manner was enough to arouse the suspicions of the police, who contacted the MI5 (the Directorate of Military Intelligence, Section 5). MI5 officer Captain Dillon questioned Mata Hari. The answers she gave to the police and the intelligence officer varied to such an extent that they had serious misgivings about her, although there was no concrete proof of wrongdoing. She told the police that she was travelling to Paris in order to sell some articles from her house in Neuilly and to sign some contracts for performances.[5] However, in her answers to Dillon she stated that she was closing up the house in Neuilly in order to then move to The Hague to be with her lover, Baron van der Capellan. As something of an afterthought, Mata Hari said that she was also signing contracts for performances in London and some provincial English theatres.[6]

The discrepancies in these two accounts could have been for a number of reasons. She was a middle-class woman, with upper-class pretensions, who may have felt that the obviously lower-class Bickers had no business knowing all of her affairs. The relationship with the baron could, however, be divulged to upper-class Major Dillon. The addition of the London and provincial English theatres may have been a complete invention because she sensed she was under suspicion and wished to appear more friendly to the British authorities. Of course, if she was working as a German spy, then the insertion of the baron's name and the invention of the London and provincial English theatres may have indeed been produced as an attempt to appear more friendly and allay British suspicions. It should be noted that no contracts for such theatres have ever been found.

After her questioning by Dillon and a review of Mata Hari's previous answers, it was noted that, 'Although she was thoroughly searched and nothing incriminating found, she is regarded by Police and Military to be not above suspicion and her subsequent movements should be watched.'[7]

The British authorities took two immediate actions. Firstly, a note was sent to all British ports, the Home Office, Scotland Yard, Military Intelligence, Havre, GHG (Intelligence Office) and the Permit Office that Mata Hari, 'appeared most unsatisfactory and should be refused permission to return to the United Kingdom'.[8]

The second action of the British authorities was to send a copy of the report that called for Mata Hari to be watched straight to the French intelligence service. She left for France on the SS *Arundell* on 9 December, under no illusions that as a suspicious foreign alien she was now *persona non grata* as far as the British authorities were concerned.

The British Nationality and Status of Aliens Act 1914 had come into force on 14 August 1914 as a direct consequence of war.[9] The act forced all aliens resident in the United Kingdom over the age of 16 to register at local police stations and to demonstrate a good character and knowledge of English. The Act gave the police and intelligence services wide-ranging powers to detain and question any adult alien who arrived in the United Kingdom. While it allowed the authorities to deport Mata Hari, their grounds for doing so appear to have amounted to little more than vague suspicions aroused by her demeanour. By December 1915, the lack of progress in the war had so heightened fears of sabotage and actions by enemy agents that the British authorities were proactively targeting anyone acting slightly suspiciously.

When Mata Hari finally arrived in Paris, she put the unpleasantness in Britain behind her. She moved into *Le Grand Hôtel Français* on the Boulevard Voltaire. She contacted Astruc, instructing him to approach Diaghilev on her behalf; Mata Hari was convinced that her new dances would be appropriate for his *Ballets Russes*. Her previous rejection by the company had, obviously, not permanently dented her confidence. However, despite her belief in herself, Diaghilev remained unconvinced and Astruc could not even secure an audition with the *Ballets Russes*.

Despite this disappointment, Mata Hari kept busy. She settled into *La Grande Hôtel Français*, where she renewed affairs with Henri de Marguérite and the Marquis de Beaufort. The former was secretary to the French legation to The Hague and the latter an officer of the Belgian Army. In addition, she had acquired a third lover, Emilio Junouy, a Spanish senator. Despite these sexual liaisons, she was soon on her travels again and in early 1916 was heading to The Hague via Spain and Portugal.

Mata Hari's behaviour at this time is difficult to analyse. The three new liaisons, all of which were initiated by Mata Hari, could have been romantic or monetary. They could of course have been a combination of the two, as despite the generosity of Capellan, Mata Hari always needed more money, and knew how to get it. They could equally have been opportunities to gather information for the German intelligence services. Her movements seem somewhat strange. The previous autumn she had been desperate to leave the Netherlands and return to her beloved Paris. Yet in early 1916, she left Paris and travelled back to the Netherlands, despite the difficulties in travel during wartime. Was this move yet another whim or did she need to make contact with her German handler in the Netherlands?

Whatever her reasons, her new liaisons were noted by British intelligence, who had put Mata Hari under surveillance. The records are unclear as to who had ordered this and whether it was initiated for a specific or general reason, but MI5 were watching Mata Hari from February 1916, and possibly since her arrival in Paris in December 1915. It is also unclear from the records whether the French intelligence services knew of the continued action of the British. However, given the fact that the British had notified the French of their suspicions about her the previous December, it is probable that both agencies were in communication in some way. Nevertheless, it must be remembered that even between friendly nations the protocols surrounding espionage work were complex and delicate, with certain operations undertaken with tacit consent that was never formalised in written communication.

On 3 February, Richard Tinsley, a British intelligence agent working in the Netherlands, sent a report on Mata Hari to London. It stated that she was in financial difficulties and his unnamed source said she had received '15,000 francs from the German Embassy via a certain Hans Sagace'.[10] The report went on to note, 'She is suspected of having been to France on an important mission for the Germans.'[11]

On 16 February, a second report was sent to London. This stated that Mata Hari had 'succeeded in her mission, and is to get now an amount, which has been deposited in a bank for her by the Germans [sic]'.[12]

How Tinsley knew what was happening inside the German Embassy is unclear. Information about Mata Hari that was useful to the Allies became conveniently available on several occasions during the British and French surveillance. On 22 February, the British intelligence services sent a note to the French intelligence services about her. The note stated that if Mata Hari was to enter Great Britain, she would be arrested immediately and sent to Scotland Yard.[13] Although it may seem curious for the British to tell the French that a Dutch citizen would be arrested if she set foot in Britain, it was probably the most effective way they had to alert the French to their suspicions, given the lack of hard evidence against her at that time. If the British were watching Mata Hari without official approval, they could not 'officially' report the results of their surveillance. The world of espionage and counter-espionage had to function within the normal diplomatic relations between countries. Even in wartime, a foreign nation conducting surveillance on a citizen of a neutral country in a third allied country would have been politically sensitive.

Mata Hari decided that life in The Hague with Capellan did not suit her after all, and wanted to return to Paris. In early April 1916, she approached the authorities in The Hague, who issued her with a new Dutch passport on 15 May. She went to the French Consulate, which issued her with a visa to enter France. The quickest and safest route from the Netherlands to France at that time was again by sea. So, despite having been told quite plainly in November that she was not to return to the United Kingdom, she went to the British Consulate in Rotterdam and applied for a visa, but the Consulate refused to issue it. Mata Hari then visited the Foreign Office in The Hague to ask them to intervene on her behalf. She presumably did not tell the officials there of her experience with the British authorities in the previous November. John Loudon, Minister of Foreign Affairs, sent a telegram to the Dutch Ambassador in London, Reneke de Marees van Swinderen, to ask for his help:

> Well known artist Mata Hari, Dutch subject whose legal name is MacLeod Zelle, wants to go for personal reasons to Paris where she has lived before the war. British consulate Rotterdam declines to put visa to passport though French consul has done so. Please beg British government to give orders to consul Rotterdam that visa may be granted.[14]

Swinderen approached the Home Office in London and was told that Mata Hari was an 'undesirable' and would not be allowed entry into the United Kingdom. He replied to The Hague, 'British have reason [to] consider entry into Britain of lady described … undesirable.'[15]

Loudon then told Mata Hari that London would not issue her with a visa and advised her to seek an alternative route. Loudon does not appear to have disclosed to her the reason for the British refusal. She should have already known why she was refused entry. This makes her decision to ask for the British visa somewhat puzzling. Had she misunderstood what had happened in November? Was her attempt to gain a visa a matter of testing the waters to see how robust the British security measures were? Or had she been instructed by the Germans to try to gain a visa in order to distract the British authorities from the activities of another of their agents?

Whatever Mata Hari's reasons for the application, the lack of a British visa forced her to make alternative travel arrangements. She approached the Spanish Consulate and obtained a visa to travel through Spain. She finally boarded the SS *Zeelandia* on 24 May. It sailed from Amsterdam bound for Vigo in Spain, from where she intended to travel by train to Madrid and then catch a connecting train to Paris.

While on the *Zeelandia*, Mata Hari was warned by a Dutch passenger, Cleyndert – a merchant from Zaandam – that another passenger by the name of Hoedemaker had been making certain claims about her conduct. Hoedemaker said he had visited Mata Hari in her cabin, strongly implying they had had sex. Mata Hari publicly confronted Hoedemaker, who admitted he had not been in her cabin but had spread the rumour. Mata Hari responded by slapping Hoedemaker across the face. The matter escalated further when another passenger, the Urugyuan Consul, warned Mata Hari that Hoedemaker was seeking revenge. Mata Hari said, 'If he wishes, I will place a slap of the sort he has already received on the other cheek.'[16]

The consul thought that Hoedemaker could cause Mata Hari problems later, and in the heightened atmosphere of the war this was not a warning to take lightly. Hoedemaker claimed to be in the pay of the British. When she disembarked at Vigo, she was followed by Hoedemaker. When she reached Madrid on 12 June, she settled into her room at the Hotel Palace and saw him outside watching her room.

Immediately after reaching the hotel, Mata Hari applied for and received her visa to cross the border into France. She travelled to the town of Irún on the border and then crossed over to Hendaye in the province of Lapurdi. Here she was stopped and questioned by French borders guards, who refused to allow her to pass. She returned to Irún and wrote to the Dutch Consul in Madrid, Royen, to complain about her treatment. Royen spoke to the French Consul in Madrid and discovered that Mata Hari was listed by the British as suspect, and therefore had been refused entry into France. His assistant wrote to Mata Hari stating that 'not even the intervention of the Minister could avail anything; neither [could] the declarations that your sympathies are pro-Ally'.[17]

Having received no help from Royen, she wrote to one of her previous lovers, Jules Cambon, who had been promoted to secretary-general of the French Ministry of Foreign Affairs. There is no record of Cambon replying to her, but the next day she returned to Hendaye and attempted to cross the border. Mata Hari used Cambon's name to intimidate the guards, who let her pass. It had taken her six weeks to complete her journey and Hoedemaker was nowhere to be seen.

He was listed on the passenger manifest of the SS *Zeelandia* as a 'salesman' and a 'Jew' of Dutch nationality. Despite his country's neutrality, he claimed to have denounced several German sympathisers to the British authorities. What his interest in Mata Hari was may never be satisfactorily explained. If he was working for the British or French intelligence services, there is no mention of him in the records. If he was an agent working under an alias, it is extremely unlikely he would then have continued to live under that name after his active service was over.

There is no evidence that Hoedemaker was involved in the incident at Hendaye. However, it remains a curious incident. Mata Hari had been issued with a visa to travel into France by the Consulate in The Hague and in Madrid, so why was she stopped at Hendaye? Had her previous application for a visa to travel into Britain raised suspicion, causing the British to notify the French of their concerns? If so, then why, after being refused entry, was she allowed to cross the border the next day?

When Mata Hari finally arrived in Paris on 15 June, she moved into a suite of rooms at the Grand Hotel on the Boulevard des Capucines. Almost immediately she realised she was being watched by two men. She complained to the hotel porter,[18] but as the men were neither hotel staff nor customers, so there was little the staff at the Grand could do. The men were Monier and Tarlet, two inspectors with the Paris Prefecture assigned to special duties. At the outbreak of the war, the French intelligence service worked closely with the Paris Prefecture under the command of Émile Marie Laurent. Several police officers were assigned to the intelligence services.

It is not known if Monier and Tarlet deliberately allowed Mata Hari to see them to ensure she knew she was under surveillance. Due to the state of France at that time, the intelligence agencies and police authorities were stretched to their limits, and although there is nothing to suggest that Monier and Tarlet were not competent police officers, they were unused to intelligence work. Between 18 June 1916 and 13 January 1917, they were tasked with following Mata Hari whenever she was in Paris. This was not always successful, as she frequently eluded them. She had money and could arrange for a taxi to be waiting for her when she left the Grand Hotel. Despite talking to the hotel staff, Monier and Tarlet were not always able to find out in advance what she was up to, and were frequently wrong-footed when she sped away in a taxi, leaving them behind. The two officers also had the problem of being on a limited police budget. While Mata Hari could walk into the front door of the most fashionable restaurants in Paris or into a box at the opera, Monier and Tarlet could find themselves barred from entry by a maître d' unimpressed by their police credentials.

Despite these problems, Monier and Tarlet amassed an impressive file on her activities, including most of the men she met. Her lovers included the Marquis de Beaufort, a 42-year-old Commandant of the Fourth Belgian Lancers, of the Division of the Cavalry of the Army of the Yser; Bernard Antoine, a French wine merchant; Jean Hallaure, a 26-year-old Second Lieutenant in the French Cavalry; and Vladimir de Masloff, a 21-year-old captain in the Special Russian Regiment of the First Brigade.

Hallaure had seen Mata Hari in the Grand Hotel in mid-July, and had sent her his card asking for a meeting. They met on 21 and 22 July, and again on the 25th.[19] Within days of the affair starting, Hallaure was warned by a fellow officer to stop seeing her. When interviewed about her, Hallaure stated:

[M]y friend Capt Christian de Mouchy … said to me one day, 'My boy, in your place, I would not go around so often with this woman. You belong to the army, where the most unfortunate rumours circulate about her. She is an alien, she was [involved] with a German before the war, and I believe she is a suspect.'[20]

On 27 July, Mata Hari decided she wanted to go to a spa town to take the waters. She had been feeling unwell for some time and had previously talked about taking the cure at Vittel, which was in Lorraine in north-eastern France. Due to its location so near to military action, she would require a permit to travel there, and needed a good reason for the pass to be issued. According to Hallaure, Mata Hari asked his advice on 27 July about approaching a physician who might testify as to her need to visit Vittel. It is not clear why Mata Hari would have needed Hallaure to give her the name of a physician. Presumably, had the illness been genuine, her own doctor could have easily written a recommendation to go to a spa town to take the waters. However, the nature of the illness was never fully explained. Hallaure's testimony stated he did not realise that Mata Hari was unwell, as he had not observed 'any change in her'.[21] It is also unclear why she wanted to go to Vittel, which was in a military zone, rather than any of the other spas available which were in safe French territory. According to Hallaure's testimony, she also asked him how to go about obtaining the permit to travel to Vittel. Hallaure told her to go to the Military Bureau for Foreigners,[22] where she would be referred to the *Deuxiéme Bureau* (French Intelligence). Hallaure then attempted to further assist Mata Hari by mentioning her request to a second lieutenant he knew slightly who worked in the bureau.[23]

For a serving military officer to have helped someone he had been warned about in such a manner was foolhardy. He was only 26 and appears to have been besotted with Mata Hari. Monier and Tarlet's reports list the dates when Hallaure and Mata Hari were together; between 21 July and 30 August, the couple met nine times and corresponded three times, despite Hallaure being on duty for most of those days. The affair appears to have been intense, although not quite reciprocal. On 29 July, Mata Hari met Vladimir de Masloff.[24] The passion that Hallaure felt for Mata Hari was apparently matched by the passion she felt for Masloff. Masloff and Mata Hari met at the salon hosted by Madame Dangeville, where Nicholas Casfield, a second lieutenant in Masloff's regiment and one of her previous suitors, introduced them. They met again on 30 July and spent most of the day and night together. This was despite the fact that she had told Hallaure that she needed to go to Vittel urgently.

Whatever the nature of Mata Hari's illness, her relationship with Hallaure and his later recollection of events, on 31 July she entered the Police Commissariat on the Rue Taitbout to ask for a permit to travel to Calais and Vittel. This was denied, as both Calais and Vittel were in military zones. It is unclear why Mata Hari had added Calais to her trip. Her visit to the police rather than the Military Bureau for Foreigners on 31 July contradicts Hallaure's testimony that he told her to go to the Military Bureau on 27 July. This anomaly may have arisen from a simple case of confusion when Hallaure was questioned in 1917, although that is unlikely as Hallaure, as a serving French Army officer, knew which departments dealt with travel permits. It is possible that when questioned, he attempted to distance himself from the suspected spy, especially as he had been warned previously about her conduct. Further contradictions and confusions arise. After she was refused permission by the police to travel, she asked the prefecture of police for a copy of her French registration papers to attach to her permit application. Presumably she had been told by the police to approach the bureau if she wished to pursue her permit application. Why she wanted a copy of her papers from the police and would not wait for the bureau to copy them is unclear. She then wrote a note to Hallaure arranging a meeting for the next day.

On 1 August, Mata Hari collected the copy of her French registration papers, attached it to her permit to travel application and went to the Military Bureau for Foreigners at 282 Boulevard Saint-Germain to ask for a permit to travel to Vittel. After speaking briefly to an official in the bureau, she was sent to the *Deuxiéme Bureau*. There, Georges Ladoux was waiting for her and she encountered for the first time the man who was to play a leading role in her fate.

10

ESPIONAGE FRANÇAIS

Georges Ladoux was head of the *Deuxiéme Bureau* of the French Army Headquarters. He had been appointed to his post on 4 August 1914 by General Joffre, Commander-in-Chief of French forces on the Western Front. In 1914, Joffre was the pre-eminent general within the French Army. He had led the retreating allied armies in a successful counter-strike against the Germans at the strategically decisive First Battle of the Marne in September 1914. Ladoux's appointment was important to both men. The previous intelligence service had presided over the disastrous Dreyfus Affair, which had jailed the completely innocent Alfred Dreyfus. In 1906, Dreyfus was exonerated and reinstated as a major in the French Army. The levels of treason, corruption and incompetence that had been exposed had vilified the intelligence service, which was disbanded and the new *Deuxiéme Bureau* created.

Despite the new personnel brought in to work there, the intelligence services remained suspect in many eyes. Espionage was thought at best to be a fruitless activity and at worst to be unethical. Ladoux and Joffre were unusual in their view that espionage could be a key weapon in winning the war. At that time, and particularly because of the Dreyfus scandal, it had to be argued that espionage could provide crucial information about enemy troop movements while feeding misinformation to the other side. In addition, the detection and interrogation of foreign agents stemmed the flow of information in the opposite direction. However, many still believed espionage to be of little value. On 10 September 1915, Ladoux wrote to Alexandre Millerand, the Minister of War, and Louis Malvy, the Minister of the Interior:

> The enemy does not limit himself to spying the details of our military operations: he searches also to dissolve all our national defence forces. His action attacks establishments working for the State, in an attempt to destroy them, or tries to debauch the personnel. He tries to injure our credit or drain our gold.[1]

Although Ladoux had written to Louis Malvy, the Minister for the Interior at that time was Théodore Steeg, who had succeeded Malvy on 1 September 1915.

This letter was important for several reasons. By September 1915, France and her allies had suffered several military defeats. The war had changed and the national mood was ugly. General Joffre was out of favour with the government and a culture of blame was starting to develop. It was at that moment that Ladoux stressed again the role of espionage, both in generating military intelligence and thwarting enemy agents. While not entirely convinced, the politicians in the government were more inclined to listen to Ladoux than before. He was given a greater degree of autonomy in running the *Deuxiéme Bureau*, and even started to take over control of counter-espionage, which had previously come under the jurisdiction of the *Sûreté*.

As Ladoux started to increase the strength of the *Deuxiéme Bureau*, he received a communication about Mata Hari from the intelligence services in Great Britain on 5 December 1915, that stated, 'Although she was thoroughly searched and nothing incriminating found, she is regarded by Police and Military to be not above suspicion, and her subsequent movements should be watched.'[2]

It is not known what Ladoux's reaction was to receiving this report from the British, but it certainly strengthened his case for the need for the *Deuxiéme Bureau*. A report from France's major ally could not be ignored, especially when it was followed up on 22 February 1916 with another. That report stated that, if Mata Hari was to enter Great Britain, she would be arrested immediately and sent to Scotland Yard.[3] This report landed on Ladoux's desk the day after the Battle of Verdun started.

The Battle of Verdun was fought on the Western Front between the German and French armies, on the hills north of Verdun-sur-Meuse in north-eastern France. The German invasion of France had faltered and then stopped at the First Battle of the Marne in September 1914. By the end of the First Battle of Ypres, in November 1914, movement on the Western Front had all but halted. The Germans dug in and built field fortifications to hold the ground they had captured. The French countered this with a series of siege offensives intended to break through the German lines and recover their lost territory. A long, bloody war of attrition developed and dragged through 1915, sapping French manpower and morale. The Chief of the German General Staff, Erich von Falkenhayn, aware of the situation in France and the state of the German troops, believed that the French Army could be defeated if it could be made to suffer a sufficiently high number of casualties.

In December 1915, he wrote to the Kaiser:

> The string in France has reached breaking point. A mass breakthrough, which in any case is beyond our means, is unnecessary. Within our reach there are objectives for the retention of which the French General Staff would be compelled to throw in every man they have. If they do so the forces of France will bleed to death.[4]

While it has been suggested that Falkenhayn actually wrote this letter after the event to defend his actions at Verdun, it accurately demonstrates the mindset of many, if not most, within the German High Command at the time. The offensive that was thus unleashed on 21 February was intended to be as bloody as possible in its execution, and was named *Unternehmen Gericht* (Operation Judgement).

The offensive began at 7.15 a.m. with an artillery bombardment by 808 guns which lasted for some ten hours. Around a million shells were fired at the French, with the main barrage concentrated on the *Région Fortifiée de Verdun* on the east bank of the Meuse River. The forts and city of Verdun came under continuous fire from dawn until midday from twenty-six super-heavy, long-range guns, the noise of which was heard 160km away. During the afternoon, the bombardment ceased temporarily while German artillery-observation aircraft flew reconnaissance over the area. At 4 p.m., the 3rd, 7th and 18th Corps attacked the French positions. The German troops used flamethrowers for the first time, and the main assault was followed by storm troopers using hand grenades to kill the remaining defenders; no prisoners were to be taken. By 22 February, the German forces had advanced 5km and captured Bois des Caures, close to the edge of Flabas. By the evening of 22 February, the French High Command realised the seriousness of the attack. The next day, that seriousness had been relayed to the intelligence services and Ladoux.

The offensive at Verdun stunned the French people, and as the battle dragged on – lasting until 18 December 1916 – it raised serious questions. Why were the German guns so accurate? How could the Germans know the French military positions so well? Had they privileged information, and if so, how had they gained it? The resistance of the troops at Verdun became a focus of pride and determination around which the French nation rallied, although this meant that anyone not vocal in their support became suspect. All of these issues came to rest in the *Deuxiéme Bureau*, as did the correspondence from British Intelligence about Mata Hari. She was, of course, not the only suspect whom Ladoux had to deal with, but by mid-June 1916, she was becoming a person of interest. The situation in Verdun remained ever-present. Mata Hari continued to have her public love affairs with various military officers, remained ostentatious in her clothing and excessive in her shopping, and despite her love of military men, remained notably silent on the issue of the bravery of the troops fighting at Verdun. On 18 June, Ladoux sent for detectives Monier and Tarlet and instructed them to keep Mata Hari under close observation.

Monier and Tarlet's initial reports about their quarry are full of the minutiae of Mata Hari's life: which costumier she visited, what hats she ordered from the milliners, which lovers she had met, where and for how long. They also detail the restaurants she visited, the cabs she took and the times she eluded them, with apparent ease and obvious amusement at their frustration. Had the reports been from 1910 or even 1920, they would have been an amusing, if somewhat tedious, portrayal of the life of a spoilt member of *La Grande Horizontale* (i.e. a prostitute). In 1916, however, with suspicions already heightened by the reports from Great Britain, every aspect of Mata Hari's behaviour became a point of concern. Loyal French women were wearing dark-coloured demure clothing; Mata Hari was still wearing bold shades and low-cut blouses. Spending on clothing had reduced across the board; who would think of buying a new hat when French sons were dying on the Western Front? Mata Hari continued to purchase more new and expensive items; where did she get her money? The fashion for wearing the French Tricolor in one's hat or as a lapel pin was prevalent. Despite her pleas that she adored Paris and the fact that she had made the city her home since 1905, there was no sign of a Tricolor on Mata Hari. Finally, there was the long list of lovers.

Love affairs were common in fashionable Paris, as in other cities across Europe in 1916, but the nuances of what was or was not acceptable were varied and subtle, and she did not conform to any notion of acceptable behaviour. Men could have dalliances in upper-middle and high-class society; indeed it was expected that men should have affairs. Respectable women were not thought to really enjoy sex. Marriage provided children and a family life, but sexual enjoyment was mostly to be sought elsewhere. Mistresses provided men with amusement and diversion from their business lives. Mistresses, unburdened by household chores or childcare, were always in a good mood. They would accompany their lovers on their less than respectable outings to places such as casinos or variety theatres. Mistresses enjoyed sex, but were still, for the most part, passive recipients of male attention. Those women who actively sought out their own lovers were few in number, but still accepted the subordinate role assigned to them. Any man could have multiple mistresses at any one time and be lauded by his male friends. No woman could think of having more than one lover at a time, and those who had several over a lifetime found their reputation ruined. In the end, all mistresses knew that when a man had finished with them and returned to his wife and family, or found another mistress, they had no option but to accept the situation.

Mata Hari did not accept it. She did not fulfil the normal role of the mistress happy to accept her fate. It had been this behaviour which had scandalised the Kiepert family. She actively sought out her lovers. She had several, sometimes seeing more than one on the same day. She was particularly fond of military men; a dangerous preference in wartime, compounded by the fact that she collected lovers from several nationalities. And, probably most damning of all, Mata Hari appeared to like sex. Within the psychology of the day, a woman who claimed to like sex and had multiple lovers had to be depraved. Depravity was a complex issue in Europe in the early twentieth century. Most scientists and psychiatrists saw such people as having a mental illness, having degenerated from normal human beings. In France in the late nineteenth century, the scientist Benedict Augustus Morel had written about the underlying 'natural forces' that shaped crime, sickness and mental disorders.[5] He suggested that psychological disorders, and generally all abnormalities of human behaviour, were an expression of an abnormal constitution in the organisms that displayed disorders. His work was highly influential in determining official attitudes to behaviours that fell outside the norm. While mental illness remained in the purview of doctors, abnormalities of human behaviour, most notably crime, were dealt with by the police. A woman who acted in a depraved manner, who liked sex, was therefore degenerate; and a degenerate could act in other criminal ways, such as betraying their country to a foreign power. What was unthinkable to a 'normal' individual was acceptable to a depraved person, and as such they would not only carry out these criminal acts but do so openly and without any expression of guilt. Such was the mindset of Ladoux when he became aware of Mata Hari.

Mata Hari walked into Ladoux's office on 1 August 1916 in pursuit of her travel permit. Ladoux noted that she was:

> [D]ressed, despite the summer weather, in a suit of a dark hue and sporting a straw hat with a large brim above which floated a grey plume. She entered into my office with the easy gait of an artist, habituated to walk into a scene, but she had in addition a graceful swing of the hips of a dancer.[6]

What then happened in Ladoux's office remains unclear, with both Mata Hari and Ladoux producing varying accounts. According to her, she had visited the *Deuxiéme Bureau* on the advice of Hallaure, who had stated that she would have to do so in order to gain the permit she required for travel to Vittel. She stated that when she arrived, 'An officer in uniform came to look for me on the ground floor and, taking my papers, led me to the second in an office where a gentleman in civilian clothes asked me to sit down facing him and received me very amiably.'[7]

Ladoux then questioned Mata Hari as to her purpose in visiting Vittel.

Ladoux: 'I see, madam, that you have asked to go to Vittel, but do you know it is in the military zone?'

Mata Hari: 'It is a resort where I have gone before. I even have a note from a doctor.'

Ladoux: 'It is very difficult for foreigners to go there.'

Mata Hari: 'If it is as difficult as that I could go near Rome, to Fiuggi, where the waters are of the same nature.'

Ladoux: 'We need not refuse you, but it is necessary to respond to certain questions, because you have been pointed out to us as a suspect.'[8]

After several more questions, Ladoux broached the subject of Mata Hari working for France.

Ladoux: 'If you love all of France, you could render us a great service. Have you thought of that?'

Mata Hari: 'Yes and no, but this is not the sort of thing for which one offers oneself.'

Ladoux: 'Would you do it?'

Mata Hari: 'I have never thought it through.'

Ladoux: 'You would have to be very expensive.'

Mata Hari: 'That, yes!'

Ladoux: 'According to you, what would it be worth?'

Mata Hari: 'All or nothing. If one rendered you services as grand as you expect? Then that is worth a great deal; if one fails, that is worth nothing.'

Ladoux: 'Reflect upon it, see if you could do something for us. I will give you your pass for Vittel, only promise me that you will not seduce any French officers.'

Mata Hari: 'There is no danger of it. I know a Russian [there] with whom I am much in love.'

Ladoux: 'I have seen you having lunch with him at Ambassadors. In any case, when you have reached a decision on the subject about which I have spoken to you, come back to see me.'[9]

If this account by Mata Hari is accurate, it means that Ladoux attempted to recruit her while admitting to her that she was known as a 'suspect'. Whatever Ladoux's motives, Mata Hari knew that in his eyes she was 'suspect'. Payment was openly discussed, although no amount was mentioned. The pass to Vittel was to be granted, despite its location in a war zone and Mata Hari being suspect, with the only restriction placed on her being not to seduce French officers.

Ladoux's account of their first meeting is somewhat different. He later wrote, '"What do you want of me?" she said to me in a French troubled only occasionally by a certain guttural inflection typical of her Oriental type.'

Ladoux: 'I don't wish anything of you, but I hear from one of our mutual acquaintances that you intend to take the waters at Vittel, and as the spa is in the military zone, you must have a *laissez-passer* to go there. Now, it is I who gives them out and I am ready to oblige you.'

Mata Hari: 'Therefore, would you like to do a great service, which is to say to the gentlemen of the police who are downstairs and who don't leave me any more than my shadow does, as it is very warm, will you authorise them to drink my health at the bistro across the street?'

Ladoux: 'I have no authority to do so, Mata Hari. But you are now under surveillance?'

Mata Hari: 'Yes, stupidly, and for several months, day and night. Everywhere I go, they follow me ... they use my absence from the hotel to search my luggage. When I return, everything is upside-down ... you know I have not the means to pay for a lady's maid.'

Ladoux then commented:

The ice is broken but not the charm, and I ask myself, at seeing my visitor's tranquil assurance and self-control, if the English service which pesters me with notes about Mata Hari, for more than a year, is not deceiving itself in telling us, without any proof, that she was a German agent.[10]

The interview continued with Ladoux openly telling Mata Hari of the suspicions about her:

'I assure you that H [Hallaure] does not believe that which our English friends say about you, that is to say, that you are ...'

'A spy,' she interrupted. 'But upon what do they base this accusation? Someone had followed me since I arrived. Has someone revealed something against me?'

'Absolutely nothing, it is why I will authorise you to go to Vittel.'

'Then, this stupid game needs to stop. Either I am dangerous, and then you will expel me, or I am nothing but a pretty little woman who, having danced all winter, wishes very much, now that the summer has come ... to be left in peace.'[11]

Ladoux concluded the meeting by assuring Mata Hari that the *laissez-passer* would be issued on the understanding that she was to meet him again on her return from Vittel. Once she had left the office, he then read over her file:

A few instants later, my faithful secretary, who was at the listening post in the bathroom where he transcribed night and day the most secret information, brought to me the collection of reports from the English police and French, a voluminous and useless packet where, during several months, we had been piling up the communications from the 'Intelligence Service' and the reports of the surveillance of our agents. I glanced through all the pieces once more. I reread the intercepted letters; most, moreover, were those exchanged by the dancer with her Russian captain at the front for several months; all had been submitted to a most minute examination and were cleared by all the chemical tests of our laboratory. There was nothing, absolutely nothing, which permitted another interpretation except a vague feeling![12]

These two accounts of the first crucial meeting between Ladoux and Mata Hari contain a great deal of detail, but care must be taken when trying to analyse this information. It must be remembered, firstly, that both accounts were recorded after the events took place, and by individuals who were justifying their actions. It should also be noted that, if Mata Hari was an active German agent, as Ladoux was head of the *Deuxiéme Bureau*, then both would have reason to lie and obfuscate within their memories of the meeting.

One element that might show his account to be the slightly more plausible of the two is the complaint about Monier and Tarlet, and Mata Hari's apparent understanding that Ladoux was their superior. She had already complained about their presence to the hotel staff, and yet in her own account of her first meeting with Ladoux she did not mention the detectives. It is a curious omission.

Mata Hari's account shows Ladoux openly admitting to her that she was suspect, but still recruiting her to work for the French Intelligence service. In Ladoux's account, Mata Hari is also admitted to being under suspicion, but no question of her working for the French arises. Moreover, Ladoux tells her he does not think she is a spy. His later rereading of her file confirms the lack of evidence against her, but leaves him uneasy. This all appears somewhat obvious. However, there are two points that indicate Ladoux was possibly more than just uneasy.

He had the files from Monier and Tarlet's surveillance of Mata Hari and her correspondence with Masloff. Although these contained no direct evidence of unfriendly activities, they all built up a picture of someone whose behaviour and actions were suspect. Ladoux's denial of responsibility for the policemen's actions was possibly an attempt to keep Mata Hari unaware of how his department worked; essential if she was an enemy agent and prudent if she was not. More puzzling are Ladoux's comments that the English had been pestering him for more than a year about Mata Hari. The first correspondence from British military intelligence to Ladoux had been in December 1915, barely six months previously, and had consisted of only two reports, rather than the multiple reports that 'pestering' suggests. Was Ladoux trying to inflate the amount of work he had been under at the time, or had he been receiving more reports about Mata Hari from a different British source? There are two possible other sources of material from the British.

After Mata Hari left Britain in December 1915, she had been put under surveillance. From February 1916, Richard Tinsley, an MI5 agent, was instructed to have Mata Hari watched. However, Tinsley was based in the Netherlands and, as that country was neutral, any active espionage work by the British breached that neutrality. As he was working on the margins of legal and political protocol, it is possible that any information he or his agents gathered could not officially be shared with allies such as the French. There was nothing to stop Tinsley or his superiors passing on information to Ladoux in less formal ways. His agents continued to watch Mata Hari when she moved to Paris. Espionage work on the soil of an ally was even more fraught with legal and political niceties. Tinsley's reports could not be official unless his actions had been approved by Ladoux's department. No note of any such approval appears in the records, but given Ladoux's attitude to his work and the considerations of war, any unofficial reports from an ally's agency would have been gratefully accepted and read, even if they were not recorded in the files. If Tinsley's information about Mata Hari had been conveyed to Ladoux, it would have certainly caused him some unease, given that it stated that since her arrival in Paris she had received '15,000 francs from the German Embassy which money was paid her by a certain Hans Sagawe'.[13] It also recorded that, 'Mata Hari left some time ago for France on a mission.'[14]

The second source of possible information from the British comes from a more unlikely section of the intelligence services. The British Library contains a letter concerning Mata Hari dated 8 August 1917, written by a Frenchman, Monsieur Folatre. The letter contains several details, most of which are incorrect. In fact, it is riddled with inaccuracies. It states that Mata Hari was born in Belgium, not the Netherlands. It claims her husband was Danish, not Dutch, and that he served in India, not the East Indies. Within the misinformation the letter mentions that, 'During her sojourn in INDIA, ZELLE Marguerite learnt the braminical danses [sic] and, in 1905, she began to produce herself on stage in several great cities in Europe.'[15]

On the surface, this letter appears to be merely a poorly informed piece of private correspondence from one individual to another, and could easily be discounted if it were not for the names of the recipient and the man who also received a copy of the letter: John Arnold Wallinger and Sir Charles Cleveland.

Wallinger was a British Indian intelligence officer who led the Indian Political Intelligence Office from 1909 onwards. He led the Indian intelligence operations from outside India, mostly in Europe, where he and his agents kept many Indian nationals under surveillance. Wallinger operated against the Indian Anarchist movement in England and the Hindu–German Conspiracy during the Great War. The conspiracy was a series of plans developed by Indian nationalist groups to undermine the British Empire in India during the Great War. A group of exiled nationalists in Germany formed part of the Indian Independence Committee, and, working with other exiles and nationalists in India, sought to foment rebellion.[16] In the decade preceding the outbreak of war in 1914, this had been one of the key concerns of the British government, much more so than events in Europe.

Wallinger was a key individual in the intelligence-gathering operations around the nascent Indian independence movement and the Hindu–German Conspiracy. As such, he was only too aware of the presence in Europe of Ustad Inayat Khan, the Indian musician who had performed with Mata Hari in 1913. Despite Khan's proclaimed intent to introduce classical Indian music and the Sufi Order to the West, he was considered a 'person of interest' by Wallinger and was under surveillance from 1910 onwards. Within that surveillance, it is unlikely that someone with Mata Hari's profile consorting with Khan would have gone unnoticed.

The work undertaken by the Indian Political Intelligence Office caused tensions between them and Scotland Yard and British military intelligence. This was based on the political tensions over Indian attempts to gain home rule. Many in the government thought there was no need to create a specialist unit to deal with the problem. However, those in the British Foreign Office and Civil Service successfully lobbied for the creation of the Indian Political Intelligence Office, which was resented by members of Scotland Yard and British military intelligence. When Wallinger arrived in London in 1910, he initially found himself cold-shouldered by members of the Yard.[17] But, by 1911, matters had improved, and by the outbreak of the war, all three departments were working reasonably well together, albeit with different targets in mind. One of Wallinger's main problems lay in the surveillance of Indian nationals outside Britain, most notably in France. When the Indian Political Intelligence Office asked the French for help in the surveillance of Indian nationals in France, the Deuxième Bureau stated that such a request would have to be made through official channels. Such surveillance would have breached the protocols of French political asylum, and as such was a dangerous move politically for the French government. Despite this setback, Wallinger received valuable assistance from the 'chief police officer of Paris'.[18] Much of the surveillance of Indian nationals being carried out in France was probably undertaken without the official knowledge of the French government, and this was down to Wallinger and his personal relationships with individuals in Paris, among whom was Ladoux. Sir Charles Cleveland noted that Wallinger was 'able to work arrangements in France in hearty co-operation with the Paris police'.[19]

Ladoux must have known of the activities of the Indian Political Intelligence Office; indeed, it is unlikely that they could have conducted their activities in France without his tacit approval and probable 'hearty co-operation'. As something of a *quid pro quo*, it is reasonable to assume that details on Mata Hari would have been passed on to Ladoux; as a non-Indian national, she was of no real interest to Wallinger. While these details may have again only hinted at her behaviour and dubious associations, they helped to build suspicion and may have added to Ladoux's sense of unease, especially as this now amounted to reports on Mata Hari from three different agencies of a friendly ally. Added to the widespread belief that depraved individuals were prone to being traitors, the reports, although giving no definitive proof, damned Mata Hari as an enemy agent.

It cannot be known for certain that any information was sent by Wallinger or any of his agents to Ladoux, but the question remains, why did Folatre write the letter to Wallinger when the information in it could have been obtained from an official department, or indeed from the various newspaper reports of her death? And why was a copy of the letter sent to Sir Charles Cleveland?

Cleveland had joined the Indian Service as Assistant Commissioner in 1887, rising rapidly to Inspector-General of the Police in 1903, then in 1910 to Director of the Indian Police Service CID. In 1913, he left India to consult with Wallinger as to his progress in Europe. By 1914, he stated that, 'During the past 12 months Wallinger's work has been more valuable than ever as his system has developed and fuller results have been secured.'[20]

In 1912, Cleveland had come under fire when an assassination attempt was made on the Viceroy's life. As a result, he needed the operations in Europe to be successful. He championed Wallinger and his work, and kept a very close watch on what was happening in Europe. Although never publicly acknowledged, Cleveland understood just how 'unofficial' some of Wallinger's operations were in France. It is not known why the Folatre letter to Wallinger was copied to Cleveland. He was in charge of the Indian police and was responsible for the suppression of Indian nationalism. He had no professional need to know about the fate of Mata Hari, and as with Wallinger, the information in the letter could have been easily obtained elsewhere;

there was no reason for him to receive it. Even if there had been a reason for Cleveland to receive such a notification from France, given his status, any letter or report should surely have come from a senior member of the *Deuxiéme Bureau* and would have been written on official stationery; the letter is written on plain paper, with no official markings.

One final small piece of evidence that indicates that Ladoux and Wallinger were in some form of communication is that Folatre was the name of a shadowy individual, occasionally – although never officially – used as an agent by Ladoux.

Had Ladoux received correspondence from Tinsley and Wallinger or their agents, and did this extra correspondence account for the 'pestering' of which he complained? Whatever information was contained in the packet Ladoux read, he was left feeling 'uneasy'. For the rest of August, Mata Hari's actions did nothing to dispel his disquiet. On 2 August, she visited Masloff, but avoided Hallaure, who had tried to visit her. On the following day, she visited the Prefecture of Police, Bureau of Aliens to try get the *laissez-passer* to visit Vittel.[21] She then twice went to the Police Commissariat, taking her registration papers with her in order to press for the *laissez-passer*. This action was despite having already been refused the travel permit by the Commissariat on 31 July, and, according to Mata Hari's testimony, she had been promised it by Ladoux, who had also already recruited her as a French spy. Later that same day, she met Masloff at the Pavillon d'Armenonville in the Bois de Boulogne. The couple spent the afternoon together before returning to the Grand Hotel, where they spent the night.[22] Ladoux had not stopped Monier and Tarlet's surveillance of Mata Hari. On the morning of 4 August, Masloff left for the Front. Mata Hari accompanied him to the station, promising to follow him as far as Vittel as soon as she received her *laissez-passer*.[23] On 9 August, Masloff wrote to her at the Grand Hotel, but she did not receive the letter. All of her mail was by that time intercepted and sent to Ladoux. Most of the correspondence came from Masloff, although there were also several pieces from Hallaure and one or two others.

Mata Hari continued to visit the *Deuxième Bureau* on 5, 7 and 11 August. She also saw the Police Commissariat on multiple occasions. All of these visits were, allegedly, to press for her *laissez-passer*. On 18 August, she spoke to Henri de Marguérie, secretary of the Ministry of Foreign Affairs at the Quai d'Orsay. He was an old friend and she sought his advice about Ladoux's offer to spy for France. Marguérie warned her about the dangers of espionage work, but is alleged to have stated that if she took up the challenge then he was certain she could render the country a great service. Quite what service Marguérie thought Mata Hari capable of was never clarified. The couple met again that evening, when Marguérie called for her at the Grand Hotel at 7 p.m. in a taxi. Monier and Tarlet lost their trail when the vehicle sped away, although they noted that the pair had still not returned by 11 p.m.[24]

On 19 August, she visited several apartments with a view to living in one with Masloff when she returned from Vittel. She signed a lease for 33 Avenue Henri-Martin.[25] She saw Marguérie again on the morning of 21 August. She then went from the Quai d'Orsay to the Police Commissariat on the Rue Taitbout. After lunch, she went to the *Deuxième Bureau* where she saw Ladoux and agreed to work for him saying, 'Captain, in principle I agree.'[26]

She agreed with Ladoux that she would go to Vittel to take the waters, and would visit him for instruction on her return. She then asked if she might send a telegram to Masloff from his office. She had not heard from Masloff since he had left on 4 August. This was refused, so she sent the telegram from the post office instead, informing Masloff that she was hoping to travel to Vittel within the week. She received no reply. On 24 August, she visited the Russian Embassy and Russian mission, but neither had any news of Masloff.[27] On 29 August, she visited the Police Commissariat and finally received her *laissez-passer*.[28] On 1 September, she left for Vittel by train, followed by Monier and Tarlet.[29]

If this catalogue of events is correct – and most of it is verified by the reports of Monier and Tarlet – then Ladoux still seemed to have had reservations about Mata Hari, despite having issued her a *laissez-passer*.

She was under constant surveillance and her mail was intercepted and read. With such concerns, Ladoux's recruitment of Mata Hari as a French spy was either foolhardy in the extreme or an attempt to flush out a possible enemy agent. Within the dangerous and complex world of espionage and counter-espionage, concrete proof was rarely found. Intelligence officers frequently had to rely on their intuition. Where individuals were suspected of being enemy agents, it was not unknown for those individuals to be allowed a degree of access to certain information under strict surveillance. What the individual did with that information could then determine their loyalties. This was a risky strategy, as an enemy agent who felt themselves under suspicion would, of course, not pass on the information. Some in the intelligence services went further and attempted to turn suspected enemy agents into counter-agents for themselves; an even riskier strategy. Within espionage, bluff and counter-bluff passed back and forth between individuals, and where the truth actually lay could, in many instances, never be determined. As Ladoux wrote in his memoirs, he suspected Mata Hari of being a German agent, but had no real proof except her depraved nature.[30] Recruiting her could determine where her loyalties truly lay, and might even give him an opportunity to 'turn her' to spy for the French.

When Mata Hari arrived in Vittel, she booked into the Grand Hotel of the Baths. She immediately saw a doctor and then waited anxiously for Masloff. She did not have to wait for long. Masloff arrived at the hotel on 3 September and booked into the room next to Mata Hari. He had been badly wounded in the left eye by phosgene gas[31] and was possibly going to lose his sight, but he asked Mata Hari to marry him; she agreed:

[Masloff] had been gravely injured by the asphyxiating gas, had completely lost the vision in his left eye and was in danger of going blind. One night, he said to me: 'If this terrible thing comes to pass, what will you do?'

'I will never leave you,' I responded to him, 'and I would be to you always the same woman.'

'Would you marry me?' he asked me.

I responded affirmatively, then I began to reflect: I said to myself, I must ask Captain Ladoux for enough money that I never have to deceive Vadime de Masloff with other men. I will let go of the Marquis of Beaufort, I will let go of the Colonel Baron [van der Capellan], I will go to Belgium to do what the captain asks, I will reclaim my furniture and my previous objects in the Netherlands. I will go to Paris and live in the apartment that I have rented; Captain Ladoux will pay me, I will marry my lover and I will be the happiest woman on earth.[32]

This recollection of Mata Hari, in which she looks to Captain Ladoux to pay her, is somewhat reminiscent of her explanation of taking money from the Germans to pay for her purloined furs and jewels. Mata Hari's actions, whatever they truly were, appear to have been carried out as much for financial gain as for any reasons of patriotism. She said she loved Masloff so much that she possibly was genuinely wanting money to set up home with him. On the other hand, on 31 August, when she was claiming to be worried about Masloff's whereabouts, Hallaure attempted to have a passionate evening liaison with her only to find that she was already in the arms of a British officer.[33] Of course, in all of these recollections it is equally likely that the mercenary element could be a front to mask the more covert activities of an active German agent.

Mata Hari was not an inconspicuous person, and as such her presence at Vittel was noted and commented upon by several other guests at the hotel. She and Masloff met Brigadier General Jules Clément Le Loup de Sancy de Rolland, known as 'Sancy', who had been involved previously in the Dreyfus Affair; it was rumoured that he had been the 'friend' mentioned in the Davignon Panizzardi letter that had been part of the evidence used against Dreyfus. He was also closely linked with Colonel Schwartzkoppen, since Sancy had served as military attaché in Berlin from 1882 to 1887. In 1916, he was no longer a serving army officer but retained many of his influential acquaintances and contacts. When Mata Hari met Sancy, she asked him to introduce her to Madame Pauline de Fleurian, the wife of the French ambassador in London; it is not known why.[34] When Sancy approached de Fleurian, she declined to make Mata Hari's acquaintance. Tarlet and Monier spoke to Sancy and de Fleurian, warning them about her. Sancy gave an account of his meeting with Mata Hari:

I was in Vittel for the season, when in the room of the restaurant of the hotel, I remarked upon a Russian officer in uniform who, knowing without a question my rank, gave me a military salute. We immediately entered into conversation, I questioned the officer on the military situation, as he was assigned to the French front, and wished him well for the grave eye wound which he had received in the services of France. I knew immediately that I was in the presence of one of those brave young Russian officers, as was indicated by his decorations.

We were conversing when a tall woman came to sit at the table with the officer, a woman whom he presented to me as his fiancée. This person gave the impression of being too old for him and I smelled right away an adventuress and I distanced myself from the false fiancée, showing the greatest reserve. What I saw next did nothing but confirm my assessment.

For six years I was the premier military attaché at the embassy in Berlin. I was in the habit of judging women of this type for I saw the enemy used them for the worst and I could tell you that the companion of the Russian officer had to me so clearly the bearing of a spy that I notified the Special Commissionaire at the station when I left Vittel.

Everything about her indicated that she wished to make the Russian officer her dupe in all regards. I knew then that she was trying to satisfy an indiscreet curiosity. It is thus that she made herself very lively and asked to visit hospitals, as I told Madame de Fleurian. It is Madame de Fleurian who unmasked her by recognising that she was a former dancer of the Folies Bergère. The former dancer did not approach me on subjects of a military character. I always kept myself on my guard.[35]

Madame de Fleurian also gave an account of additional knowledge of Mata Hari:

My doctor, Dr Boulommier, was the first to alert me that a very beautiful woman was staying at the same hotel as I and asked me with a certain enthusiasm if I had seen her. I said no. A few days later, I was taking tea in the park with … the doctor and his wife, when the person in question passed.

I found her to be of the gaudy type which showed me her social background. I became aware that this person had inflamed the masculine element at the hotel. Most of the men found this woman elegant and pretty.

Me, I was of a little different opinion, I noticed that she was of a certain age and that she had the air of a person who used morphine or cocaine. Her style throughout (I do not criticise otherwise her sense of propriety) rarely pleased me. For example, she said to the maid that she was a Dutch princess and I knew that this sort of title did not exist.

For the other part, she held conversations with a nun, in front of several people, saying for example that she had a château in Touraine and that she danced in Russia. I finally understood when, one evening, I found myself entering by accident into the salon of the hotel where she was finishing singing; she made a great bow as if she were in the theatre. Then a name was pronounced, that of Mata Hari, and a memory came to me of a dancer spoken of by the young people, perhaps my nephews. This woman was most often with a young Russian officer.

When I was leaving Vittel, one morning Brigadier General de Sancy introduced to me an officer of the gendarmerie … We spoke of Mata Hari and he told me that this woman was under suspicion. As far as I was concerned, I had no suspicion of espionage, I had taken her for a schemer, one of the cosmopolitan women that one saw in the spa towns before the war.[36]

Brigadier General de Sancy's recollection of Mata Hari as having the 'bearing of a spy' may seem, on the surface, to be evidence of his astute perception, although it must be remembered that he had already been spoken to by Tarlet and Monier. His statement that he contacted the Special Commissionaire when he left Vittel indicates that, despite the presence of the detectives, Sancy still felt the need to report his encounter to the intelligence services. This may have been due to his connection to the Dreyfus scandal. For an individual who had previously been involved in one espionage affair, Sancy probably felt he could not afford to be linked to another. By reporting the incident, he was no doubt attempting to ensure that no suspicion fell on him. However, despite his previous Dreyfus connection, Sancy's opinion of Mata Hari as the sort of woman who would spy would still carry some weight, given his previous military experience. It would have added to the general belief in her guilt, even if it did not carry any proof.

Madame de Fleurian's assertion that Mata Hari was the type to use drugs is curious. There is no evidence that Mata Hari ever took drugs. She probably took mercury at several times in her life when she was suffering from the symptoms of her syphilis. She may also have taken a medical concoction known to prostitutes to prevent pregnancy – astringent lavages of various chemicals such as pennyroyal or aloes. In combination with the mercury, this may have given her a particular pallor which Fleurian mistook for the taking of morphine or cocaine.

The description of Mata Hari as a 'schemer' and a 'cosmopolitan woman' is perhaps more striking, and chimed with Sancy's characterisation of her as an 'adventuress'. A cosmopolitan woman was a polite term for a courtesan, and was used by the upper classes to denote those who were known, or suspected, to be in the 'oldest profession'. The other phrase occasionally used was that of an 'international woman', one that Mata Hari used about herself. It may be that Fleurian was using the terms in a disparaging manner and without any proof; however, the depravity of such women and their predisposition for treason was well known. As Sancy said, 'I saw the enemy used them for the worst.' These remarks served to confirm Ladoux's suspicions that Mata Hari was an enemy agent.

Madame de Fleurian and Brigadier General de Sancy finally made their opinion of Mata Hari known to the other guests at the Grand Hotel, possibly encouraged by Tarlet and Monier. The guests started to shun them to such an extent that Mata Hari and Masloff socialised very little and mostly kept to their own company. Their time together was limited, and by 7 September, Masloff's leave was over. Once he had left, those other hotel guests who had socialised with her and Masloff now avoided Mata Hari altogether, and she was left more or less alone. The only individuals she spent any time with were her doctor, Dr

Boulommier, and Monsieur and Madame Roux. The Rouxs were also staying at the hotel and had previously socialised with Mata Hari and Masloff. During their brief friendship, Mata Hari had given them a keepsake photograph of her and Masloff. Now that she was alone, Mata Hari dined again with the Rouxs and interestingly asked for the photograph to be returned. She remained at Vittel until 17 September, when she returned to Paris.

On 13 September, Ladoux suspended Tarlet and Monier's surveillance of Mata Hari, but was recommenced on 13 October. This followed Ladoux's usual practise when matters of surveillance became indiscreet. One of the main criticisms frequently levelled against espionage was that it was unethical. The real concern was that surveillance could uncover that which many did not want exposed. Following an alleged traitor to discover to whom they were betraying secrets was one thing, but discovering that in reality the minister involved was merely paying off a young prostitute was quite another. Many of the files in the *Deuxiéme Bureau* contained gaps where surveillance was suspended or blanks where names were omitted to save embarrassment. The work Ladoux undertook was vital, but he still had to operate in a milieu of upper-class hypocrisy, where scandal and retaining one's good name lay side by side. Many of the files in the Dreyfus Affair refer to individuals simply by their initials. In Mata Hari's case, for example, Hallaure was referred to as 'Lieutenant X' in deference to his family and in some instances surveillance was missing on the occasions she met with ministers of state such as Henri de Marguérie. Given Mata Hari's normal behaviour, it is more than likely that she had at least one sexual liaison during the period with no surveillance that could have compromised someone in the French government.

Although what Mata Hari was doing during that missing month cannot be known for certain, the reasons can. She needed money. Although she had decided to renounce her other lovers to remain faithful to Masloff, she still needed to make money. She was no longer dancing because she was too old. In addition to her day-to-day expenses, she had an ever-increasing mountain of debt. She owed money to the Grand Hotel in Vittel, and had neglected to settle her bill before leaving. She had an outstanding debt with the Hotel Meurice of some 1,300 francs, which was owed since 1913 and for which the management of the hotel was threatening to sue her. She had started to buy, on credit, some furniture for the apartment at 33 avenue Henri-Martin. She also had several smaller debts to a variety of costumiers, milliners and perfumiers that needed settling. She had never shown any capacity for keeping her finances in order, and this had been exacerbated by the outbreak of war.

Prior to 1914, the upper classes frequently ran accounts with trades people that were paid years later. This was a commonly accepted practice, with credit extended to those from 'good' families by tradesmen, secure in the knowledge that the debt would be repaid at some point in the future and that an association with such a family was good for business. As long as one's credit remained good there was no problem, and it was said that no true member of the upper classes knew how much he owed to tradesmen. The outbreak of the war changed everything. Who knew if the young marquis who owed several thousand francs would return from the Front? There was also a degree of anger among many shopkeepers that their sons were dying in cold, wet trenches while upper-class women still did not pay their bills for luxury items. These changed attitudes were a particular problem for Mata Hari. Despite all her pretensions, she was not upper class; many of her lovers may have been, but she was definitely middle class. Under the strain of war, her class mattered. The little patience that was given to upper-class patrons by the more deferential tradesmen was not extended to her, and she was becoming increasingly beset by trades people demanding payment. As Mata Hari had stated, 'I must ask Captain Ladoux for enough money that I never have to deceive Vadime de Masloff with other men.'[37]

So on 18 September she went to see Ladoux.

The details of this meeting were recorded by Ladoux in his memoirs, and, read with the usual caution for any account written after the event and for publication, contain several important details. After some initial pleasantries Mata Hari talked of her longing to marry Masloff but said that, 'he is from an aristocratic family and his father the admiral forbids this mismatch … If only I had money.'[38]

Ladoux then asked her how much she needed, to which she replied, 'You could not pay me so much … a million.'[39]

It was an astonishing amount of money to ask for. Ladoux replied that to earn such a sum would require her to produce extremely important secret information from within the German High Command, but that such a task would be almost impossible. Mata Hari replied that she could, claiming she knew someone who could help her. She said, '[O]ne man could, and he was also my lover, he is one of the biggest suppliers of the German army and could come and go as he liked at the grand headquarters.' Asked what his name was, Ladoux says she replied, 'Craemer.'[40]

Did Mata Hari mean Karl Kroemer, the honorary German Consul in Amsterdam who had initially recruited her as a German spy? If so, it seems somewhat cavalier of her to mention his name to Ladoux, although Kroemer would indeed be able to come and go relatively easily at the German High Command. It must be remembered, however, that Craemer and all of its variations was a relatively common name across Germany and Austria, and may thus be unrelated to the German Consul.

The conversation continued. Ladoux asked Mata Hari, 'You really wish to enter into our service? Take care; the profession is dangerous.'

Mata Hari: 'I don't doubt it.'

Ladoux: 'And next, that is not all … Let's say that you succeed. But when you have your information, what will you do? It is necessary that we receive it in our turn.'

Mata Hari: 'Oh! You must have a means of doing that. An agent … in Amsterdam … for example?'

Ladoux: 'But no, alas! We have no one in the Netherlands and it is for that reason that you would be precious to us. You do not know how to use invisible inks?'

Mata Hari: 'No, but I will learn.'

Ladoux: 'Yes, but if one is pinched, it is the end.'

Mata Hari: 'Nobody pinches Mata Hari, she knows how to protect herself.'

Ladoux: 'So we have observed!'
Mata Hari: 'What! Always these vile suspicions?'
Ladoux then said:

> Listen well, I am certain, absolutely certain, that you are an agent in the service of Germany. But I will overlook this at this moment, because you have come to me to make me this proposition which will put you in such a situation, if I accept, that you will proceed to betray Germany or us. You are a gambler, Mata Hari, and you must play. Rouge et noir ... Red it is us, over the line that you see there, that of the front, where the blood flows night and day, for two years already. Black, it is your German friends. I warn you, red wins, black loses. Reflect well before placing your bet. Tomorrow it will be too late. I will leave you this night to think it over.

Mata Hari replied: 'I have thought it over. I will play red. I am a gambler, but I am superstitious also, and I am sure, in coming to you, that it would bring me happiness.'[41]

Ladoux's admission to Mata Hari that he suspected her of being a German agent appears a somewhat startling statement to have been made to someone whom he was contemplating using as a French spy. However, he had told Mata Hari on their first meeting of the suspicions that the British held about her. If she was an active German agent, then Ladoux's statement left her unmasked and of no further use to the Germans. In that case, his denial to her of the presence of any French agents in the Netherlands was only prudent. The mention of the dangers of espionage work was probably meant as a genuine warning to one who was to become an agent, but possibly also a veiled threat to an enemy agent.

Just like their first meeting, Mata Hari's recollection of this varies from that of Ladoux. She wanted to work to earn the money to marry Masloff, but did not want to be sent to Germany, which was understandable considering that she had already agreed to act for them and received an initial payment. Ladoux apparently agreed and said that she would be sent to Belgium. Mata Hari knew Monsieur Wurfbain, a Belgian banker who was friendly with

General Moritz Ferdinand Freiherr von Bissing, the governor-general of occupied Belgium. Wurfbain had been introduced to her by the Dutch banker Schelk, who had helped her in August 1914. Von Bissing was deputy commander of the VII Army Corps from August 1914 until November 1914. After the fall of Belgium, he was promoted to *Generaloberst* and appointed governor-general in December 1914. He had numerous friends and colleagues within the German general staff in Belgium. If Mata Hari had been able to engineer an introduction to von Bissing, she might well have procured information that could have proved highly advantageous for the French.

Ladoux asked Mata Hari why she wanted to work for the French. Her answer was quite frank. She said, 'I have no other interest, except that of becoming able to marry my lover and be independent.'

Ladoux: 'The reward will be worth the trouble. And the question of money? Have you thought of it?'

Mata Hari: 'I ask a million francs, but you can pay me after when you have recognised the value of my services.'

Ladoux: 'Oh! Oh! That is a great deal of money, but if you truly render us a service that we ask of you, then we will pay it.'[42]

Although somewhat different from Ladoux's version of events, this interview reinforces what Mata Hari consistently said about her work; it was purely a financial transaction. She had taken money from the Germans because they had taken her money, furs and jewels; she would take money from the French because she needed it in order to marry her lover. The problem with such a financial approach was that her loyalty remained under suspicion. Mata Hari had told the Germans she would work for them, but had not done so. What was to stop her from saying she would work for the French, but then do nothing? If her motives were purely financial and not patriotic, and she was available for hire to the highest bidder, then she remained suspect.

The truth of the actual conversation probably contains elements from the two accounts. Mata Hari was now engaged either as a French agent or pseudo-French agent in order to uncover her true identity as a German agent. She started to prepare for her task. However, she still had the problem of having little cash, with multiple creditors chasing her, and she needed a new wardrobe. It may seem frivolous to be concerned about clothes, but if Mata Hari was to attempt a seduction of von Bissing, she would need a variety of costumes to attend the sort of social events at which she might pursue him. Two days after her meeting with Ladoux, she sent him a letter asking for an advance on her payment to allow her to buy new clothes.[43] The letter was uncoded and was sent through the ordinary post, where it could have been intercepted by anyone. Why did Mata Hari contact Ladoux in such a manner? Did she not realise what she was doing? She had, by this time, been recruited by two different intelligence agencies. It seems unlikely, therefore, that she would not have been warned about open methods of communication. Was it a genuine mistake, or was the letter to Ladoux deliberately sent in an open manner? If Mata Hari was an active German agent, did she write that letter knowing it would be intercepted, to notify the German intelligence services that she had been recruited by Ladoux? As she probably realised that Ladoux still regarded her as suspect, a coded letter to the Germans might have been intercepted by the French and thus confirmed Ladoux's suspicions about her. An open letter to Ladoux that could be intercepted by the Germans could, possibly, just be explained as a mistake.

In any event, Ladoux failed to answer the letter and on 20 September Mata Hari returned to his office. He admitted that he had received her letter requesting the advance, but that his superior, André Goubet, had said that no payment was to be made.[44] Mata Hari explained that she could not provide herself with a wardrobe without funds, and that if she attempted to ask Capellan for funds she might well permanently alienate his affections. Ladoux stood firm on the subject of money and Mata Hari was left with no option but to back down.

The conversation then changed, with Ladoux again asking Mata Hari to use invisible ink in her communications, but she refused, stating, 'No. That sort of trickery goes against my nature.'[45] This contradicted her previous agreement to learn how to use the ink. She also refused to inform on other agents, which she found unethical. It is noticeable that Ladoux made no direct mention of her foolhardiness in having sent the uncoded letter via the ordinary post. Was it considered too trivial a matter to bother with? Or had it merely added to the proof of her suspect actions?

Ladoux then told her she would receive instructions from an agent, codename AF44, who would visit her in The Hague. He asked her if she recognised the number, as it was 'hers'. Mata Hari replied, 'Captain, I beg you once more, drop these insinuations that irritate me with the informations from your little agents and all these dirty tricks, this will only harden my character, there will come a moment when I will no longer want to do anything [for you].'[46]

Ladoux's confrontation of Mata Hari with the codename AF44 showed his continued suspicion of her. He did not know, at that point, of her code number H21. At their previous meeting, he had asked her about Antwerp, indicating that he had proof of her visits there. Antwerp was important in that it was believed to be the location of a German spying hub run by a Fräulein Doktor Schragmüller. It was here that German agents were trained and given codenames, with A for Antwerp followed by the initial of the country to which they were sent: F for France, GB for Great Britain etc. The evidence for the hub in Antwerp is somewhat sketchy, although such German espionage units certainly existed. Mata Hari was living in The Hague when Ladoux suspected her of being in Antwerp, despite not having any actual proof. Antwerp was the closest German hub to The Hague that the French were aware of at the time. As the distance between the two cities is less than 130km, with a frequent train service, it was a reasonable assumption on Ladoux's part that she would have been assigned to Antwerp, although how he had uncovered the code AF44 is unknown.

Ladoux appears to have accepted Mata Hari's protestations of innocence, or at least gave the impression of having done so, and sent her to see Henri Maunoury at the Prefecture of Police to obtain a visa to return to the Netherlands, travelling via Spain. While she awaited the visa, Mata Hari attempted to deal with her continuing money troubles while also providing herself with a new wardrobe.

By the beginning of October, matters were becoming desperate. She was finding it increasingly difficult to get credit at her usual costumiers and milliners, and the threats of Johannes-Frederich Schwenker, the manager of the Hotel Meurice, to sue her for her outstanding debt were becoming all too real. The money she normally received from Capellan allowed her to live, but did not cover any extra expense. She decided, nevertheless, to write to him with a direct appeal for more. As the baron was married, she could not write to him directly, and so wrote to Otto Bunge,[47] the Dutch Consul in Paris, to ask him to write to Lintjens to ask her to request some 6,000 francs from Capellan. Mata Hari stressed the need for urgency.

That feeling of urgency was not misplaced. On 14 October, Schwenker obtained a court order of seizure of goods against her. The hotel seized several of her trunks in surety against her debts. Mata Hari managed to find some 200 francs to pay the management, but they still refused to release the trunks. She went to speak to the managers and, after a further payment of 300 francs, her trunks were returned.[48] On receiving the trunks, she took them to the apartment on the avenue Henri-Martin for safe keeping. She was unable to move in, as the entry date on the lease was not until the autumn, although the manager was willing to allow her to use the apartment to store her luggage. She moved into cheaper rooms in the Grand Hotel and started earning money again by receiving gentlemen callers.[49]

She visited Ladoux[50] on 17 and 19 October to plead again for an advance. At the same time, she visited her bank to ascertain if any funds had been deposited by Capellan. On 23 October, Masloff arrived in Paris on a three-day pass.[51] He and Mata Hari spent the entire time together and visited the new apartment at avenue Henri-Martin. On 26 October, Masloff left Paris. Mata Hari spent the next two days writing him three letters, which she posted on 28 October. All three were seized and instantly sent to Ladoux in his office.[52] Despite all of her protestations in Ladoux's office on 18 September, he had not stopped the surveillance of her.

Mata Hari remained short of cash and visited Ladoux once more, on 31 October, to plead for an advance; it was again refused. However, by 4 November, money had been deposited in her bank account by Capellan. Curiously, on the same day, Mata Hari sent Masloff a money order for 500 francs.[53] It is not known why she did this, because Masloff was no more in debt than any other young Russian Army officer at that time. As the son of a wealthy aristocratic family, he had no problem in gaining credit.

On 5 November, Mata Hari left Paris on her first mission for Ladoux. She took the night train for Madrid. The express set off at 9.50 p.m., with Mata Hari in sleeping car 2492a, berth 8, followed by two *Deuxiéme Bureau* agents and a series of telegrams sent to border guards and agents along her route.[54]

Margaretha and Rudolf
MacLeod, marriage photo,
11 July 1895. (Collection Fries
Museum, Leeuwarden)

Rudolf MacLeod and Non
MacLeod, 1905. (Collection
Fries Museum, Leeuwarden)

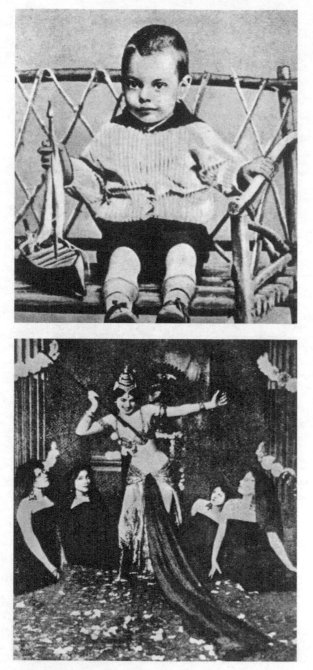

Norman John
MacLeod, 1899.
(Collection Fries
Museum, Leeuwarden)

Mata Hari dancing at
the Guimet museum
in Paris, 13 March
1905. (Collection Fries
Museum, Leeuwarden)

Mata Hari in full oriental headdress in Vienna, 1 January 1907. (Collection Fries Museum, Leeuwarden)

Mata Hari Javanese dancing in Paris, 1905. (Collection Fries Museum, Leeuwarden)

Above left: Mata Hari in her furs in Paris, 1908. (Collection Fries Museum, Leeuwarden)

Above: Mata Hari in her furs at the races, 11 January 1911. (Collection Fries Museum, Leeuwarden)

Left: Mata Hari in one of the scandalous photos from Paris, 1905. (Collection Fries Museum, Leeuwarden)

Above: Mata Hari dancing with Inayat Khan in Neuilly, 1913. (Collection Fries Museum, Leeuwarden)

Below: Mata Hari in Berlin, 1906. (Collection Fries Museum, Leeuwarden)

Above: Mata Hari in rare demure pose in Berlin, 1914. (Collection Fries Museum, Leeuwarden)

Above: Mata Hari in portrait pose, February 1915. (Collection Fries Museum, Leeuwarden)

Left: Mata Hari in the Netherlands, 13 March 1915. (Collection Fries Museum, Leeuwarden)

Below: Mata Hari in oriental pose, 1906. (Collection Fries Museum, Leeuwarden)

Above: Mata Hari and Vadime Massloff, 1916.

Above: Mata Hari in fashionable pose in Paris, 1915. (Collection Fries Museum, Leeuwarden)

Right: Mata Hari at the time of her arrest, 13 February 1917. (Collection Fries Museum, Leeuwarden)

Above: Pierrre Bouchardon. (Collection Fries Museum, Leeuwarden)

Left: Georges Ladoux. (Collection Fries Museum, Leeuwarden)

Below: Mata Hari's final photo, 14 October 1917. (Collection Fries Museum, Leeuwarden)

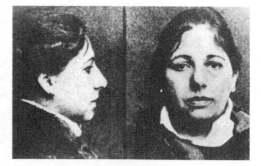

11

CONFUSION AND COLLUSION

When she reached Madrid, Mata Hari took the connecting train to Vigo and then waited for her steamer for the Netherlands. On 9 November, she boarded the SS *Hollandia* bound for Amsterdam via Falmouth in Cornwall. Both Mata Hari and Ladoux knew that any ship passing through British waters would be required to dock at a British port to be checked. They also both knew that the British intelligence services considered Mata Hari to be suspect, and that she was liable to be questioned at the very least, if not arrested, when the ship docked. So why did Ladoux send her to the Netherlands via that route without notifying his British counterparts? Did he hope that the British might uncover more evidence of her alleged activities for Germany? Nothing in any of the records indicates that Mata Hari questioned the route. Did she expect to be above suspicion now that she was working for Ladoux, or at least that the British authorities would know of her new status?

While she was on board the *Hollandia*, Mata Hari grew friendly with the captain, who told her that the gossip on board ship was that there were a couple of spies among the passengers. Mr and Mrs Allard, who were Belgian, were, allegedly, spies for England and Germany respectively. Mata Hari would later pass this information on to Allied[1] and, allegedly, German agents.

On 14 November, the *Hollandia* docked at Falmouth and the ship was boarded by several British officials. Mata Hari remembered the details in a later statement:

> Upon our arrival in this English port, the boat was invaded by marine officers, police, soldiers, and suffragettes, the last charged with searching the women. Two suffragettes searched my trunks and my cabin with an unheard-of thoroughness. They were unfastening the mirror from the walls and looking under my bed with an electric lamp. Then an officer submitted me to a formal interrogation. He asked me if I indeed carried the names written in my passport and if I never travelled under another identity. Then, he stared at me fixedly for at least two minutes. Seeing that I did not lower my eyes, he took from his pocket an amateur photograph, representing a woman dressed in Spanish style, with a white mantilla, having a fan in her right hand and her left hand on her hip. Overall, the woman was a bit too small and more strongly built than I. I laughed, but my protestations did not convince the officer. He told me that the photo was taken in Malaga where I swore I had never been. The captain of the boat and certain Dutch passengers were kind in attesting to my identity, but nothing doing. The officer made me disembark and sent me to London with my baggage.[2]

The official who interrogated Mata Hari was George Reid Grant, an MI5 agent stationed at Falmouth. Grant was assisted by his wife, Janet, who was also an MI5 agent and who had strip-searched Mata Hari. The Grants had found 'nothing incriminating'[3] in her luggage. However, they had mistakenly identified her as a woman called Clara Benedix, who, like Mata Hari, was suspect and on the intelligence services' list of those to be watched. Grant questioned Mata Hari, who flatly denied being Benedix, but said that she had briefly met the woman on a train. The MI5 man was not satisfied.[4] Something in Mata Hari's general manner and the similarity between her and the photograph of Benedix were sufficient for Grant to telegram his superiors in London stating, 'MARGARETHA ZELLE MacLEOD, travelling on Dutch passport

No 2603, issued at The Hague, 12-5-16 ... It is believed that she is the woman "CLARA BENEDIX", a German agent, circulated by MI5 and DID [the Department of Interior Defence].'[5]

In his report, Grant wrote that, 'As Madame MacLeod's story seems altogether very strange, it was decided to remove her and to send her to London for further examination. She is being sent to C.O. tonight under escort.'[6]

The Grants accompanied Mata Hari to London. She was taken to Scotland Yard and handed over to Chief Inspector Edward Parker. Once she was formally booked in, she was taken into an interrogation room to await the arrival of Sir Basil Thomson, Assistant Commissioner of Police and head of Special Branch at Scotland Yard.

When Thomson met her, she asked to be allowed to write to the Dutch legation. Her letter read:

> May I beg your Excellency with all deference urgently to do everything possible to help me. A terrible accident has happened to me. I am the divorced Mrs Mac-Leod [sic] born Zelle. I am travelling from Spain to the Netherlands with my very own passport. The English police claim that it is false, that I am not Mrs Zelle. I am at my wit's end; am imprisoned here since this morning at Scotland Yard and I pray you, come and help me. I live in The Hague, at 16 Nieuwe Uitleg, and I am as well known there as in Paris where I have lived for years. I am all alone here and I swear that everything is absolutely in order. It is a misunderstanding, but I pray you, help me.
>
> Sincerely,
>
> M.G. Zelle McLeod [sic][7]

After she had written the letter, Mata Hari handed it over to Thomson, who retained it for two days before forwarding it to the Dutch legation.[8] It is noticeable that she chose to approach the Dutch authorities for help rather than the French, despite her having made Paris her home for most of her adult life. It is also curious that she did not instantly contact Ladoux for help. Although all agents were instructed not to expect help from their superiors if caught by an enemy power, this did not apply to a friendly ally. Once the matter of the letter was dealt with,

Thomson began to interrogate Mata Hari. The questioning initially took place in Dutch, through a Belgian translator. Mata Hari disliked the translator:

> For four days, three men in uniform interrogated me. They questioned me in Dutch through a Belgian who had a visible horror of the people of my country. He spoke my language like a dirty Flamand and he had the audacity to say to the three men that I had a German accent. Then he asked me insidious questions about Dutch cities where I had lived, trying to catch me out.[9]

The interrogation was led by Thomson, assisted by Captain Reginald Hall and Lord Herschell, both of whom worked for the DID. The questioning centred on Mata Hari's identity and whether or not she was the German woman Clara Benedix. Thomson started with questions about her passport:

> Thomson: 'Are you ready to account for the fact that the seal does not meet?'
> (Mata Hari's passport had a break in the seal across the photograph.)
> Mata Hari: 'I did nothing with my passport, sir.'
> Thomson: 'Can you account in any way for that seal not meeting? Do you wish to say anything about the writing coming under the photograph?'
> Mata Hari: 'That is my passport.'
> Thomson: 'You wish to say nothing?'
> Mata Hari: 'Nothing.'
> Thomson: 'You never went under the name Clara Benedix?'
> Mata Hari: 'Never, but I have been in the same compartment in a train with that woman.'
> Thomson: 'When was that?'
> Mata Hari: 'As I went from Madrid to Lisbon.'
> Thomson: 'Was that the 24 of January of this year?'
> Mata Hari: 'Yes, it must have been.'
> Thomson: 'Did you ever have inflammation of the left eye?'
> Mata Hari: 'No, I have never had anything the matter with my eyes.'
> Thomson: 'You know that one of your eyes is more closed than the other?'
> Mata Hari: 'Yes, it has always been so.'

Thomson: 'This photograph [Clara Benedix] also has that peculiarity.'

Mata Hari: 'It is possible, but that is not me.'[10]

Thomson: 'You went to Barcelona in February for a fortnight, then to Madrid and on to Lisbon?'

Mata Hari: 'That was not with this passport. The passport is in Holland.'

Thomson: 'Have you any proof at all of your alleged movements in Spain other than this passport?'

Mata Hari: 'No. The other passport is in The Hague at the Passport Bureau.'

Thomson: 'What we propose to do is to bring somebody across from Barcelona who knew you there under the other name.'

Mata Hari: 'You cannot do that.'

Thomson: 'If you are going to be put on your trial as a spy you can then send for any witnesses you like from Holland, but in the meantime we shall keep you in custody on suspicion of espionage and on the charge of having a forged passport.'[11]

Thomson continued to press the issue of Mata Hari's similarity to the photograph of Benedix:

Thomson: 'It is a very rare thing that two people should have a droop in the left eye and the peculiarity in the left eyebrow is exactly identical, as they are in this photograph and yourself.'

Mata Hari: 'That is not my photograph.'

Thomson: 'Then you are a victim of circumstances. There is another circumstance in which you are the victim. There is handwriting under the photograph on the passport, and if it is forged it is a very clumsy forgery.'

Mata Hari: 'It is not a forgery. Can I be visited by the Dutch Ambassador?'

Thomson: 'You can communicate with the Consul. I am going to write to the Dutch Embassy as we have grave doubts about your passport. I shall also tell him that I believe you to be Clara Benedix, a German. Can you tell me what Clara Benedix is like?'

Mata Hari: 'She is younger than me – much the same height or a little shorter, of stout build. I could not see the colour of her hair.'

Thomson: 'Did she talk to you?'

Mata Hari: 'Yes, we talked together all the time.'

Thomson: 'What did she say she was doing?'
Mata Hari: 'I did not ask her.'[12]

Thomson then returned to the question of her passport:

Thomson: 'Is this the passport you signed?'
Mata Hari: 'Yes.'
Thomson: 'Did you sign it when it had the photograph on it?'
Mata Hari: 'Yes.'
Thomson: 'Very well, you explain the fact the writing goes up underneath it.'
Mata Hari: 'That is my passport: that is all I can tell you.'[13]

At the end of the day's questioning, Mata Hari was told to write her signature, which was found to be the same as that on the passport. She was then sent to Cannon Row police station, and instructions were given that writing materials were to be given to her.[14]

The confusion over Mata Hari's identity, and whether or not she was the German agent Clara Benedix, was of vital importance to the British: Benedix was a known agent, Mata Hari was only a suspected one. Benedix, who was possibly originally from Hamburg, was dark in appearance and worked as a flamenco dancer in Madrid, collecting military information which she sent back to Berlin. When the authorities boarded the SS *Hollandia* at Falmouth, they were looking for Benedix. It appears, although the records are frustratingly incomplete at this point, that the British authorities had been alerted by their agents in Spain that Benedix was on the move and heading for Britain. The train journey with Mata Hari seems to confirm that. When the *Hollandia* docked, Benedix was, therefore, uppermost in their mind rather than Mata Hari. The mis-identification of Mata Hari as Benedix is curious, and within the world of espionage the true events may never be fully known. Benedix was a German agent at a much higher level than Mata Hari. Had Mata Hari's mis-identification as Benedix really come about from a British agent's report? Or had it come from German agents happy to see Mata Hari detained and questioned, as she had nothing important to tell, while Benedix continued on her work undisturbed? The meeting of Mata Hari and Benedix on the train was also just too coincidental. Had that been arranged by German intelligence? Had Mata Hari told her German handler what her movements were to be when she left Ladoux's office? The appearance of Mata Hari on the same train as Benedix was certainly fortuitous for the Germans. The confusion over the woman caused the British to stop and question Mata Hari while Benedix continued on her way undisturbed. If part of Mata Hari's role as a German agent was to deflect attention from Benedix, it worked perfectly. It did, however, leave Mata Hari in a somewhat dangerous position. What is equally likely is that the Germans used Mata Hari as a distraction without her knowledge. The ease with which certain damaging information about Mata Hari appeared would prove increasingly common.

After a night spent in the cells in Cannon Row, Mata Hari returned for a further day of questioning. Thomson initially focussed on her apparent payment from the Germans:

Thomson: 'Just before you went to Paris, did you receive the sum of 15,000 francs from anybody?'

Mata Hari: 'No.'

Thomson: 'That was in Holland.'

Mata Hari: 'No, but I took 15,000 francs from a bank and gave it to another bank. I have two banks in The Hague.'

Thomson: 'What was the bank you took it from?'

Mata Hari: 'Londres, and I have another bank Sch [sic].'

Thomson: 'Londres bank is the bank of the German Embassy.'

Mata Hari: 'I do not know.'

Thomson: 'We have information that Mata Hari received 15,000 francs from the German Embassy.'

Mata Hari: 'That was the amount I took to go to Paris.'[15]

This line of questioning would seem to indicate that Thomson was starting to believe Mata Hari over her identity. It is unclear how the

British authorities knew about her bank transactions or payments from the German Embassy. Had this information about her been conveniently supplied by the Germans? The banks would not have given this information voluntarily. Indeed, throughout the Great War, bank privacy was almost uniformly respected. It is unlikely that the German Embassy in The Hague had been infiltrated by a British agent, so how did the British know that Mata Hari had been paid and the amount of that payment?

The questioning continued until Mata Hari finally confessed to Thomson about her role as a French agent:

> Now I have something to tell you that will surprise you. I thought it was too big a secret. This captain, Captain Ladoux, asked me to go into his service, and I promised to do something for him. I was to meet him in my home in The Hague. That is why I sent a telegram.

> Thomson: 'You ought to have mentioned this to me yesterday. Where did you meet Captain Ladoux?'
> Mata Hari: 'That is old history. In my lawyer's office.'[16]

She continued to explain her recruitment by Ladoux:

> One day the Captain said to me 'You can do so many things for us if you like', and he looked me in the eyes. I understood. I thought a long time. I said 'I can'. He said 'Would you'. I said 'I would'. 'Would you ask much money?' he said. I said 'Yes, I would'. 'What would you ask?' I said 'If I give plenty of satisfaction I ask you 1,000,000'. He said 'Go to Holland, and you will receive my instructions.' 'If it is for Germany I do not like to do'. 'No' he said, 'it is for Belgium'. So I awaited his instructions in my home.[17]

Mata Hari's explanation failed to convince Thomson. It was riddled with pointless inconsistencies and lies, which he could have easily checked with Ladoux. On 16 November, he sent his own message to the Dutch minister, Reneke de Marees van Swinderen:

I have the honour to inform you that a woman carrying a French [*sic*] passport bearing the name of Margaretha Zelle MacLeod, No. 2608 issued at The Hague on the 12 of May 1916, has been detained here on suspicion that she is a German agent of German nationality named Clara Benedix of Hamburg. She denies her identity with this woman, and steps are being taken to establish it. The passport bears signs of having been tampered with. She has applied to be allowed to write to your Excellency, and materials for the letter have been furnished to her.[18]

After a few hours of reflection and continued comparison of Mata Hari to the Benedix photograph, Thomson sent a second message to the Dutch legation:

We have the honour to inform you that a lady bearing a Dutch passport, named Madame Zelle MacLeod, has been removed from the Dutch ship *Hollandia* on her arrival at Falmouth, there being great suspicion of un-neutral acts against her. She has asked me to forward to you the enclosed letter. Inquiries are being made as quickly as possible by cable, and she will not be detained longer than necessary. If, however, she proves to be a person suspected of un-neutral acts, it may be necessary to take further action against her.[19]

It seemed that Thomson was finally convinced that Mata Hari was not Benedix. However, he did not appear convinced of her role as a French agent, or at least not convinced enough to stop his grave suspicions of her. The problem that Mata Hari faced, although she did not know it, was that she could not prove her claim of working for the French. Thomson knew from her file that she had been questioned previously and placed on the watch list by the British authorities. Furthermore, he knew that the British had relayed their suspicions to the French. If Mata Hari had genuinely been recruited by the French, Thomson would have expected the British authorities to have been notified of this development and that Mata Hari would then have no longer been considered suspect. Notwithstanding any lack of communications from the French about this alleged change in her status, Thomson telegraphed the *Deuxiéme Bureau* on 16 November to ascertain the truth of Mata Hari's claim.[20] Ladoux replied almost instantly that Mata Hari was not employed by him. He further stated that he suspected her of being an enemy agent, and he had merely pretended to employ her in order to 'prove' her guilt. He also wrote that he would be glad to hear if the British had definitively established her guilt.[21]

However, Thomson had not established her guilt. None of her answers while being questioned revealed her guilt, and even a search of her extensive luggage had found nothing incriminating. The reply telegrams from those individuals she had named as witnesses to her identity started to arrive in Thomson's office. Baron van der Capellan, the Marquis of Beaufort and Otto Bunge, among others, all testified that she was, indeed, Mata Hari. With her identity confirmed and no physical proof against her, Thomson decided to release her: he had no real grounds on which to detain her. The release had stringent conditions imposed, probably because she remained suspect due in part to Ladoux's message. After four days of questioning, Mata Hari was released but told she must return to Spain. She was refused permission to journey onwards to the Netherlands.[22]

The Dutch were becoming increasingly concerned about her. In addition to the correspondence sent to the consul in London by Mata Hari and Thomson, which had been forwarded to the authorities in The Hague, they had also received a letter from Ladoux warning them about Mata Hari and the French and British suspicions about her.

Upon her release from Cannon Row, Mata Hari went to the Savoy Hotel and booked into room 261. Ignoring Thomson's statement that she must return to Spain, she applied for a permit to travel to The Hague to marry Captain Vadime de Masslof. As she was a foreign national, the permit office checked with the police if there were any restrictions on her movements. Thomson's office was notified, and reported to the permit office on her status. Permission to travel to The Hague was denied on the grounds that she was suspected of being an enemy agent employed by the Deutsche Bank.[23] After the refusal, Mata Hari visited Thomson to ask for the permit; a ship leaving on 25 November was bound for Rotterdam. Thomson repeated that she could not travel to the Netherlands but must return to Spain. Mata Hari returned to the Savoy and waited for a ship bound for Spain. On 1 December, she boarded the SS *Araguaya* bound for the port of Vigo.

That same day, the Dutch Minister for Foreign Affairs in The Hague, Reneke de Marees van Swinderen, sent a letter to Van Royen, the Dutch envoy in Madrid, warning him of Mata Hari's imminent arrival in Spain:

> The compatriot had originally been stopped because one thought her passport was a fake and it was suspected her real nationality was German and that she was a certain Clara Benedix from Hamburg. However, these suspicions were soon proved unfounded but our official messages from Paris gave reason to believe that Mrs MacLeod had indeed been carrying out activities in ways that the police look on unfavourably …
>
> She said that allies in Paris trusted her to convey messages and she had to do this in the Netherlands. The police were suspicious about these communications and this was confirmed from information gained from Paris from which it became clear that the orders had not gone out from the allies but the enemy … She declared she was willing to return to Spain of her own free will … I detect she wants to avoid anything which could spread rumours about this 'adventure' (I quote) of hers.[24]

The SS *Araguaya* docked in Vigo on 11 December. Mata Hari disembarked and went straight to the Hotel Continental. Once she was settled in the hotel, she wrote to Lintjens asking her to apologise to Capellan and to explain her absence and, no doubt, the full story behind the telegram he had received from Thomson about her identity. She also needed more money, and once again Lintjens was asked to approach Capellan for funds. After sorting out her finances, Mata Hari then met Martin Cazeaux, the Dutch Consul in Vigo. Mata Hari had originally met Cazeaux, a Frenchman, in Paris before the war, where they had a brief affair. She told Cazeaux what had happened at Falmouth and London, and he expressed surprise that she had been mistaken for Benedix: 'You'd have to be English to make such an idiotic mistake.'[25]

Cazeaux then asked if she would be willing to spy for the Russians.[26] This allegation about Cazeaux is surprising, to say the least. Even if he had not received word from the Dutch Consul in Madrid warning him about Mata Hari, why was he asking her to spy for the Russians? Or had this offer come from France? Many of the *Deuxiéme Bureau* agents working in Spain were well known to Cazeaux, and it was alleged that many of his activities, official as well as extra-curricular, benefitted France equally as much as they did the neutral Netherlands, and always benefitted Cazeaux. The Great War was an opportunity for many to make money. Information was valuable, and for every patriotic agent selflessly working for their country there were as many working for whoever paid them. Wherever the initial idea to spy for Russia had been generated, Mata Hari declined to give a definite answer either way, and journeyed on to Madrid. Cazeaux told Mata Hari that if she agreed, an agent would contact her at the city's Ritz Hotel.

She arrived in Madrid and moved into the Ritz. From there she sent a telegram to Capellan to ask for money – she was becoming desperate – and wrote to Ladoux for instructions. While she was waiting to hear back from either, Mata Hari tried to find Diego de Léon, a friend who had asked her to act as a broker for him in the sale of some paintings in Paris. Despite being thought to be in Tortoza, de Léon could not be found. Money was becoming extremely short, so she sent a telegram to Cazeaux asking when the Russian agent would contact her. Cazeaux replied that the agent was in Switzerland but would return shortly. At this point two things happened simultaneously, although independently of one another, both of which would prove disastrous for Mata Hari.

In late 1914, Ladoux had celebrated the fact that the British, with French help, had broken one of the encryption codes the Germans used for transmitting messages. The British 'Room 40' team had broken the code and informed their counterparts in the Eiffel Tower, the station that monitored several strands of German communication, most notably the one between Berlin and Madrid. In December 1916, Ladoux ordered that all communication between Berlin and Madrid was to be monitored and sent to him.[27] Why this was not done until December 1916 is unclear, although it is possible that the monitoring was being carried out by another member of his team and Ladoux only took an active interest once the situation with Mata Hari intensified. There were, after all, multiple communication strands being decoded and deciphered, and multiple active agents to be watched.

After a few days in Madrid, Mata Hari had still not received any instructions from Ladoux, so decided to take matters into her own hands. She asked the manager of the Ritz if she might see the list of diplomats currently residing in Madrid. Most hotels held an up-to-date list of diplomats resident in the city to enable them to send out correct invitations for any social events being held. Mata Hari used the list to find a German officer from whom she could either extract secrets to pass to Ladoux or make further contacts. She saw the name of one Captain Kalle and sent him a short letter asking for a meeting. The letter also contained her visiting card, embellished with an embossed crown and the aristocratic title, Vrouwe Zelle-MacLeod; a title to which she had no right.[28]

Arnold Kalle was a newly promoted army major and had been an attaché in the German Embassy in Madrid since 1912. A career soldier, he had previously served as a cavalry captain in the German general staff. Kalle was in charge of German intelligence operations. One of his main tasks was to disrupt friendly relations between Spain and the Allies. He also participated in some of the arms trafficking that took place in Morocco. He was the head of the mission in Madrid, and the man to whom all German agents working in Spain and Portugal were instructed to send their reports. This chain of command had been determined by Nicolai and Roepell, and was relayed to German agents when they attended training with the German intelligence Service in Cologne. Her choice of Kalle as the one person to make contact with was strange. She may have remembered his name and thought she could therefore make an initial friendly contact; or, as a German spy, she was, quite rightly, making contact with her German superior.

The problem for Mata Hari, the French spy, was that she had received no instructions from Ladoux. When she had set out from Paris, her aim was to go to Belgium and befriend Bissing, and through him the German general staff. Once in position, she would gather as much information as possible to give to Ladoux to earn her one million francs and marry Masloff. Thwarted in that attempt by the British, she had to find another way to earn her money. Kalle and Mata Hari met at his home in Madrid on 23 December:

> Kalle: 'Why do you come to see me?'
>
> Mata Hari: 'I was held four days in England; I was stopped and taken for German during the voyage, it would appear, with a false Dutch passport. They wished very much that I was Clara Benedix, what is the full story?'
>
> Kalle: 'How well you speak German! How is that?'
>
> Mata Hari: 'I lived three years in Berlin.'
>
> Kalle: 'You must know some officers [there].'
>
> Mata Hari: 'Yes, many.'
>
> Kalle: 'Give me some names.'
>
> Mata Hari gave him some names and added that she was the mistress of Alfred de Kiepert.
>
> Kalle: 'Now I know who you are. You are the woman of whom Kiepert was so jealous. That reminds me. I saw you at dinner with him at the Carlton Hotel [in Berlin]. You had come from the Silesian mountains.'
>
> Mata Hari: 'It is easier for you to recognise me than it is for me to recognise you.'
>
> Kalle: 'I will tell you. What happened to you on your trip was not my concern. I am not occupied with such things since the king personally asked me to abstain [from espionage]. What was done was ordered at Barcelona but I went immediately to ask for the explanation from the Baron de Roland.'[29]

This initial conversation between Mata Hari and Kalle may be interpreted in several ways. Was she, as a seemingly active German agent, trying to give Ladoux the impression she was challenging Kalle by implying he had engineered her arrest at Falmouth? Did Kalle play along with the charade, giving her de Roland's name with the almost certain knowledge that the French already knew all about him? Or was she, as a French agent, genuinely challenging Kalle? The fact that Kalle stated that 'What was done was ordered in Barcelona' would give credence to the theory that the Germans had supplied some information about her to the British; possibly the details about the financial transactions, for their own reasons. It would also support the belief that she was an active German agent. Kalle would have been unlikely to tell an enemy agent that they had engineered her arrest. Kalle then went on to confide even more information to Mata Hari: 'I am tired. I concern myself for the moment with the disembarkation of a submarine of German officers and Turks and munitions on the coast of Morocco, in the French zone. This takes all my time and my brain.'[30]

If Kalle knew Mata Hari was a German agent, he would know that she was a low-ranking one and from what had happened in England it seems possible that the Germans were already starting to use her as a diversion from more effective agents such as Benedix. To tell her about a submarine landing was risky, but not overly so, as the information was non-specific. Although the ability to land a submarine of officers and munitions on the coast of French Morocco undetected was serious, it was only one submarine. Furthermore, Kalle had failed to mention where in Morocco this had happened, when, how many officers landed, what sort of munitions and for what purpose. Was Kalle giving her information that, if questioned, she could reveal to the Allies, who would then conveniently occupy their time on a piece of non-specific information while other German activities went unnoticed? If, on the other hand, she was a French agent, then the information could still fulfil its purpose of distracting the Allies. It was certainly a very convenient piece of information for she to have discovered within a matter of minutes of an initial brief visit.

Whether acting for Germany or France, or both, on the evening of 23 December, Mata Hari wrote to Ladoux informing him that she had made contact with Kalle, that he had informed her that the head of German intelligence was Baron de Roland and that a submarine with German and Turkish officers had landed in French Morocco.[31] No copy of this letter survives in the archives of the *Deuxiéme Bureau*.

In a later meeting with her, Ladoux vaguely alluded to the information about the submarine.

The following day, Mata Hari dined with de heer de Wirth, one of the attachés from the Dutch legation. De Wirth introduced her to Colonel Joseph-Cyrill Denvignes, one of the senior attachés at the French Embassy. Denvignes was fascinated by Mata Hari, seeking her out the next evening at a ball at the Ritz Hotel. Despite barely knowing Denvignes, while the two of them were sitting chatting at the ball, Mata Hari told him of her recent travels and her experience with the British police. Denvignes then asked Mata Hari her purpose in visiting Madrid, to which she replied, 'My colonel, calm down, I am one of yours … If only I had known you one day earlier, I would not have had to go to the trouble of sending my information to Paris, I could give you the letter yourself and that would have been quicker.'[32]

Why did Mata Hari say to Denvignes that she was 'one of yours'? Did she believe Denvignes suspected her? Denvignes then asked Mata Hari what information she meant, and she told him everything that Kalle had told her.[33] Why did she do this? She had been recruited by the Germans and the French; she had received some basic instruction in sending messages and secrecy; she was an intelligent woman and had had enough experience of men to be able to judge their characters; and yet she spoke openly to a man she barely knew in a crowded ballroom, where she could have been easily overheard. Had Denvignes' name been mentioned to her by Ladoux as someone she could trust? Or had the lack of contact with Ladoux unsettled Mata Hari so much that she used Denvignes to allay any suspicions about her and her contact with Kalle?

On Christmas Day, Mata Hari dined with de Léon, who had finally arrived back in Madrid. She then met with Denvignes – although they had made no formal arrangement to do so – who asked her all about de Léon. It seems Denvignes was becoming enamoured of Mata Hari. Once reassured about de Léon, Denvignes asked her more questions about the information she had spoken about the previous day. This time the conversation took place at Denvignes' request, in a discreet part of the hotel's reading room. Denvignes wanted to know specific details; details that could prove useful, rather than the vague statements that Kalle had originally made. She agreed to return to Kalle and seek out the information Denvignes wanted.

Mata Hari then visited Kalle again. She told Kalle that she intended to return to the Netherlands as soon as possible, and as the route by boat had proved impossible she wanted to try the land route through Switzerland and Germany. Obviously she would have to pass through several borders and would require the requisite travel permit to do so. She hoped that Kalle might help her. Kalle replied that he could not. She then tackled Kalle about the information Denvignes had asked her to obtain. She said to Kalle, 'It must be so very difficult to disembark troops from a submarine on the coast of Morocco. Where do you have to bring off this coup?'

Kalle replied that 'beautiful women must not ask too much'.[34]

Mata Hari claimed that the request for help in travelling to the Netherlands was merely an excuse to visit Kalle again. She did not explain why she asked Kalle such a direct question. The conversation sounded rather too direct coming from someone used to talking with men. When Mata Hari met with Denvignes later that day, she said that she had aroused Kalle's suspicions by following Denvignes' instructions. Or had she? There is no record of the meetings with Kalle from any source other than Mata Hari herself, and her recollections were given as part of her interrogation when under suspicion of espionage by the French authorities.

Mata Hari met and dined with Denvignes over the next two days, when he told her he was returning to Paris. Despite her disquiet at what had happened with Kalle, and possibly feeling that Denvignes was partly to blame, she asked him to go to see Ladoux and Colonel Goubet, his superior, on her behalf. She wished Denvignes to stress how well her work was going. Denvignes advised her to write a letter with all her information in it and to leave it with the Marquis de Paladines, his replacement at the embassy, when he was gone. This, obviously, presumed that she would gather new information, despite having antagonised Kalle on her last visit. It is not clear exactly why

Denvignes advised her in this manner. But the simplest explanation might be that if she wrote a letter and then left it at the French Embassy, it would stop the danger in her sending information in uncoded letters through the ordinary posts, as she continued to do. Throughout her time as a spy for the French, Mata Hari sent most if not all of her messages in unencrypted open form, such that any agent from any country could easily intercept and read. This was despite being repeatedly told not to do so and to use either encryption or invisible ink.

Before Denvignes left, he arranged to meet Mata Hari at his hotel in Paris, the grand Hotel d'Orsay. After he departed, Mata Hari received an invitation from Kalle to visit him at his home. Their conversation is revealing.

Kalle: 'Come here into the light. You have certainly repeated what I told you, for the French send their radio messages everywhere asking where the officers will alight [in Morocco].'

Mata Hari: 'They might easily know from another source than me. And then, the radio messages! How do you know what they are telegraphing?'

Kalle: 'We have the key to their radio!'

Mata Hari: 'Ah, that is something else! How clever you are.'

Kalle: 'With a beautiful woman all is forgiven, but if they knew it was me who told you, it would cost me a great deal in Berlin.'[35]

The conversation was then interrupted while they had sex, or as Mata Hari brazenly put it, 'I let him do what he wanted.'[36] They then resumed talking as Mata Hari stated that the German Army had very many brave men.

Kalle: 'But the French do also. The aviators notably. They have one right now who flies over our lines and deposits among us a passenger that we must search for. But we are informed and one of these days we will see him. We know everything; we have agents in France who are very well informed.'

Mata Hari: 'How do they warn you?'

Kalle: 'There are many means.'

Mata Hari: 'Well, that astonishes me very much. I have travelled a good deal during this war and judging by the inspections to which I have been subjected, I ask myself how one could pass the frontiers with secret things. One cannot even pass with a hairpin. In England, they checked the ribbons on my chemises.'

Kalle: 'But it is surely not with women like you that one transports such things. That would be the biggest stupidity in the world. We use people who are a little dirty, those whom one doesn't notice. They carry ink formed into little white balls under their fingernails and in their ears.'

Mata Hari: 'My God, what inventions!'[37]

The visit ended with Kalle giving Mata Hari 3,500 francs.[38] Was this, as she later insisted, a gift? Was it payment for her sexual favours? Or was it a further payment as a German spy? Although the conversation was, on the surface, full of information, was it really anything the French did not know? In effect, Kalle was telling the French that the Germans knew about the passenger that had been dropped behind their lines. The fact of German agents being in France was not news. Neither was the news of the ink pellets particularly of note. The use of minute ink pellets was a method favoured by agents from several countries, and had been in use for some time. What was curious was Kalle's comment that 'it is surely not with women like you that one transports such things'. Had Kalle let slip the truth that Mata Hari, if a German agent, was not used for important work? That would be given to others who were less ostentatious? The only point of real information from Kalle was the claim that the Germans had broken the French radio encryption codes.

At the beginning of the Great War, a British ship had secretly cut off the German transatlantic cables near the German coast. All transatlantic communication had, therefore, to be carried out via radio transmission or via cables of other nations. The British had then broken the German radio codes in the early autumn of 1914, and the French unit at the Eiffel Tower was intercepting and decoding all messages sent via that code. However, the Germans had broken one of the French codes by the late summer of 1916, and so knew that the French had broken one of their codes. The Germans continued to use the broken code to send misinformation, but also developed a different second code with which to send true information. The second code was also broken in late 1916. The messages sent back and forth between Berlin and Madrid were sent via radio transmission. These were intercepted by the antennae that sat on top of the Eiffel Tower.

The fact that the Germans knew their continental code system had been broken but were continuing to use it to send misinformation is important, as it was details sent via the continental system that gave Ladoux his 'proof' that Mata Hari was a German agent.

Mata Hari could not have fully known what the situation was regarding the various radio codes, and so this information could support her claim that she was a spy for the French. That said, within the smoke and mirrors of wartime espionage, what each side knew about the other side and vice versa remains unclear. Was the information that the Germans had broken the French code really news, or did the French already know that? The German deciphering of the French code required the French to create a new code and worry about how to relay information in the interim. Were the Germans trying to force the French into unnecessarily abandoning an unbroken code in order to waste time and resources in creating a new one? Was this information true? Or was it misinformation being spread by German agents, bearing in mind that one of the easiest methods of codebreaking was to gain information while a code was being created. Had Kalle been indiscreet, or had he spread misinformation, with or without Mata Hari's knowledge and assistance? The question remains unanswered.

Whether what she had gained was information or misinformation, Mata Hari's method of delivery remained as insecure as ever. She wrote a letter to Denvignes detailing what she had gleaned from Kalle, and took the letter to the French Embassy to give to the Marquis de Paladines. Unfortunately, the marquis was not at the embassy, so she left the letter with another attaché, asking that it be sent on to Denvignes. Despite having learned about codebreaking from Kalle, the contents of the letter remained unencrypted and the letter itself was left in the possession of a brief acquaintance.

When Mata Hari had returned to Spain, she had been followed by Ladoux's agents. Her visits to Kalle were monitored, as was her relationship with Denvignes. Although not under any suspicion of acting for the enemy, Denvignes was a worry for Ladoux. As a member of the French diplomatic service, Denvignes represented the respectable establishment face of international *entente cordiale*, carried out at embassy receptions and gala balls. Ladoux, working as head of the *Deuxiéme Bureau*, had to contend with the grubby world of espionage, with its lies and subterfuge, a world that examined ladies' chemises and checked what was under people's fingernails. Politically, Denvignes was in a much stronger position and with more influential friends than Ladoux. If Mata Hari was the German spy that Ladoux thought she was, her relationship with Denvignes could prove problematic. If Denvignes finally unmasked her, then he gained the credit and Ladoux would be left having to justify why his department existed, especially given most politicians' antipathy towards the *Deuxiéme Bureau*. On the other hand, if Denvignes became overly enamoured of her, Ladoux could be called on to explain why he had not warned the attaché as to the suspicions around the dancer, particularly if there was any suggestion that French secrets had been obtained and passed to the Germans. This may explain, in part, why Mata Hari had not heard from Ladoux since her return from England. Ladoux was receiving reports on her activity and was considering what to do.

Ladoux had in fact been receiving information about Mata Hari from the agents following her, but also from the team in the Eiffel Tower. On 13 December, a message sent by Berlin to Madrid was intercepted that referred to the activities of agent H21.[39] These general messages continued. They contained little precise detail, but identified H21 as an agent in Madrid and in contact with Kalle.[40] On 25 December, another message from Berlin was intercepted. This instructed Kalle to pay H21 3,000 francs.[41] A message was sent in reply on the following day, stating that H21 had been paid 3,500 pesetas but that a further payment should be made to H21's staff in Roermond (where Anna Lintjens lived).[42] Kalle sent another message on 28 December that H21 would arrive in Paris on 29 December, and asked for 5,000 francs to be paid to her via Lintjens and Bunge, the Dutch Consul.[43]

These messages certainly appeared to identify an agent H21 in Spain, but did they identify Mata Hari? Some of the details were correct: Lintjens, Mata Hari's maid, did live in Roermond. Some details were incorrect: Mata Hari did not arrive in Paris until 3 January, not 29 December; had she perhaps changed her mind about when she would leave Madrid? But why were the Germans sending messages about one of their agents in a code they knew was broken? Was she a low-level spy, useful as an expendable distraction while other more important agents went about their business?

While this exchange of messages was going on, Mata Hari was considering what to do. She decided that she had obtained as much information as she could from Kalle and would return to Paris in the New Year. On 1 January 1917, she received a letter from one of her former lovers, Senator Emilio Junoy. The senator told her that he had been questioned by a *Deuxiéme Bureau* agent about their relationship. Furthermore, the agent had warned Junoy to be on his guard against her, as she was 'a person known to be hostile to the Allies'.[44] On receiving this letter, Mata Hari went at once to the French Embassy. The embassy was closed, so she went to the home of the Marquis de Paladines to try to find out what was happening. The marquis replied that he knew nothing about the matter.

On 3 January, Mata Hari arrived in Paris, moving into a room at the Hotel Plaza Athénée. She then wrote a letter to Masloff, whom she mistakenly thought was at Verdun; his regiment was actually in Champagne. Next she tried to meet with Denvignes. She telephoned the Hôtel d'Orsay, where Denvignes had told her he would be staying, but was told that no one of that name was there. She then telephoned the Ministry of War to enquire about him there. The official she spoke to told her that he did not know anyone called Denvignes. Mata Hari then wrote Denvignes a letter, posting it to him care of the Ministry of War.[45] Without bothering to wait for a reply, she went to the *Deuxiéme Bureau*, but no one was available to see her. Left standing outside the *Bureau* office, she met an officer she knew slightly who was leaving the building. She explained her predicament about Denvignes, and the officer replied, 'Ah, yes, the military attaché, but he leaves this evening for Madrid.'[46] She rushed to the railway station to attempt to see Denvignes.

After a desperate chase across Paris to the Orsay station, and then on to the station at Austerlitz, Mata Hari finally met Denvignes. She confronted him on his behaviour, saying, 'And so this is the way you leave, my colonel, without warning me. And our business! Have you seen Captain Ladoux?'[47]

Denvignes replied that he had seen Ladoux and his superior, Colonel Goubet, who had been impressed by Mata Hari's information. Denvignes then revealed that when asked by Goubet if he was in a relationship with her, he had said no. Mata Hari challenged Denvignes on the lie and he could not answer.[48]

It has never been established exactly what conversations Denvignes had with Ladoux and Goubet, but from his avoidance of Mata Hari it would seem that he had been strongly warned about his association with her. The following day, 4 January, she went to the *Deuxiéme Bureau* to find out what was happening. She asked to speak to Ladoux and handed over the pass he had given her before she had left for Spain. The pass, which should have enabled her to have been seen instantly, was returned to her with the word 'absent' written upon it. She returned the next day, and having been kept waiting for an hour was told to return the following day at 6 p.m. Mata Hari finally saw Ladoux on 5 January. The meeting was tense. Ladoux gave no explanation for his lack of contact while Mata Hari had been in Spain. He told her that Denvignes had paid the *Bureau* a short visit, but had not reported any information from Mata Hari. Ladoux also denied knowing anything about any agents' questioning of Senator Junoy.

Ladoux: 'In any case, you must never forget that you do not know me and I do not know you. It is certainly not we who have sent someone to the senator, and if an agent did this stupid thing, he will be sent to the front.'

Mata Hari responded:

> It is all the same to me, but I suppose that you have no interest in spoiling my
> work by the intervention of little secret agents. If a real French secret agent
> sees something that he does not understand, he runs to the embassy of France
> and not to the house of a Spanish senator. What's more, I was astonished by the
> reception you gave me. Where are the thanks for the services I have rendered
> you?

Ladoux: 'What services? That about the Baron de Roland and the submarine?'

Mata Hari: 'You forget that about the radio, the aviator and the secret ink.'

Ladoux: 'That is the first news of it I have heard.'

Mata Hari: 'What, the colonel told you nothing!'

Ladoux: 'I repeat to you that he did nothing except pass through here. What! You say that they have the code for our radios. The military attaché is pulling your leg.'

Mata Hari: 'Is there not one chance in a hundred that his information is correct and that this would repay the pain of verifying it?'

Ladoux: 'Evidently, but I am open-mouthed in astonishment.'

Mata Hari: 'Me too.'[49]

Ladoux's treatment of Mata Hari had, of course, been changed by the receipt of the radio messages about agent H21. Where before he had merely suspected her of being a German agent, after receiving the radio messages, Ladoux believed he had his proof. But if so, why not arrest her immediately? Was it because he knew that the Germans had used the broken code to send the messages, and therefore this might be misinformation? If this was the case, it still might have meant that she was a German agent, albeit not a very important one, but someone they were willing to sacrifice. Arrested and detained, she might reveal some information. Followed and watched, however, she might lead Ladoux and his men to more senior agents or her handler. From the moment Mata Hari left Ladoux's office, she was followed, her telephone conversations were listened to and her correspondence was intercepted, read and frequently taken away. His comment that 'you do not know me and I do not know you' was the typical instruction from a handler to an agent, and was the standard response to be used if arrested by the other side. It was, however, a curious comment for Ladoux to make at this point in their relationship; especially as he considered her an enemy agent. Was it, in this instance, a genuine remark that Ladoux and Mata Hari did not know each other?

The main French cryptographer during the Great War was Dr Edmond Locard. He was the man who had broken the second German code. In his memoirs, Locard stated that he had only realised that the Germans were using the broken code to send the messages about Mata Hari around 15 January, when it was brought to his attention by a junior member of staff.[50] If this is true, it would not explain why Ladoux had not contacted Mata Hari when she was in Spain. However, Locard's memoirs were written in 1954, some thirty-seven years after the event, so Locard may have mistaken the date. They were also written at a time when doubts were raised about Mata Hari's conviction and many involved in her trials sought to correct the record regarding their own involvement.

There is one possible explanation why Ladoux had ignored Mata Hari when she was in Madrid, and that was the lack of Allied progress in the war: 1916 had been a brutal year for the Allies, with the French possibly suffering more than most. Some 350,000 men had lost their lives at Verdun. The war was territorially bogged down, the Germans remained on French soil and the Russians had political problems at home. General Joffre, who had recommended Ladoux for his role in the *Deuxième Bureau*, had been dismissed as chief of staff on 12 December 1916, replaced by General Robert-Georges Nivelle. Prime Minister Aristide Briand was under immense political pressure and was replaced in March 1917 by Alexandre Ribot. Ladoux and the *Deuxième Bureau*, along with the rest of the political and military leadership of the country, were desperately trying to explain what was going wrong and to find answers to the lack of progress in the war. Ladoux's department, which was viewed with suspicion by many, was coming under increasing pressure to catch foreign spies and saboteurs, while also supplying useful information from their own agents. Although strongly suspected of being a German agent, in December 1916 and January 1917 Mata Hari was not the sole focus of Ladoux's work.

While being ignored by Ladoux, Mata Hari turned to her great love, Masloff, and wrote to him as soon as she arrived in Paris that January, 'My dear, will I soon hear from you? Could you come? Kisses from your Marina.'[51]

Masloff replied that he would arrive on 8 January. The day before he was due to arrive, Mata Hari wrote to Masloff again, 'Tomorrow evening – My God, it is your Christmas today [Russian Orthodox Christmas]. I hold you for a long time. See you soon, Your Marina.'[52]

Masloff did not arrive the next day, and Mata Hari received no letter or telegram explaining his absence. Worried, she wrote to Count Alexis Ignatieff, a senior Russian military attaché at the embassy in Paris, asking if he knew of Masloff's whereabouts. From then onwards, Mata Hari wrote to Masloff daily,[53] but received no reply. She started to realise that she was being followed again, and on 12 January went to the Dutch Consulate to ask for help.[54] It is unclear which consulate official she spoke to, but it may well have been Bunge, who had been mentioned in the Berlin telegrams.

To add to her worries about Ladoux's changed attitude, Masloff's absence and the men following her, Mata Hari was running low on cash again and wrote several times to Capellan, via Lintjens, to ask for money. He did not reply. Mata Hari moved from the Plaza Athénée to the cheaper Hotel Castiglione. Ladoux's agents followed her. She started to try to evade the agents. She changed direction frequently when travelling, using several taxis for one trip.[55] Despite these precautions, she was still followed and her letters were still intercepted and stolen. Staff in the hotel collaborated with the police, handing over any letters and telegrams she sent or received. On 14 January, a reply from Masloff finally arrived. The hotel concierge handed it straight to the police without Mata Hari knowing of its existence.[56] It was a situation that could not go on indefinitely.

Finally, Mata Hari wrote to Ladoux:

What do you want of me? I am disposed to do all that you ask. I do not ask
you your secrets and I do not wish to know your agents. I am an international
woman. Do not discuss my methods, do not ruin my work with secret agents
who cannot understand me. That I desire to be paid is legitimate, but I wish
to go.[57]

She did not, however, send the letter immediately to Ladoux, but
instead showed it first to her lawyer, Clunet. The old lawyer thought
the letter's tone to be brusque and the request for payment mercenary.
Mata Hari was pragmatic, saying, 'If I am not ashamed to accept money,
then I must not be ashamed to say so.'[58]

Mata Hari no longer trusted the staff in the hotels in which she
stayed, and posted the letter herself. Despite Clunet's misgivings about
the mercenary nature of the letter, she had little option as she was very
short of money. Capellan had still not sent any funds, she owed money
to various dressmakers and milliners across Paris and was unable to pay
her hotel bill. She moved out of the Hotel Castiglione and into the
even cheaper Elysée Palace Hotel.[59]

It is not clear why she showed Clunet the letter. Perhaps it was
to ensure that Ladoux could not claim he had not received it, as he
had done with the correspondence from Spain. It is noticeable that
Mata Hari describes herself as an 'international woman' in the letter,
the particular term for a high-class courtesan, but one that hinted
at her international connections. In addition to not asking Ladoux
about his secrets or not wishing to know his agents, was she trying to
distance herself from espionage work? Although she frequently made
some incredibly stupid decisions, Mata Hari was not unintelligent.
She had been warned repeatedly by Ladoux and several others that
she was suspected of being an enemy agent; she had been detained
and questioned at length by the British security services; she knew she
was being followed; and she suspected her mail was tampered with. It
is extremely unlikely that she did not realise that she was in danger. It
is also noticeable that she had again made contact with Clunet, her
lawyer, after such a long absence.

Once Mata Hari had sent the letter to Ladoux, she received one from Capellan. The baron had finally sent her some money, but warned that he could not continue to maintain her house in The Hague if she had no intention of returning there. She went to the Dutch Consulate to collect the 3,000 francs that Capellan had deposited; she sent 1,000 francs to Masloff. The Russian had still not arrived to see her; she had not received his letters; she had still not been paid by Ladoux; Capellan was threatening to cut off her funds; and she was followed wherever she went. She therefore decided to leave Paris, but that required money.

Very little is known about Mata Hari's movements between 15 January and 13 February, when she was arrested. The Mata Hari dossier in the *Service Historique de l'Armeé de Terre* archive in Vincennes holds no papers for that period. Whether they have been lost or deliberately removed cannot be known. Although some have speculated that Ladoux stopped the surveillance on her at that point, there seems no reason why he should. In addition, both Henri Maunoury, from the Prefecture of Police, and Albert Priolet, the Police Commissioner, stated categorically that the surveillance on her was not removed.[60]

Despite the absence of these files, some of Mata Hari's activities can be uncovered which give a clue as to the reason why they might have been removed. She was working to raise the money to leave Paris by 'entertaining' as many men as she could, and she had returned to the *maisons de rendezvous* of her earlier Parisian life. It is noticeable how far she had tumbled down the social scale, as merely a few months previously she had been meeting gentlemen in high-class hotels. In addition, she had formerly preferred senior ranking army officers, but her conquests now included individuals such as Paul Bourgeois, who was merely a military nurse. Bourgeois was interviewed by Ladoux's staff:

> The 6 or 7 of February, I cannot be precise about which of the two days, having permission, I went to Paris and in mid-afternoon found myself on the Rue de Castiglione. I entered into the garden of the Tuileries to take photos

of the snow. It was then that I saw, walking before me, a pretty young woman, extremely elegant, about thirty-two years old. I approached her and asked if she would pose for my photos to animate the scene. We fell into conversation and finally, we went together to take tea in a house in Rue Caumartin, near the place de L'Opera at the left, and going toward this street. I do not know the name of the place because I had never been there before. If I remember correctly, the facade is painted blue. My new friend, she seemed to know the house and it was she who chose it and we were directed to a table on the right that she was particularly fond of.

There, we continued to chat about everything but not military matters. This woman posed not a single indiscreet question of that type, she never asked me where I was [stationed]. The conversation was very gay and mostly superficial. I wanted to see this young woman again and asked her if she would be my marrine [sweetheart] and naturally she accepted ... In leaving I arranged a rendezvous with her for the next day.[61]

Bourgeois' testimony clears Mata Hari from carrying out any enemy activities, but his statement that she 'seemed to know the house' and the table that she was 'particularly fond of' seems to confirm that she was frequenting *maisons de rendezvous*. Bourgeois is of course keen to point out that he had never been to the *maisons de rendezvous* before.

Mata Hari had still not heard from Masloff, and continued to write to him daily – sometimes twice daily. The letters were confiscated by Ladoux's agents, as was any correspondence from Masloff to Mata Hari. In desperation, she turned to her old friend Adam Tadeusz Wieniawski, a Polish composer. Wieniawski had joined the French Army at the start of the Great War, and in January 1917 was seconded to the Russian Red Cross in Paris. Mata Hari hoped that Wieniawski might be able to get word to Masloff, or at least tell her where the Russian was stationed. Wieniawski was also interviewed by Ladoux:

Of all her questions, the only one that shocked me was when she asked, 'Was Masloff grievously wounded at Verdun?' However, the Russian troops were never in that sector. I told her that her friend, as far as I knew, was simply bruised. And on her demand I gave my word to inform her if something serious happened to Masloff. I had promised also to recommend to his boss, General Netchvofodoff, to give him permission for a convalescent leave if he needed it. I had soon thereafter to telephone the general several times, he responded to me: 'She is a tall, brown woman, an exotic type? In that case, I counsel you to have nothing to do with her, I have had very bad reports of her.' ... At about this time, Madame Zelle found a way of telegraphing me at Chalons [where he was based]. I do not know how she had my address, I believe that she asked me for news of Masloff. I did not respond and have not heard further from her.[62]

This testimony from Wieniawski shows quite clearly the suspicion in which Mata Hari was held by senior members of the Russian Army. While obviously not proof of any wrongdoing, it indicates the level of suspicion which she had, by this time, generated across all of the Allied forces. Her mannerisms and conduct were such that despite having been in Spain, France and England, a Russian general claimed to have received bad reports about her. The question she posed about Masloff would have done nothing to allay suspicions. The fighting at Verdun had finished in December 1916, and no Russian units had been involved. This had been plainly reported in every newspaper across France. Mata Hari could not have been ignorant of these facts. Even if she had not read any papers, the talk in the hotels and cafes was all about the glorious victory at Verdun. She could not have failed to know what had happened. Why, then, had she asked about Masloff's injuries at Verdun? Had she not read a sole newspaper, not seen a single headline at a newspaper stand or overhead at least one conversation since her arrival in Paris? Or had she deliberately asked such a foolish question in the hope that Wieniawski would be so taken aback at its stupidity that he would have replied with details of where Masloff and the Russian troops were actually stationed? The question remains unanswered.

Finally, around the middle of January, Masloff arrived in Paris. Initially elated, Mata Hari was soon to be disappointed as Masloff explained he could not marry her as they had previously planned; he had been refused permission. Masloff had received a letter from his colonel's military attaché, in which the colonel had expressly forbidden Masloff from marrying her or having any further contact with her. The colonel had been sent a report by Count Ignatieff from the Russian Embassy in Paris, informing him about reports Ignatieff had received about Mata Hari. A French officer, unnamed in the letter, had written to Ignatieff, warning him that she was a 'dangerous adventuress'.[63] This warning from the unnamed Frenchman had probably reinforced the rumours already circulating amongst the senior Russian military about her and had resulted in Masloff's colonel forbidding the marriage and any further association. After a few days, Masloff had to leave Paris and return to his unit.

Mata Hari had not had any contact with Ladoux since their meeting on 5 January, and he had not replied to her letter. She visited the Prefecture of Police, where she asked Maunoury for a permit to return to the Netherlands, travelling through Switzerland. Maunoury informed her that Ladoux was on leave at the French Riviera, and would not return for some three weeks. As only Ladoux could authorise a travel permit, she would have to wait until his return. Mata Hari was undaunted by this refusal, and went to the Ministry of Foreign Affairs to ask if anyone in that office could grant her a travel permit. She was told the pass could only be authorised once her papers were checked, and was advised to return a few days later.

On 10 February, a request for a warrant to arrest Mata Hari was sent from the War Ministry to the Office of Military Justice:

I WISH TO MAKE KNOWN that the herenamed Zelle, divorced spouse of MacLeod, a.k.a. Mata Hari, dancer, Dutch subject, strongly suspected of being an agent in the service of Germany.

This information came from a very reliable secret source and the following indications have become known to the counterespionage service of the Army Headquarters.

Zelle MacLeod belongs to the Cologne intelligence service where she is known by the designation H21.

She has been twice in France since the onset of hostilities, undoubtedly to receive intelligence for Germany.

During her second voyage, she offered her services to French intelligence, when in fact, as she showed later, she would share whatever she learned with German intelligence.

Arrested by the English on her attempted return to the Netherlands she was returned by them to Spain where she entered into relations with the German military attaché at Madrid, at the same time she offered to the French military attaché to pass on information about the activities of German intelligence in Spain.

She confessed the points mentioned in the paragraph above to the German military attaché, as is established by a secret document from her, and further that she had received 5,000 francs from the German intelligence service at the beginning of November in Paris.

She has, further, remitted to the German military attaché a series of intelligence reports about military and diplomatic orders which were then transmitted by the headquarters to Berlin.

She finally agreed to return to France where a sum on 5,000 francs was sent to her by successive transmissions from the German ambassador in the Netherlands at the general consulate of the Netherlands in Paris. This sum effectively reached Zelle on January 16, 1917, and then she had made a photo of the receipt signed M. Bunge, consul of the Netherlands, whose exact role in this affair could not be established except by questioning.

I communicate to you the information which will permit you to appreciate the opportunity that is offered by issuing an order of denunciation against Zelle MacLeod, on the strength of which two dossiers of information have been constituted, one by the Army Headquarters and the other by the Prefecture of Police, dossiers which they could use for investigation.[64]

This long missive was sent by Hubert Lyautey, the Minister of War, from his office at the Army Headquarters, *Cinquième Bureau*, Section of the Centralisation of Information. Marked 'secret', it was sent to Général Augustin Dubail, General of the Division, Military Governor of Paris, at the office of Military Justice. The request was robust in its list of Mata Hari's alleged offences. While her actual guilt or innocence was still to be established, the strength of the request was such that it was something of a foregone conclusion that an arrest warrant would be issued.

On 12 February, Mata Hari returned to the Ministry of Foreign Affairs. She was told that her papers had still not arrived, so they were unable to issue her with a travel permit. On the same day, the warrant was issued for her arrest:

> Woman Zelle, Marguerite, known as Mata Hari, residing at the Palace Hotel, of the Protestant religion, born in the Netherlands August 7 1876, 1 metre 75 centimetres tall, able to read and write, is arrested for espionage, attempted espionage, complicity in espionage and intelligence with the enemy, in his favour.

Albert Priolet, the Police Commissioner, was instructed to have Mata Hari arrested, her belongings and correspondence were to be seized and searched, any and all ongoing correspondence to be intercepted and seized and all bank details to be sought. The investigation was to be carried out by Captain Pierre Bouchardon, investigating magistrate of the Third Council of War: the military court that investigated espionage cases.[65]

12

ARREST AND
INTERROGATION

On the morning of 13 February 1917, Mata Hari was arrested in room 131 at the Hotel Elysée Palace. Priolet read the arrest warrant to her while his team of five inspectors searched the room, collecting up her possessions and sealing them into their evidence bags, as follows:

Seal number one:

A French visa issued at The Hague on 27 November 1915 to Madam Zelle (Register 312), issued for Paris for the last time 4 January 1916 for the Low Countries via Spain and Portugal.

A travel permit issued under the number 1498 E to Madame Zelle for a trip to Vittel.

A residence permit in the name of Madame Zelle, issued in Paris 13 December 1915.

An extract from the registry of enrolment for aliens in the name of Zelle (Registry 41.13, volume 32).

An addendum to the visa number 312 issued in London 2 December 1915, to go to Hendaye 11 January 1916.

A visa issued in The Hague 12 May 1916 in the name of Madame Zelle (Dutch passport).

Seal number two (wrapped):
One lot of correspondence.

Seal number three (wrapped):
Different receipts, bills and diverse papers.

Seal number four (wrapped):
Ten papers dealing with the sending of money, the rental of a safety deposit box, bank matters, the rental of an apartment, 33 Rue Henri-Martin.

Seal number five (wrapped):
A chequebook for Credit Lyonnais, account number 147045, in the name of MacLeod, Mata Hari.

Seal number six (wrapped):
Fifty-three diverse addresses.

Seal number seven (wrapped):
Thirty photographs.

Seal number eight (wrapped):
A valise containing books, brochures, programmes and various objects.

Seal number nine (wrapped):
A box containing a pendulum clock and addressed as a gift from Mme. Zelle.

Seal number ten (wrapped):
A box containing various objects that Mme. Zelle intended to take to the Netherlands as gifts for her servants.

Seal number eleven (wrapped):

A travelling bag containing toilet products being submitted for examination by the judicial identification service.

Seal number twelve (wrapped):

An envelope containing six bank notes in the value of 100 francs, numbers 79885324, 06968003, 28148089, 58349558, 67750343; a bill for 60 florins, number AA094887; a bill for 40 florins, number UB2363; a Russian bill, number 609466. (Separate from this, a sum of 100 francs was left with the aforementioned Zelle.)[1]

Mata Hari was then taken by Priolet to the Palace of Justice, where she would be interrogated by Pierre Bouchardon, the investigating magistrate of the Third Council of War.

Bouchardon was a lawyer who had become a substitute judge and then assistant director of criminal law in the Ministry of Justice. He had an excellent legal mind and an almost obsessive attention to detail in the cases in which he worked. When the new department of the Third Council of War was created, Bouchardon was asked to become its sole investigating magistrate. His main investigative techniques were repetition and persistence. He would ask suspects the same questions repeatedly until he gained the truth, and would investigate every aspect of a case until it was solved. His nickname amongst his colleagues was, allegedly, 'The Grand Inquisitor'.[2]

Mata Hari's first interview with Bouchardon took place at 11 a.m. on 13 February. Present were Bouchardon, Mata Hari and Sergeant Emmanuel Baudouin, who took notes of the proceedings. Bouchardon started by going through the legal formalities of the situation. He asked Mata Hari if she had read the arrest warrant issued against her and she replied that she had. He then informed her of her right to have a lawyer present and asked if she wanted one called. Mata Hari declined, stating that she did not need a lawyer as she was innocent of all charges. She formally waived her right to have her lawyer present at her first and last questioning. Mata Hari was then asked if she wished to make any statement regarding the charges laid against her. She replied, 'I am innocent. Someone is playing with me, French counter-espionage, since I am in its service, and I have only acted on instructions.'[3]

The rest of the questioning followed closely the list of charges as laid out in the arrest warrant. To every accusation put to her, Mata Hari proclaimed her innocence. At the end of the interview, Bouchardon told her that she was to be held in Saint-Lazare prison. She was visibly shocked. Bouchardon later recalled:

> I saw a tall woman with thick lips, dark skin, and imitation pearls in her ears, who somewhat resembled a savage … [When I informed her she was to stay in prison] she turned to me, a haggard look came into her eyes, which were dumb with fear; bits of dyed hair stuck out at her temples.[4]

Bouchardon believed Mata Hari guilty from the start and treated her accordingly. The French justice system, as laid down in 1789, presumed those arrested to be innocent until proven guilty, 'Any man being presumed innocent until he has been declared guilty.'[5] Despite this law, as the justice system combined the roles of investigator and magistrate, many working within the system adopted the attitude of presumed guilt in the late nineteenth and early twentieth centuries. This was doubly so in the case of women. The mindset of most was that innocent women would not get arrested; therefore a women who was arrested could not be innocent.

Bouchardon recalled, 'From the first interview, I had the intuition that I was in the presence of a person in the pay of our enemies. From that time, I had but one thought: to unmask her.'[6]

Although this may seem somewhat prematurely judgemental by Bouchardon, in February 1917 France was a country nearing collapse. The war that had been supposed to last a few months had dragged on for over two years; almost a million French troops had been killed and injured; hundreds of civilians had been killed and injured; many more had been made homeless; enemy forces had occupied the north of the country, harming daily life in the rural economy and affecting food supplies to the cities; industry was disrupted, as all efforts were now directed to the war; and the economy was teetering on the edge of bankruptcy. Morale in the country had plummeted, and was so bad that some French troops were on the brink of mutiny. In May 1917, troops in thirteen of the divisions of the army had mutinied. Revolts occurred in a further twenty-one divisions and over 27,000 French soldiers deserted throughout 1917.[7]

The abnormal situation of the French in 1917 rendered normal rational responses null and void. The psychology of the country was dangerously close to despair, and the government and the armed forces, and those of the Allies, could not afford to see the French will break. Official propaganda from the *Maison de la Presse*, of the Ministry of Foreign Affairs, worked overtime to rally the nation around the brave fighting men, but could only go so far to counter the reality on the ground. The claim that defeats and stalemate were the result of the work of saboteurs and spies could explain what was happening without apportioning blame to the French themselves. It was, however, a risky stratagem; if the spy or saboteur was not caught, then the admission of the success of enemy agents could result in panic. The Ministries of War, Foreign Affairs and Justice did not agree on how to raise morale. Even within each department there was disagreement, with some favouring increasing discipline amongst the troops, while others proposed trapping possible agents – as Ladoux had done – and some suggested blanket suppression of any bad news reports. This disparate and piecemeal approach left officials such as Bouchardon to negotiate the politics of the situation while undertaking a full investigation of Mata Hari's alleged espionage activities.

When the first interview was over, Mata Hari was taken to a cell in Saint-Lazare prison. Saint-Lazare had been originally built on the boundary of marshland on the banks of the Seine in the twelfth century, and been founded as a leprosarium (leper colony). By the seventeenth century, it was used to house individuals of low morals, and by the eighteenth century was a prison hospital for prostitutes with venereal disease. The nineteenth century saw its use change again when it was used as a prison for female prisoners, usually working-class and those convicted of serious crimes. Due to the prisoners housed there, Saint-Lazare had a very bad reputation.

Because of its marshland location, Saint-Lazare was notoriously cold and damp. In addition, most cells had a permanent population of fleas, lice, bedbugs, cockroaches and rats. On her first night in Saint-Lazare, Mata Hari was placed in the padded suicide cell. This was normal procedure for all new arrivals, as the shock of arrest and subsequent confinement in Saint-Lazare could undermine the most solid of constitutions. The cells in Saint-Lazare were dark. The lavatory was a metal bucket, and washing had to be done with a single bowl of cold water every morning. The food was minimal and poor, and had to be paid for by the prisoners: the daily ration was of low-quality coffee, bread, soup and vegetables; a small meat portion was served once a week. The prisoners were cared for by nuns from the Order of Marie-Joseph. Mata Hari was placed under the care of Sister Marie and Sister Léonide.

She was seen on her first night by the prison doctor, Léon Bizard. When asked if she required anything, Mata Hari replied, 'Yes! A telephone and a bath.'[8] Neither was available to prisoners, even those not convicted of any crime. She spent the next twenty-four hours alone in her cell, and it was 15 February before Bouchardon began his interrogation of her. His pen portrait of his prisoner shows the stress that she had obviously been under with the recent surveillance and subsequent arrest and imprisonment. It is honest to the point of brutality:

Was she, had she been pretty? Without a doubt, if one consulted the portrait taken in her youth which was the one in her passport. But the woman who was led to me in my office at the Third Council of War had suffered much at the hands of time. Her eyes large as eggs, bulbous, yellow and disfigured with red veins, the snub nose, the skin showing the application of too much rouge, the mouth stretched almost to the ears, lips like the fat rolls of a Negro, large teeth like paddles with a space between the incisors, hair greying at the temples where the dye had not lasted as long; in the pallid light that infiltrated the courtyard of the gaol, she did not resemble the dancer who had bewitched so many men. But she had kept the harmony of her figure, the slenderness and a certain swing of the hips that was not devoid of grace, a little like the undulation of a tigress in the jungle. Feline, supple, and artificial, used to gambling everything and anything without scruple, without pity, always ready to devour fortunes, leaving her ruined lovers to blow their brains out, she was a born spy … She squandered money with such frenzy that she was often reduced to penury. Then she frequented the houses of assignation. Dr Léon Bizard, doctor of the prefecture of police, encountered her in the course of his visits [to check the prostitutes for venereal disease], in an establishment in the quarter of L'Etoile. In addition, she had prohibitive rates, fifty louis for a 'passing fancy' [a quick sexual act].[9]

The comment that Dr Bizard had previously seen Mata Hari in one of the *maisons de rendezvous* is telling. With the prevalent attitudes towards women, depravity and criminality, it did not aid her case for Bouchardon to be told by Bizard that he had seen her before while examining prostitutes. Bouchardon had been tasked with finding a spy, and his first report by the prison doctor was confirming Mata Hari's depravity and potential criminality even before the questioning had begun.

Bouchardon started the interview on 15 February by again asking if Mata Hari wanted a lawyer. She again declined, and signed a statement to that effect, 'I expressly renounce, for the present interrogation, all of the formalities of the law which concern the assistance of legal counsel and the benefit of procedures at his disposition.'[10]

Once the point regarding legal representation was settled, Bouchardon began questioning Mata Hari. He started by asking about her childhood, then moved on to her marriage to MacLeod, her divorce and her life as a dancer and a courtesan. Slowly, Bouchardon attempted to build up a picture of her life. Initially, she co-operated, giving Bouchardon as much detail as she could. However, not all of the detail she recounted was strictly accurate; details were muddled and obfuscated; dates were never remembered with accuracy; her lovers were given elevated titles; and her times in the *maisons de rendezvous* were not mentioned. She did not know, apparently, of Dr Bizard's previous recognition of her. Had Mata Hari been arrested by an ordinary policeman for an ordinary crime, these lies and half-truths would have counted for very little. As she had been arrested on a charge of espionage, her evasion merely added to Bouchardon's suspicions about her, especially as the truth about her 'titled' lovers and even the *maisons* were revealed as the interrogation continued. Mata Hari finally admitted to having worked at *maisons de rendezvous* at 5 Rue de Galilée, 86 Avenue Kléber, 14 Rue Lord-Byron and in the Rue de Caumartin. These confessions confirmed her depraved and thus criminal nature.

The interrogation lasted the entire day, and at some point she seemed to have realised the seriousness of her situation. At the end of the day's questions, she finally asked for legal assistance:

> I wish, for the rest of the questioning, that Maître Clunet, who is already occupied with my affairs, should be designated as my lawyer. As for the rest, I ask you to permit me to have my linen dressing gown, which is indispensable to me. Finally, I am in Saint-Lazare under conditions that I cannot withstand and I ask that you have me examined from the point of view of health. I am suffering greatly and I need special care.[11]

Mata Hari's assertion that she was suffering may have been merely due to the stress she was under because of her circumstances. In addition, she may have been ill with the complaint that had caused her to seek the waters in Vittel in 1916. Alternatively, the need for 'special care' may have hinted at syphilis, for which particular mercury compounds would be required. Bouchardon arranged for her to be seen that evening by Jules Socquet, one of the prison doctors. Socquet examined her in her cell and reported that the prisoner was:

> 40 years, tall, well-formed and seemingly vigorous. Because of the emotions caused by her arrest, she says, and the rules to which she was subjected since that day, she vomited blood that night. This frightening state is heightened by the fact that she finds herself in a cell that is dark and airless. The cell where we visited her is spacious; the walls are padded, but it is aerated by only a single circular window with a grill measuring about 25 centimetres in diameter, in the middle of which is an electric lamp.

At the time of our examination, we were able to verify that she was menstruating. The accused had no fever; her tongue was clean and not coated. She was very emotional and nervous. Auscultation of her chest revealed no unusual sounds; it was the same with the sounds of the heart.

CONCLUSION: The accused Zelle is not actually suffering from any organic disease or complaint or fever. She can without any serious inconvenience withstand a regime of preventative detention. As soon as possible, as a means of humanity, we suggest it would be necessary to change this cell for a lighter and more airy one.[12]

Despite Doctor Socquet's report that Mata Hari was 'vigorous', on 19 February she was admitted to the prison infirmary. No specific illness was reported and she was soon discharged, but returned to a new and, relatively, better cell. On 21 February, Bouchardon resumed his questioning. When she was brought to Bouchardon's office she was joined by her lawyer, Clunet.[13] Although a noted expert on international business law and a devoted admirer of Mata Hari, Clunet was out of his depth in this case of alleged espionage. Bouchardon commented that Clunet was:

> an old and somewhat naive admirer of the dancer … He carries out his defence of his client with an ardour of a neophyte and he has a tenderness towards her that I cannot explain to myself, for he knows that at the outbreak of war, the accused was in Berlin itself, the mistress of two officers and of the chief of police. It was Madame Zelle herself who told him this.[14]

The interrogation then commenced. After the previous interview, which had established the narrative of her life, with its many truths and half-lies, Bouchardon concentrated on the details of her actions as a spy. He questioned her about her return to Paris from The Hague in 1916. At one point, she said that she needed to buy certain toilette items that were unavailable in the Netherlands. This was a somewhat strange statement to have made. What was available in France, a country partly occupied by foreign troops, that was not available in the neutral Netherlands? What was so important about that toilette item that a substitute could not be used? Was this some kind of a mercury compound that she was able to get under a long-standing doctor's prescription, due to her long residency in Paris? To obtain the same compound in The Hague may have required an embarrassing medical examination with an unknown doctor. Given her personality, it is entirely possible that she would have rather travelled to Paris than submit to a strange doctor. Of course, the return to Paris would also have been of benefit to a German agent.

Mata Hari also told Bouchardon about Masloff. It was, she stated, a 'grand love on both sides'.[15] Bouchardon doubted this. He reported that:

> Already the official mistress of Colonel van der Capellan, of the Dutch army, she was also the mistress of the Belgian commandant the Marquis de Beaufort and of the Russian Captain de Masloff, who presented her as his fiancée and for whom she played the comedy of great love. This triple liaison did not stop her from having fleeting relations with one Montenegrin officer, one Italian, one Irish, three or four English and five French officers. Far from being ashamed, she flattered herself about it. 'I love officers,' she declared, 'I have loved them all my life. I would rather be the mistress of a poor officer than a rich banker. My greatest pleasure is to go to bed with them without thinking of money, and then, I like to make comparisons among the different nationalities.'[16]

The interrogation continued. Mata Hari told Bouchardon that she had wanted to visit Masloff at Vittel, required a travel permit and thus met Ladoux, who asked her to spy for France. The problem that she had, and may well not have been aware of, was that Bouchardon, in keeping with the beliefs of many of the time, thought of her as basically immoral. The standards of behaviour to which women were expected to adhere had no flexibility: one was either a respectable woman or an immoral one. Ladoux's initial reports of Mata Hari and her eventual admission over the *maisons de rendezvous* left Bouchardon in no doubt she was definitely not in the first category.

Given Bouchardon's opinion of Mata Hari, it was extremely unlikely that he would have believed her version of events; notwithstanding the obvious and verifiable lies she had told him during her first interrogation. In every element of her testimony, he was unlikely to give her the benefit of the doubt. However, Bouchardon was an extremely professional man, and although his questioning was rigorous, he gave little away about his personal feelings. Mata Hari was not stupid, she knew that the charges she faced were serious, but it is possible that she still, at that stage, did not realise how serious. She was also hampered by a lawyer whose attitude was that of a solicitous lover who told her what she wanted to hear rather than the reality of the situation, although it is possible that Clunet also failed to recognise the gravity of her circumstances.

After the day's interrogation, Mata Hari returned to her cell and wrote a letter to Bouchardon:

I again ask for my provisional liberty from the military governor of Paris. I beg you, please help me to obtain it. You see that neither my trunks or my letters contain anything improper and never, never, have I done the slightest thing like espionage against you. I suffer too much. Until I am freed, I beg you for the following:

My couturier Madame Chartier; 5, Rue Delambre, has at her shop a cloak of white cloth, decorated with black fox. I have 25 or 30 francs yet to pay her for a small repair to it. Could you get this garment and pay her 50 francs?

The chambermaid of the first floor of the Elysée Palace Hotel must have received my lingerie back from the laundress. There are 5 or 6 francs to pay. Would you please go look for this?

Would you ask the agents who searched my room what they have done with my toilet articles and my gold earrings, the large Portuguese rings, which were found in the drawer to the right of my dressing table.

Madame Dalodier, milliner; 14 Rue Duphot, for my boa with white plumes. There are 15 francs to pay.

Would you like to arrange all this? I would be grateful. And then there is something close to my heart. It is the permission to go see my fiancé Captain de Masloff. I cannot finds words to ask you for more.

I have never – never – done anything bad towards you. Give me my freedom.[17]

Bouchardon's response to this letter was pragmatic. He sent a police inspector, Curnier, to collect Mata Hari's possessions and pay off her outstanding bills.[18] This was probably a routine procedure for prisoners without family members to settle their affairs in the matter of small debts. Alternatively, it may have been thought necessary by Bouchardon to have dealt with this trivia in order to concentrate solely on her interrogation. As for her request for 'provisional liberty', that was ignored completely.

It is noticeable that Mata Hari had not asked Clunet to deal with these matters for her. Their relationship is somewhat difficult to analyse. He adored her, and had done so since he had first met her in 1906, although they had only very briefly been lovers. He had acted on her behalf on several occasions, usually unsuccessfully, so when she had finally realised that she needed a lawyer, it was natural for her to ask Clunet for help.

What is curious is why Clunet did not advise her to seek another lawyer. Did he not realise the gravity of the situation, the complexity of the law in matters of espionage and his own lack of experience and knowledge in that field? There is no record of Clunet advising Mata Hari to employ a lawyer with relevant experience. Was it a matter of pride on Clunet's part that he thought he could defend her? Or was he still the besotted lover that wanted to be in her presence, no matter what the circumstances? Equally, there is no record of Mata Hari questioning Clunet's ability to act on her behalf. Was this blind faith on her part, a belief in her own innocence or sheer stupidity? There was no requirement on the part of Bouchardon to advise her that she needed proper legal advice. The law only required Bouchardon to advise her of her right to have a lawyer present. On 22 February, Clunet filed a petition for Mata Hari to be given 'provisional liberty' during Bouchardon's investigation of the case on the grounds that there was no hard evidence of espionage activity on her part.

While the petition was being considered, Bouchardon received the report on Mata Hari's belongings that had been seized upon her arrest and subsequently examined. The report, dated 23 February, stated that an initial search had revealed nothing incriminating. The monies and jewellery found in her hotel room and deposit box were sent to the court clerk for safe keeping. She was then allowed to draw funds from the clerk to pay for incidentals during her imprisonment. Bouchardon ordered financial checks to be made at the banks in which Mata Hari held accounts in order to ascertain if she held any further accounts, safety deposit boxes with large sums of money, or money that could not be accounted for. Nothing was found. Bouchardon widened the search and sent inquiries to banks across Paris for any accounts or safety deposit boxes in her name; none were found. Turning to her make-up and toiletries, Bouchardon ordered chemical analysis to be carried out on everything.[19]

The analysis was carried out by the chemist Edouard Bayle. All of Mata Hari's make-up, toiletries and medicines were examined; two were of particular interest. One was a cream of oxycyanide of mercury which she had obtained on prescription in Madrid. The other was a lotion of mercury bi-iodine and potassium iodine.[20] Both were relatively standard treatments for syphilis. They could also be diluted to use as invisible ink. Mata Hari claimed to use them as a vaginal douche to prevent pregnancy. Their presence was suspicious but not conclusive; Bouchardon still had no physical evidence.

The next interrogation began on 24 February. Bouchardon questioned Mata Hari again about her visit to Ladoux's office.[21] She told Bouchardon that Ladoux suspected her of being a German agent, but still recruited her to spy for France. She then went on to relate her arrest and questioning by the Metropolitan police in London and how they had mistaken her for Clara Benedix.

Mata Hari did not, or course, know that Ladoux had told the British that he had suspected her of being an enemy agent, so he had merely pretended to employ her in order to 'prove' her guilt.[22] Bouchardon, having been given her file by Ladoux, was aware of this ruse by his colleague. After a long day of questions, she was again returned to her cell.

Two days later, on 26 February, the petition to give Mata Hari provisional liberty was denied. The petition was returned to Clunet with the word 'REJET' written across the top of the page.[23] She was informed of the decision in a letter from Clunet. At that point, the letter she got from Clunet was the only correspondence she was receiving, Masloff's letters and postcards going directly to Bouchardon. On 12 February, Masloff had written to her informing her that he was in the Marguerite Hospital at Épernay and asking her to visit him. Masloff had previously been gassed and required an operation on his throat. He wrote again on 13 February:

> For five days I have been in hospital at Épernay. You would not believe how this life brings me down. I need so much to have you close to me to whisper words of love in my ear until my heart is full. Alas the distance that separates us obliges me to do nothing except think of you. I visit you in dreams that are so strong that I forget it is only a dream and I am seized by a sudden foolish thought that I wish to embrace you. I open my arms and suddenly the vision disappears leaving me saddened. In these painful moments your photograph, which never leaves me even on the day of battle, is a sweet consolation. I have already expedited a letter to ask you if it is possible for you to visit me. What would it take for you to do it? Please upon receipt of this, telegraph me your response. Épernay is a small city where you will not need to bring all of your trunks, because you could come only for three or four days. My kisses and thoughts. I cover your splendid body with kisses.[24]

Masloff wrote twice more: once to tell Mata Hari that he had been moved to a hospital in Paris, and then on 18 February stating that he was 'astonished by your silence'.[25]

While Masloff was in hospital in Paris, Mata Hari continued to be questioned by Bouchardon. The next interrogation took place on 28 February. Bouchardon concentrated on her relationship with Kalle in Madrid. This was a crucial part of her interrogation. If she was a genuine French agent, as she stated, then she would have been working under Ladoux's instructions regarding Kalle. However, Ladoux had not instructed her to approach Kalle. Furthermore, when Mata Hari gained information from Kalle, it should have been passed securely back to Ladoux via a pre-arranged system. Mata Hari had initially sent the information to Ladoux in an unsecured , open letter, and then when she had received no reply, gave her subsequent information to Denvignes at the French Embassy. Finally, she wrote information in a letter which she then left with a casual acquaintance at the embassy for that individual to pass to Denvignes to pass to Ladoux.

If Mata Hari was to be believed, then she appeared to have been the most careless of French spies with the information she gathered. In addition, if her statement was to be accepted, then Ladoux, the head of the *Deuxiéme Bureau*, had recruited and then sent into the field an incompetent and poorly prepared agent with no pre-arranged method of securely sending information back to headquarters. Indeed, Mata Hari had consistently refused to use invisible ink. Ladoux had clearly stated to British intelligence that he had merely 'recruited' her as a foreign agent. She had been sent out on her 'mission', under surveillance, in order to trap her. No method for sending information was arranged because no method was considered necessary.

A further interrogation on 1 March saw Mata Hari continue to relate her activities in Madrid. She concentrated on Denvignes' behaviour towards her. She explained that Denvignes had flattered her, used her sexually and then rejected her, despite promising to help her. For Bouchardon to believe this, he had to admit to the unchivalrous behaviour – driven by lust – of a senior attaché in the French diplomatic service. While this in all probability may have been true, Denvignes, in his statement to Ladoux's agents, would, no doubt, have given an alternative version. Denvignes' statement would probably have been more flattering to himself and painted her in a negative light.

Bouchardon continued to interrogate Mata Hari alone; the system allowed lawyers to attend only the first and last interviews. Despite this, she continued to write to Clunet a series of letters complaining of her treatment and the conditions in Saint-Lazare. As the petition to give Mata Hari her provisional liberty had failed, Clunet wrote to Bouchardon requesting that she be transferred to the prison hospital. The letter of 7 March stated that Mata Hari was ill with a high fever and breathing difficulties. Bouchardon ordered Socquet to examine the prisoner. Socquet made his report on 10 March:

At the time of the examination, we found the accused in bed complaining of a headache in the occipital region, a respiratory complaint, and a sore throat. She was in a very extreme state of nervousness and never stopped crying. Upon examination, we found nothing in particular: the patient had no fever, no temperature, and ascultation of her chest revealed nothing abnormal; her tongue was clean and had no coating. In fact she was being treated by the physician of Saint-Lazare.

CONCLUSIONS: The woman Zelle, of a very nervous temperament, preoccupied with her situation as a defendant, is not currently suffering from anything serious. The prolongation of her detention at Saint-Lazare, under the current conditions, is not likely to present any serious inconveniences.[26]

The unsympathetic tone of this report is a clear reflection of the attitudes of the time towards prisoners, especially those held to be traitors. What is somewhat less clear is the mention of the fact that Mata Hari was being treated by the physician of Saint-Lazare, Bizard. If she was being treated by Bizard, why did Bouchardon ask Socquet to examine her? It is probable, given the mercury-based cream and lotion found amongst her toiletries, that Bizard was treating Mata Hari for syphilis. It was a recurring chronic illness that did not necessarily require admission to the prison hospital. That does not, however, explain why Socquet, rather than Bizard, was asked to examine Mata Hari at that point.

Despite her not being considered ill enough to be admitted to the hospital, Mata Hari sent a short note to Bouchardon asking if her next interrogation could be postponed for a few days as she felt too ill to get out of bed. Bouchardon allowed her this small respite, and he did not interrogate her again until 12 March. At that interrogation, Bouchardon examined the various letters and papers that had been found in her hotel room when she had been arrested. Each item was examined in turn, and she was asked questions. Who was the individual, what was her relationship to them? What was the meaning behind this phrase? How had she known where Masloff was stationed? Finally, Bouchardon asked her if she had returned to Germany at all during the war. She replied, 'No, I absolutely did not.'[27]

Clunet applied again to the Military Governor of Paris to ask for Mata Hari's release on provisional liberty.

The papers found in Mata Hari's room gave Bouchardon the names of fifty-three men of various nationalities who appeared to have had some kind of relationship with her. Detectives were sent to interview as many as possible. Most spoke of her as a charming and amusing female companion, with no apparent interest in military matters. While this may have been true, the men were faced with an embarrassing situation. To have admitted to spending time with a courtesan was one thing, to have been associated with a suspected enemy spy was quite another. This was especially true for those who were in the army. Warnings from senior officers about Mata Hari had been circulated for some time now, so ignorance of her was not an option. Many downplayed their association with Mata Hari; none spoke of her asking anything about the war.

On 16 March, Clunet wrote again to Bouchardon about Mata Hari's health:

> I receive pitiful letters from Mata Hari. She is in a pathological state of anxiety; she coughs up blood and feels her life is in danger. Excuse me for insisting, but it would be a minor inconvenience to grant a hospital room to this sick one who poses no risk of flight. It would be common humanity to arrange this.[28]

This was quickly followed by a note from Mata Hari, 'I cried from fear in the night and no one could hear me. Take pity on me. The shock has upset me so much that I no longer feel myself. I think I am going mad. I beg you not to leave me locked up in this cell.'[29]

Bouchardon took no action over these two letters. On the same day, the latest request for provisional liberty was again refused. On 21 March, Clunet wrote again about Mata Hari's health. She was, he wrote, coughing up blood, wasting away and 'physiologically depressed'. He pleaded with Bouchardon for her to be moved to the prison infirmary, or at least to be seen by another doctor.[30] A second doctor was called and stated that her health was 'satisfactory'.[31] Mata Hari remained in her cell. On 23 March, Mata Hari wrote to the Military Governor of Paris to ask to be released on provisional liberty. On the same day, Clunet wrote to Bouchardon with the same request. Both appeals were denied.

While Mata Hari continued to assert that she had never spied against France, and indeed had spied on behalf of France, Bouchardon finally took a formal statement from Ladoux. Several extracts are of interest:

> MacLeod had liaisons with several officers without regard to their rank, from all armies, of all ages and nationalities ...[32]
>
> It was very shortly evident that MacLeod was in the service of our enemies, but it was necessary to prove it, and for this is was necessary that MacLeod spent a long time in Spain where our intelligence service is particularly well organised. After the voyage to England and the Netherlands was interrupted, she acted like a good agent and went to place herself at the disposition of the German military attaché in Madrid. This put the proofs of MacLeod's guilt into the hands of the head of the army and he could place her under arrest a few days after her return to Paris ...[33]
>
> In case it should seem to you that the documents of a particular secret nature to which these proofs refer are indispensable to your interrogations, you would have to ask for permission from the Minister of War who alone could authorise their release.[34]

Ladoux's statement contains two noteworthy elements. Firstly, there is the question of Mata Hari's sexual conquests. It cannot be stressed strongly enough how much this mattered in 1917 European society. The moral codes of the day were more than just the social norms: they indicated the deeper moral fibre of an individual. A sexual woman was deviant, with no moral compass and open to all kinds of criminal activity, including the ultimate: betrayal of a country through espionage. Ladoux's belief that her sexual activity was a central element in her guilt as an enemy agent was not a mere idiosyncrasy on his part, but was shared equally by Bouchardon as well as the rest of the French and indeed British intelligence services.

There is also the lack of any concrete evidence of Mata Hari's guilt in Ladoux's statement. No specific details are given, and indeed Ladoux stated that if Bouchardon wished to receive such evidence then he had to apply to the Ministry of War for its release. As it had been Lyautey, the Minister of War, who had initially requested a warrant for Mata Hari's arrest, it followed that his department held the evidence that had triggered the request in the first place. The policy within the Third Council of War was that the investigating magistrate should not see any evidence in advance of his inquiries, unless absolutely necessary. This procedure, another result of the Dreyfus Affair, was to ensure that the magistrates followed where their interrogation led, rather than be drawn into seeking to corroborate existing evidence.

While Bouchardon continued searching for evidence of Mata Hari's espionage activities, she wrote to the Dutch Consul for assistance. When she had been arrested, Clunet had been informed that he was not allowed to contact the Dutch Consul. Clunet barely protested; he was not sure of the legal situation. In fact, Bouchardon was in a delicate diplomatic situation. Normally, a non-French national arrested on suspicion of espionage would have had the right to have their consul or embassy notified immediately. However, France was at war and the emergency powers were somewhat hazy as to the legal situation regarding nationals of a neutral country. Diplomatic courtesy dictated that the Dutch Consul should be notified, but what if members at that consul were also involved in enemy activities? Rumours about the true German loyalties of Otto Bunge, the consul, were well known. In addition, if the Dutch Consul was informed, questions might be asked as to why Mata Hari's only legal representation was an elderly lawyer with no experience in such matters. Possibly hoping to have finished the interrogation quickly, Bouchardon and his superiors had not notified the consul when she was arrested. As each week went past, the problem grew of explaining the delay in notifying the consul.

Matters came to a head on 26 March when Mata Hari herself wrote a joint letter to Count Limberg-Styrum, the secretary of the Dutch legation in Paris, and Otto Bunge. She told them of her arrest, declared her innocence, requested that they do everything in their power to obtain her release and also notify her maid Lintjens to inform Capellan what had happened. As all of her correspondence was intercepted, Bouchardon read the letter on the morning of 27 March. Unsure as to how to proceed, Bouchardon sought advice from his superiors including Lyautey and Jules Cambon, one of Mata Hari's ex-lovers.

By 1917, Cambon had been promoted to secretary-general of the Ministry of Foreign Affairs. He wrote to Bouchardon with some advice:

> After studying the question, I believe we cannot prevent the accused from addressing an appeal to a representative of her country. [If we did], when the situation of the Dutch woman is finally known, we would have exposed ourselves to claims by the legation of the Netherlands and from the Dutch government.[35]

Cambon then offered Bouchardon a course of action to address the situation. The letter could be sent to His Excellency, Alphonse Lambert Eugène ridder de Stuers, the Dutch Envoy Extraordinary and Minister Plenipotentiary in Paris. De Stuers, whose role as Queen Wilhelmina's representative in Paris was a high diplomatic one, was known personally to Cambon. The proposal was for Cambon to then discreetly inform de Stuers of Mata Hari's guilt and persuade him to act to dissuade the staff at the consulate from acting on her behalf.

This suggestion required a deft touch and relied on the co-operation of de Stuers. Although Cambon knew His Excellency, he could not know what other matters were pressing within the Dutch diplomatic community and could not therefore be sure of de Stuers' actions. It was decided to merely misdirect the letter. Bouchardon was able to bury the letter within the bureaucracy of his department, such that it did not reach Bunge until 22 April.

Mata Hari had not been interrogated by Bouchardon since 12 March, during which time she had been confined in her cell. On 6 April, she wrote to Bouchardon to ask again for provisional liberty:

I beg you, stop making me suffer in this prison. I am so weakened by this system and the cell is driving me mad. I have never carried out any espionage in France and I have nothing bad in my luggage, neither in my bottles nor in my safety deposit box. Give me my provisional liberty, then you can search but do not torture me here. I am a dancer, you cannot expect that I think and laugh calmly as before. Stop, I entreat you. I will not abuse [your kindness].[36]

This latest appeal for liberty was denied on 10 April.

While Mata Hari had been in custody, Capellan had been puzzled by her absence. He approached Loudon, the Dutch Foreign Minister, to ask if he had any news of her. Loudon sent a telegram to Bunge, and received the reply that she had been arrested and was in Saint-Lazare prison under interrogation for espionage.[37] On ascertaining Mata Hari's whereabouts, Capellan and her maid Lintjens wrote to her; their letters were intercepted and read by Bouchardon.

Despite Bunge being aware of Mata Hari's imprisonment, there is no record of any action on his part. No member of the consulate sought permission to visit her and no records exist of any correspondence from the consulate about her situation. It is not known why Bunge had not acted. If, as strongly suspected, Bunge was himself a German agent, and if Mata Hari was a convenient distraction from other German spies, then that might explain his lack of action.

On 12 April, the interrogation began again. Bouchardon concentrated on Mata Hari's recruitment as a French spy. He asked her again if she had not already been a German agent when she was recruited by Ladoux:

Our question should not surprise you. Have you not told us yourself that you were an international woman and haven't you acknowledged that there was a time before the war when you were in Berlin and had intimate relations with Lieutenant Alfred Kiepert of the 11th Hussars of Crefeld, with Captain Lieutenant Kuntze, chief of the seaplane station and with the chief of police Griebel?[38]

Mata Hari replied:

> The fact that I had relations with these people does not imply at all that I
> committed espionage. I never did anything for Germany nor for any country
> except France. In my profession as a dancer, I could easily have relations with
> the important men of Berlin, without any mental reservations that you would
> later suspect something. Besides, it is I who gave you their names.[39]

This emphasis on Mata Hari's sexuality as an 'international woman' is
another example of how central an issue this was for the interrogation
and the suspicion in which she was held. What is curious is her
apparent lack of understanding that this was so. She was an intelligent
woman. She knew that as a member of *La Grande Horizontale* she was
not a 'respectable woman' like all the wives of her lovers. She knew
how she had been treated in her divorce case and over the custody of
her daughter. Yet, for some reason, she could not understand how her
status now left her condemned as a depraved woman and vulnerable to
the accusation of espionage. Bouchardon was not holding a personal
prejudice against her, but simply reflecting the social understanding
of the day. Had Bouchardon not questioned her about her sexual
activities, had he not realised that as a sexual woman she was depraved
and thus the very person that would make an excellent enemy agent,
it is unlikely he would have attained the position he had within the
Third Council of War.

On the evening of 12 April, Mata Hari wrote again to Bouchardon:

> I am very astonished and saddened that you have refused my provisional liberty.
> I am not abused but the conditions under which I must live here are … so
> dirty. I do not know how I can bear them. Realise that I am quite a different
> sort of woman than those around me and yet I am treated like them. I beg of
> you, review this decision and permit me to live outside of prison. It is not very
> difficult and I will make no trouble. Also I beg you in the name of humanity,
> send the letter I have written to Captain de Masloff. Do not leave him in
> uncertainty. Do not make him suffer needlessly.[40]

Although Boudhardon had refused to forward Mata Hari's correspondence to Masloff, she may not have been aware that he was also withholding any letters from Masloff to her. This continued silence from Masloff was, in addition to her imprisonment, causing Mata Hari to become increasingly agitated. Her complaint that she was 'a different sort of woman than those around me and yet I am treated like them' is possibly symptomatic of that agitation. Although there was a considerable difference between courtesans like Mata Hari and the girls who worked as streetwalkers in Paris, it was only a difference of social degree; under the law, they were all prostitutes. Mata Hari, whose adult life had frequently been a fantasy, was trying to create the illusion that she was different from and better than the other female prisoners in Saint-Lazare. This was despite the fact that she had at times worked in places such as the *maisons de rendezvous*. Had she finally recognised the danger she was in with regard to Bouchardon's notion of her depravity, and was this an attempt to distance herself from that notion? Whatever the reason, the request fell on deaf ears.

The following day, 13 April, she wrote to Bouchardon again:

As for the three officers about whom you spoke to me yesterday Kiepert, Kuntze and Griebel. Do you understand that I knew them in February or March of 1914, well before the war? When I was in Berlin to prepare for my engagement at the Metropol Theatre where I had signed for six months? Never did I hear from them again. What wrong is there in that? Have I told you that, after war was declared [my engagement at the theatre was cancelled], I filed a lawsuit against a couturier in Berlin? And that I had lost the suit in two instances by default? The proofs of this suit can be found in the Ministry of Foreign Affairs at The Hague and in the office of my lawyer, Maître Hijmens [in The Hague] ... Also in Berlin they seized my magnificent furs which were worth from sixty to eighty thousand francs? Perhaps I will never be able to buy their likes again. You see, my captain, that my relations with Germany were not very happy and the only way I could save ... my jewels and my money was by the intervention of my government and a lawyer. Because the appeals were not yet lost, I did not know in which bank my possessions were held. This judgement could not be enforced outside of Germany but if I travelled there, I risked my trunks being seized and it was for this reason that I did not follow the advice or the wish of Captain Ladoux to go to the Netherlands in November by Switzerland and Germany.[41]

This letter appears to be an attempt by Mata Hari to clarify her situation with the three officers and what had happened to her in Berlin with the confiscation of her furs and jewels. The letter, however, contains a crucial error; Mata Hari certainly saw Griebel again and was in Berlin with him when the July crisis arose. This could be considered part of her usual lack of accuracy with the truth, were it not for the second letter she wrote on the same day covering the same points. She was starting to break psychologically.

Mata Hari had been in Saint-Lazare for sixty days. She started to write Bouchardon multiple letters. She wrote explaining her innocence, what she had done and what her motives were. Then she wrote complaining of her treatment, pleading for her freedom or for clean lingerie. She wrote directly to Bouchardon and at the same time she wrote to Bouchardon through Clunet. She also wrote to Clunet constantly, asking for help.

On 23 April, Clunet wrote to Bouchardon:

I must insist most energetically of you that the questioning of my client must come to an end. It has been two months since she was imprisoned in Saint-Lazare under suspicion of espionage. No proof has been furnished against her that supports this indictment. It is not possible any longer to maintain such a state of things against this unhappy woman, or at least it is necessary to give her provisional liberty. This accusation came from the Minster of War, so it is this department which is obliged to produce some proof immediately. It would be unjust and cruel to prolong this situation.[42]

This letter highlights how little Clunet understood about cases involving espionage. In ordinary criminal cases, the police would collect evidence of a crime and then arrest an individual. The investigating magistrate would investigate the police department's case and could instruct the police to pursue further lines of inquiry. In cases of espionage, the process was different. The Ministry of War could, acting on suspicions alone, but more usually with some evidence, make a charge of alleged espionage. Once the allegation was made, it was Bouchardon's role, as investigating magistrate, to pursue the allegation and find evidence of Mata Hari's guilt. The investigation could take as long as necessary and could collect evidence from any source, including the Ministry. However, the Ministry of War was under no obligation to produce proof of her guilt – that was Bouchardon's role. The weight of evidence required for an allegation and arrest to be made in espionage cases was also different from that in criminal cases. This was allowed as espionage cases, by their very nature, rarely had solid physical evidence, relying more heavily on witness testimony and inference and the character of the accused. Clunet seems to have been unaware of these facts, which was not surprising as he was a civil lawyer. What is surprising is that at no point did he ever suggest to Mata Hari that she might benefit from a different lawyer or appear to seek advice on the matter himself. Despite this lack of knowledge or expert advice, Clunet started to prepare another attack in Mata Hari's defence.

At the end of April, Bouchardon informed Mata Hari that he intended to interview Masloff. He further told her that Masloff had been injured and hospitalised. That evening, she wrote to Bouchardon about Masloff:

I thank you very much for the information about Captain de Masloff but I do not understand. Captain de Masloff has nothing to do with the Third Council of War. Does he even know that I have been arrested? Because you have forbidden me to write to him, he thinks I have left. Wouldn't you let me write to him now? Captain de Masloff was my lover. He knows nothing of my life or projects. He knows nothing of my visits to Captain Ladoux. I have never spoken to him of that. We amused ourselves together and that was all. I beg you likewise never to ask him to appear before the Council of War. He is a very brave officer, who has before him too beautiful a career to let it be the least bit damaged by this. But I desire absolutely and I beg you again to permit me to let him know what has happened to me by a word from me. I do not want him to think of me things that are not true. He could think I have left Paris without saying anything to him. He does not deserve to suffer because of me in any way.[43]

This strange letter is probably the clearest evidence that Mata Hari was in love with Masloff, or at least had reasonably strong feelings about him. The letter is her attempt to protect Masloff. It is stretching credulity somewhat to describe Masloff as her lover but then declare that he knew nothing of her life; but if he knew nothing, then he would not be involved. Whatever her guilt, or otherwise, she certainly seems to have genuinely tried to save Masloff from any involvement in her case.

13

THE BREAKTHROUGH

I t is not known what Bouchardon thought of Mata Hari's latest letter, as it was written just as there was a breakthrough in the case. On 21 April, Ladoux had sent a report to governor Dubail informing him of the existence of fourteen telegrams between Kalle and Berlin regarding Mata Hari.[1] At the same time, Ladoux sent transcripts of nine of the telegrams to Bouchardon. The first telegram, sent on 13 December 1916, appeared to identify Mata Hari as a German agent, 'Agent H21 from the intelligence office in Cologne, sent in March for the second time to France, has arrived here. She has pretended to accept offers of service for the French Intelligence and to carry out two trips to Belgium for the head of the service.'[2]

The telegram, which was very long and detailed, reported on agent H21's arrest in Falmouth, the order for her to return to Spain and payments to her by Kalle. It identified H21 as a female agent, but was it Mata Hari? She had originally been detained by the British because they thought she was Clara Benedix. So was H21 possibly Benedix?

A second telegram from Kalle to Madrid indicated that H21 was giving information to the Germans:

H21 informs us: Princess George of Greece, Marie Bonaparte, is using her 'intimate relations' with Briand [Aristide Briand, the French prime minister] to get French support for her husband's access to the Greek throne. She says Briand's enemies … would welcome further defeats in the war to overthrow him. Britain has political and military control of France. French are afraid to speak up. General offensive planned for next spring.[3]

If H21 was indeed Mata Hari's code, then the timing of these telegrams – December 1916 – and the familiarity of tone with which Berlin and Madrid used the code H21 would strongly suggest that Mata Hari had received this number before she arrived in Madrid, possibly before or just after she had met Ladoux for the first time. While this seems a fairly obvious and mundane point, it is significant. When Mata Hari was 'recruited' by Ladoux, she was not given a code number by him. The common practice across most European intelligence services – although the Russian intelligence service had a different system – was not to give code numbers to new agents until they had received some form of training or had carried out some basic work. If Mata Hari was H21, then she had either received training from or had undertaken some work for the Germans. The fact of her having a German code number but no French code number would be noted as highly significant during her trial.

In addition, if Mata Hari was H21, then she does appear to have given information to the Germans, but how significant was it? Marie Bonaparte's affair with Briand was well-known gossip in Paris, as was Prince George's desire for his father's throne. The idea that the British controlled the French was a widely held belief. A general offensive in the spring was true; every army in the war planned a general offensive each spring. So was this information general gossip that Mata Hari had passed on as a low-ranking German agent, or was it general gossip that Mata Hari had passed on as a French double agent?

On Christmas Day, Berlin sent Kalle a telegram:

Give H21 3,000 francs and tell her that:
1) The results received are not satisfactory;

2) The ink which H21 received cannot be developed by the French if the correspondence paper is treated in conformity with instructions before and after the use of invisible ink;

3) If, in spite of that, H21 does not want to work with invisible ink, the agent should come to Switzerland and, from there, communicate her address to A.278

This telegram raises more questions than it answers. The statement that the results received were 'not satisfactory' corroborates the fact that the information in the previous telegram was merely widely held gossip. The fact that the results were unsatisfactory does not necessarily mean that they were not the actions of an active agent. Mata Hari consistently maintained that she had not given any information to the Germans. On the other hand, this was exactly the sort of gossip that she was widely known to have talked about to her lovers before the war. It was also the sort of low-level gossip that Nicolai of German intelligence had sent an army of German agents out into the field to gather as early as July 1914. Known as *spannungsreisende*, or 'tension travellers', these were individuals who would travel across Europe as holidaymakers or commercial travellers, listening to gossip and conversations about activities in France and Russia.[4] While some concentrated on military matters, others would report innocuous seeming information about public opinion, which could, in its way, inform political decisions.

The telegram raised other points. H21 is obviously working for the Germans, but was H21 Mata Hari? In German, the gender of pronouns are obvious, as the words are different. However, Ladoux did not send the original telegram to Bouchardon, only the French transcript in which the pronouns are the same. It is also unclear if the original, German telegram used the letter 'A', or if this was inserted in the French transcription in place of another name. It is also unclear if 'A' meant the German control centre at Antwerp or an individual. What is more damning for Mata Hari is the mention of H21's dislike of using invisible ink, something which Mata Hari had previously stated to Ladoux.

On 26 December, Kalle sent another telegram to Berlin:

H21 has received 3,500 pesetas. She will request, by a telegram from the Dutch consul in Paris, that a further sum of money be made available to her domestic servants [sic] in Roermond and she requests you to advise Consul Kroemer in Amsterdam about this.[5]

This telegram certainly seemed to confirm that H21 was Mata Hari, linking her directly to Kroemer. It was followed by another on 28 December:

H21 will arrive tomorrow in Paris. She will ask to be sent at once, by telegram, through Consul Kroemer in Amsterdam and her servant Anna Lintjens in Ruremond [sic], 5,000 francs to the Compton National d'Escompte de Paris, to be handed over, in that city, to the Dutch consul Bunge.[6]

Here, Mata Hari's identity is definitively confirmed from the mention of her maid Lintjens. Equally damning is the receipt of another payment from the Germans. She did receive 5,000 francs from Bunge, and although the money may have come from another source such as Capellan, that was never verified.

The telegrams were strong evidence against Mata Hari. However, their existence, their content and the manner in which they were dealt with and reported raises several questions.

Why was Bouchardon not informed of the existence of these telegrams until the middle of April? Why did Ladoux mention fourteen telegrams to Dubail and speak of twelve intercepted messages, and yet only produce transcripts of nine? Why were the originals never sent to Bouchardon, only transcripts? Why were the original telegrams never produced, or asked for, in the court martial? Why was the situation regarding the broken German code never mentioned in relation to the telegrams? Why are none of the originals of these telegrams in the Paris archives? Why are only some of the transcripts in the Paris archives?

There are in effect three sets of telegrams: the twelve original telegrams intercepted by the staff at the Eiffel Tower, the fourteen transcriptions that Ladoux gave to Dubail and the nine transcriptions that Ladoux gave to Bouchardon. Allowing for their de-encryptions by Locard's team, translation from German to French and genuine human error – the team at the Eiffel Tower was working back-to-back twelve-hour shifts – there are still several discrepancies between the contents of the three sets. The most obvious of these is in the number of telegrams in each set. As well as a mismatch in numbers, certain errors appear between the Tower originals and the Dubail and Bouchardon sets. Individual names are changed: Consul Kroemer becomes Krämer. Place names are misspelled: Roermond becomes Ruremond. Dates are confused. There are other discrepancies. The eighth 'Dubail' telegram, which corresponds to the seventh 'Tower' telegram, stated that Mata Hari is 'unwilling to go to France'. This statement is not in the original copy of the Tower telegram, which was then transcribed. The eleventh 'Dubail' telegram corresponds to the tenth 'Tower' telegram; both are dated 31 December and stated that 'Agent H21 has already left'. Was Kalle so incompetent that he did not know where she was? Or had he forgotten that she had not yet left Madrid, but for the purposes of framing her in the broken code the actual date was irrelevant? Of course Mata Hari may have told Kalle she intended to leave on 30 December and then may have changed her mind without telling him. She actually left on 2 January. However, the statement 'Agent H21 has already left' was, apparently, not in the original telegram. The first 'Bouchardon', 'Tower' and 'Dubail' telegrams all correspond. All seem to identify H21 as Mata Hari, but there the similarity ends. In the 'Dubail' telegram, Kalle identifies Clara Benedix as the individual Mata Hari was mistaken for in Falmouth. That was not in the original 'Tower' telegram, nor in the 'Bouchardon' version. The original 'Tower' telegram stated that she would carry out 'two trips to Belgium'; in the 'Dubail' and 'Bouchardon' telegrams that was changed to 'trial trips'.[7] This might seem trivial, but an indeterminate number of trial trips could, therefore, account for any discrepancies in dates within the telegrams. It also increased the potential amount of espionage work Mata Hari had allegedly undertaken. None of the telegrams are available as a complete set in the French archives. The Eiffel telegrams only exist as the transcriptions, not the originals.

Because Ladoux only produced the telegrams after several weeks of Bouchardon's interrogation, because he never produced the originals – only his transcriptions – and because no originals and only partial transcriptions survive, it is difficult to fully assess the authenticity of the telegrams and their contents. The fact that they were sent via the broken German code could indicate that the Germans used this to 'create' Mata Hari the spy to distract attention from the activities of other agents. Equally, if she was a German agent but a low-ranking one, her superiors may have sacrificed her to distract attention from other agents. Either way, whatever the Germans had sent, Ladoux knew that it had been sent by the code that the Germans knew was broken. If the telegrams had been produced in their original form as soon as Bouchardon had started his investigation, and with the knowledge about the broken code, they could still have formed part of Bouchardon's work. They may not have 'proved' Mata Hari was a spy, but under French law at the time her admission of taking money from the Germans, her association with Kalle and the possession of a code number would probably have been enough to convict her anyway. The production of the three different sets of telegrams and the manner in which they were produced by Ladoux has never been fully explained. Was Ladoux trying to ensure her conviction because he was convinced of her guilt, or was he acting to distract attention from others? Events after Mata Hari's execution would call his actions into question, including his own activities.

Locard's report about the telegrams stated that Kalle had 'specifically used an old cipher which he knew was cracked'.[8] If this was true, then it would indicate that the Germans were deliberately using Mata Hari for their own purposes; presumably to distract from their more important agents. Once Ladoux read Locard's report, he would realise that the Germans had been deliberately sending misinformation about her. However, there are several points to consider here. Did Kalle actually know the code was broken? This might seem obvious, but encryption work was extremely specialised and many working in the intelligence services outside the encryption teams were not sure how their own codes worked. The fact that the Germans had two codes – one of which was broken and was known about but was still used, and one that was thought not broken but was – confused many, especially as those involved were embarrassed by the situation and sought to cover their mistakes. In addition, Kalle was a career soldier posted in Madrid away from the centre of the German Army in Berlin and the vital command in Belgium. There were plenty of German officers happy to keep other rival officers 'out of the loop' over what was going on. Kalle could have used the broken code in complete ignorance that it had been broken in the previous August. Although an unlikely scenario, this was a possibility; it is notable that Locard, despite being head of his department, had been unaware the broken code was being used until a junior colleague informed him.

A second, more likely possibility was that although the Germans had sent information about Mata Hari in the known broken code, that did not mean that she was not a German agent. All agents of all intelligence services were expendable, and Ladoux knew this: witness his 'you do not know me and I do not know you' statement. All active agents knew that they could be abandoned by their bosses if necessary. If the Germans were 'using' Mata Hari to deflect attention from other activities, she was still therefore a tool being used by the enemy. She had signed up as a German agent; how they chose to employ her was their business. Locard's report did not clear Mata Hari, but merely increased the confusion around her status as a German agent.

On 1 May, Bouchardon interrogated Mata Hari again, concentrating on the information contained in the telegrams. Mata Hari replied reasonably robustly, if not entirely honestly:

> Von Kalle can say what he likes [in the telegrams]. It could well be that he knew about the exchange between my domestic in the Netherlands and me. When I telegraph, I give the paper to the porter at the hotel without going myself to the post office. In any case, I am not agent H21, von Kalle did not give me one sou and the 5,000 francs I received in November, like that which I received in January 1917, came to me from my lover the Baron van der Capellan.[9]

Moreover, as Mata Hari pointed out, she was not the only one who had been arrested and detained on the SS *Hollandia*. After an inquiry by Bouchardon, Scotland Yard later confirmed that a couple, the Allards, from the *Hollandia* had been detained along with Mata Hari, and that the woman, who was in reality named Ilse Blüme, had been interned as a German agent.[10]

The discovery of another German agent on the *Hollandia* could have cast doubt on Mata Hari's identity, but only if Blüme had also been recruited by Ladoux, which she had not. Furthermore, Mata Hari's assertion that Kalle had not given her any money was a blatant and stupid lie. Kalle had given her money; 3,500 francs. She later admitted this, but claimed the money was a gift.[11] Of course, the money could well have been a gift, but as she had already denied having received the payment, Bouchardon was unlikely to have given her the benefit of the doubt.

The telegrams, whatever their provenance, were fatal to Mata Hari's defence. Previously, she had been able, up to a point, to dissemble her way past the hearsay of others; there had been no real physical evidence linking her to the German intelligence service. The telegrams, however, gave Bouchardon an entirely new way of catching her out in her testimony. A misremembered date could previously be shrugged off as the result of a poor memory. With the production of the telegrams, that was no longer an option. As a career civil servant fighting for his country in the midst of a war, Bouchardon was much more likely to believe the written content of an official telegram of another civil servant, even an enemy civil servant, rather than the word of a suspected spy.

In addition to the telegrams, Bouchardon had been engaged in correspondence with Ladoux and Goubet, Ladoux's superior, seeking clarification of several of Mata Hari's answers to his interrogation. Ladoux confirmed he had only 'pretended' to employ her. He also explained that German agents in Spain were noted to be concerned about their submarine movements near Morocco being detected by the French. Goubet confirmed Mata Hari's connections with Kroemer and Wurfbein, the Amsterdam representative of the Deutsch Bank.

While none of this information damned Mata Hari, it gave further support to the case against her. Mata Hari was trapped: whatever she said was assumed to be a lie; whatever Ladoux said supported the assumption of her guilt.

Goubet, working from the telegram transcriptions he had received from Ladoux, wrote a general statement which he forwarded to Bouchardon. He considered Mata Hari to be 'one of the most dangerous that counterespionage ever encountered'.[12] He concluded that:

> If Zelle, through an intermediary at whose identity it is perhaps not difficult to guess, had procured nothing for Krämer, if she had swindled him out of the twenty thousand francs in May without giving him any further sign of existence, this consul would not have sent her another five thousand francs in November through Anne Litjens [sic] and Bunge. What is more, Zelle would not have presented herself in December to von Kalée [sic], under her number as agent H21, thus permitting the military attaché to unmask her and learn of her treason.[13]

This is a fair point by Goubet. Mata Hari had stated that she had accepted her first payment of 20,000 francs from Kroemer as compensation for her furs; she had initially denied her second payment of 3,500 pesetas from Kalle, and then tried to pass that off as a 'gift', and she had then received the third payment of 5,000 from the Dutch Consul, which she claimed had come from Capellan. If the third payment had come from Kroemer, as the telegrams stated, then it was difficult to see why the Germans would continue to pay her if she was not giving them some information, or at least acting as a distraction from other agents. If, however, the payment had come from Capellan, it would corroborate her version of events. Although no proof was ever produced, Otto Bunge was strongly rumoured to have German sympathies and was suspected by many to possibly be a German agent. His handling of the payments for Mata Hari was, therefore, suspect.

While Mata Hari's interrogation by Bouchardon continued, the police attempted to track down and interview all those whose addresses and visiting cards had been found amongst her belongings when she was arrested. Amongst those interviewed by the police were: Berthe Boucher, a manicurist; Anna Baron, a hotel chambermaid; Lieutenant Henri Mège; Eugénie Soreuil, a fortune teller; Henri Liévin, a money lender; Sublieutenant Emile-Louis Thiry; Ernest Molier, retired stables and circus owner; Annette Borillot, a nurse; Fernand Bloch, a businessman; Julie-Clothilde Breton, a dressmaker; reserve lieutenant Henri Raphérer; Sergeant-Major Georges Louis; and Lieutenent-General Maurice-François Baumgarten. Most gave little useful information, other than to confirm her highly sexual and thus depraved nature. Proof again of her aptitude for espionage.

On 4 May, Clunet launched his defence of Mata Hari, which he had been preparing since 23 April. Despite, or perhaps because of, his lack of experience in espionage cases, he had gone back to the law in preparing a case to aid her defence. The law of 1899 concerning the procedures and processes of military tribunals stated that a defendant had the right to have legal representation present on every occasion when they were questioned. However, a wartime decree had been passed in 1916 which had amended this right, stating that legal representation had only to be present at the first and last occasion that a defendant was questioned. However, reasoned Clunet, the 1916 law did not explicitly bar legal representation from attending every questioning. Clunet further argued that as military tribunals dealt with the most serious of cases and imposed more severe penalties, then defendants needed to have more legal protection rather than less. Clunet used this legal point to argue that he should be present at all of Bouchardon's interrogation of Mata Hari, and also to gain access to the papers of her case.[14]

Clunet wrote a long letter outlining his legal argument and sent copies to Bouchardon, Commandant Schedlin, chief of the Bureau of Military Justice of the Military Governor of Paris, and Général Auguste Dubail, General of the Division, Military Governor of Paris.[15] Bouchardon forwarded a copy of the letter to the chief military prosecutor, Major Julien, with a brief confidential note outlining his position. Bouchardon believed that national security was his prime motive, and as such his understanding of the 1916 law was that legal representation was allowed only at the first and last interrogation. In addition, in any espionage case, the details that emerged had to be kept secret, so the fewer individuals present during questioning the better.[16]

A delicate legal argument between Bouchardon, Schedlin, Dubail and Julien ensued. The 1916 law had been passed as part of a raft of emergency measures enacted to deal with the exigencies of the war. Bouchardon argued that the intent of the 1916 law was the protection of the state from enemy agents, rather than the safeguarding of the rights of the accused. The presence of legal representation was guaranteed at the first and last interrogation, but there was no right for it to be present at all interrogations. But had the 1916 law amended and thus superseded the 1899 act? The law had been drafted quickly. Had it failed to amend the relevant sections? What had been the intention? State security was indeed the intent of the law, but at what costs to the rights of the accused? Finally, Julien decided he would follow the spirit rather than the letter of the law. Clunet was not to be allowed to be present at any interrogations until the last, and was not to be given access to the papers on the case.[17]

A few days after Clunet was informed that his legal challenge had failed, Mata Hari wrote to Bouchardon:

I understand perfectly the game that Captain Ladoux has played in his profession, but he had strayed too far with his promises and his words. I believed he was sincere. An officer does not lie and I was so persuaded that my life had nothing suspect, because I did not concern myself with espionage, that I could not even imagine that you would consider someone who had done nothing to be as guilty as one who had done something. It never entered my head. I swear to you again that I never carried out any espionage and I never wrote a letter [to the enemy?]. Me, I am not guilty. I am Dutch. Obviously I know some Germans. I am a dancer and after the war, I will be obliged, perhaps, to take some engagement in the theatre in Berlin and Vienna, as in Paris. I am not married. I am a woman who travels and amuses herself a great deal. I can be excused for sometimes forgetting about money. Sometimes I win, sometimes I lose. And the money concerned is nothing but a win, as I will again. The loss of my furs grieves me. I lost them because I was engaged in the theatre in Germany. The war thus caused all these bad things and I think that [the Germans] should reimburse me, at least in part. I recall also the conversation that I had with my visitors, after my return to Paris. I will tell you about it. I beg you, my captain, to be less hard with me. I am not guilty of espionage. And now that my love for Masloff has become the sentiment that rules my life, because he is the man for whom I would do anything, and for whom I would lose everything. Captain Ladoux can calm himself. There are appearances, it is true, but not any serious actions. I swear to you. If Captain Ladoux gives me freedom I will still keep my word. He will want and need it. I always told him true information about the Germans. Never did he wish to believe me. There are little agents who can provide little information. And since he wanted for great information, it is only the great women who can get them. There is no need for revenge because I have done nothing against his country and never even intended to.[18]

This letter shows the first real signs that Mata Hari was losing her control. She blames Ladoux, tells him to remain calm and then appeals to him for her freedom. She writes of her love for Masloff, but fails to explain its relevance. Mata Hari states that she will tell of the conversation with her visitors, and then does not do so. It is difficult to determine what the point of the letter was, other than to continue to plead her innocence in a somewhat rambling manner. She then wrote to Clunet, asking him to ask Bouchardon to allow her to confront Ladoux, Denvignes and Hallaure. This request, which Clunet sent to Bouchardon, was completely inappropriate. Accused prisoners had no right to demand to confront their accusers. Even if Mata Hari was sufficiently stressed not to realise that the request was completely fanciful, it is somewhat strange that Clunet did not attempt to reason with her and explain the situation. Whatever Clunet's motives were in passing this request to Bouchardon, the examining magistrate ignored the little lawyer. On 10 May, Mata Hari wrote to Bouchardon again:

This is what I will ask of Captain Ladoux, when I see him. He arranged for me to come to his office in the Ministry of War. He asked me if I wanted to enter his espionage service. He gave me the idea to be of service to France and Germany at the same time [become a double agent] in order to do great things. He promised me, if I succeeded on the mission completely, one million [francs] as payment. He knew that I frequented the German headquarters. He was up to date on my visit to Spain. He was not opposed to my passage across France, when I was asking for my passport at the French consulate in Madrid. He refused three times to see me when I went to the Ministry of War in Paris, in order to explain to him all that I had written. He seeks to avoid a confrontation now? Then, my captain, it smells very much as if he has acted against me and I beg you to give me my liberty, as he has done nothing other than assure me passage across two enemy countries, that which was impossible.[19]

Just as he had done with the initial request from Clunet, Bouchardon ignored her letter.

Mata Hari tried to persuade Bouchardon of her innocence in yet another letter written on 15 May, in which she again begs for her freedom:

For three months I am imprisoned in this cell. Morally and physically, you have done me such harm that I beg you to end it. I cannot support any longer the filth, the lack of care for my body, and the disgusting food to which I am not used. You cannot degrade a woman, day after day, as you have ordered. I am here because of a misunderstanding. I beseech you: stop making me suffer. I cannot take any more, truly, truly. Whether the confrontation that I asked for is the cause of the waiting. Whether this wounds the vanity or another sentiment of Captain Ladoux. Beg him to give me my liberty. I will speak to no-one about what had happened to me here in Paris, but let me leave this terrible prison Saint-Lazare. I cannot stand any longer this wretched life to which you have condemned me. Stop, I beg you.[20]

Later that same day, Mata Hari wrote another letter to Bouchardon:

I beg you, my Captain. I have always been an honest woman and well received everywhere. Do not make me suffer in Saint-Lazare, it is frightful. I am losing my sanity here. I told you what I believed on the first day. I say it again. A candid interview with Captain Ladoux will be enough. What is the point of driving me insane in this cell where I lose my head and my word? I cannot bear it. I have done nothing that merits this and I beg you again, speak with Captain Ladoux, give me my liberty. I will go and never speak of what has happened here. Tell him. I beg you ... Captain Ladoux was wrong to mistrust me. He wanted me to bring off something great, he wanted me to rise high. If he wanted me to tell him all my plans at the beginning, he would have had to pay me in advance, as I asked. Time would not have been wasted, and I swear to you that I alone would have given him such services that no other person ever will. I was so in love with my lover, and this made me work with the illusion of being able to win what would be my only happiness, and that I believe still [21]

Neither letter elicited any response from Bouchardon. The examining magistrate was continuing to have inquiries made wherever he could about Mata Hari, her lovers and her finances. At the same time, by leaving Mata Hari in her cell unaware of what was going on, Bouchardon hoped that she would break down and confess her guilt. Mata Hari, who was becoming increasingly stressed, wrote to Clunet:

The brusque change, the horrible food and the lack of cleanliness, these are the cause of the blemishes on my body. I grow more and more unhappy. I cannot stand this life, I would rather hang myself from the bars of my window than to live like this. I beg you, please speak to the investigating magistrate and tell him that he cannot degrade a woman used to cleanliness and care, from one day until the next, until she lives in dirty misery. When will it end? Does he wish to kill me? Must he kill me? Or give me liberty? One day it will be too late, there will be nothing left to do. It is horrible, horrible. If you could see how I am forced to live here! It is shameful, shameful. Have pity on me, I beseech you. [22]

A few days later, Mata Hari wrote yet another letter to Bouchardon, saying, 'That which I feared for several days arrived last night. I have a fever in my head. You have made me suffer too much in this cell. I am completely mad. Do you wish to end it all? I am a woman, I cannot bear more than my strength.'[23]

At last Bouchardon responded. He requested Dr Socquet examine Mata Hari. Socquet reported back she had:

> An extremely nervous temperament … One does not observe in the Zelle woman any appreciable stigmata on the different parts of the body permitting to a current diagnosis of progressive syphilis. She says she never had any vulvar lesions, eruptions on her body, not placques on her lips. Since her incarceration in Saint-Lazare, she has been following a treatment for syphilis.[24]

Despite Mata Hari being extremely nervous and calling herself 'mad', Socquet did not recommend she be moved to the infirmary or that Bouchardon's interrogation of her be mitigated in any way. On 21 May, Bouchardon interrogated her again. She told Bouchardon, 'I have decided today to tell you the truth. If I have not told everything before, it was because of certain doubts which I will explain.'[25]

This was exactly the breakthrough that Bouchardon had been waiting for. He asked Mata Hari for more details, which she willingly supplied. She told him about the visit from Kroemer and his recruitment of her as a spy for Germany. She then detailed the three small numbered flasks she had received. Two contained a white fluid, while the contents of the third were a 'bluish-green, absinthe colour'. Kroemer had shown her how to use the fluids. He had then told her to write to him at the Hotel de L'Europe in Amsterdam. She had, she claimed, thrown the flasks overboard as she sailed out of Amsterdam. Mata Hari then said she was paid 20,000 francs in advance and that she took this with a clear conscience, but with no intention of doing anything for Germany. The Germans had confiscated her furs, so they owed her; thus reasoned Mata Hari.[26] As she had no intention of working for the Germans, she had not told Ladoux of her meeting with Kroemer; she did not think it relevant.

There was a major problem with Mata Hari's tale. While logical to her, it confirmed to the French that she had been recruited and paid by the Germans, and was therefore a German agent. It also explained why the Germans had sent the information about her in the broken code to the French. If she had taken their money and not done the work, then she was expendable.

Mata Hari had assumed that when Ladoux had recruited her, she would again be paid in advance, but this had not been forthcoming. When she was in Falmouth, he had failed to help her. When she arrived in Spain, he failed to contact her in any way. Mata Hari did not know what to do and she had little money, so she decided to approach Kalle for help. She told Kalle about her recruitment by Ladoux, offered him some information she had gleaned from the newspapers and asked for payment of 10,000 francs. Kalle sent a telegram to Berlin for permission to release a payment to agent H21, but Berlin refused. The payment of 3,500 pesetas came, as far as Mata Hari knew, from Kalle himself. She had sent a telegram to her maid Lintjens to ask Capellan for money. Unfortunately, she had also said that if Capellan could not pay, then Lintjens was to ask Kroemer, Mata Hari's initial German contact, for some money. Mata Hari admitted that she had received money in Paris from the Dutch Consulate, but did not know from whom that money had come.[27] These were the payments that Colonel Goubet, Ladoux's superior, had thought damning proof of her activities as a German agent.

Bouchardon instantly sought more details from Mata Hari. He questioned her on one key point, 'Whom have you served? Whom have you betrayed? France or Germany?'[28] Mata Hari replied that she had wanted to aid France and damage Germany, and had succeeded in both aims.

Bouchardon then informed Mata Hari that he had previously interviewed Hallaure, and that her former lover contradicted her version of events on several points. Bouchardon related how Hallaure had said that he had broken off his relationship with Mara Hari after having received a warning about her from a friend.[29] Furthermore, Hallaure said that he was confused by Mata Hari's need for a permit to go to Vittel, as she did not seem to be ill in any way.[30] Hallaure continued by stating that he had not suggested she go to Vittel and had not sent her to the office at Boulevard Saint-Germain. Mata Hari countered this by saying that she had not said that Hallaure had suggested she go to Vittel, but that he had sent her to 282, Boulevard Saint-Germain. Bouchardon finished the day's questioning by listing all of the officers Mata Hari had seen in Paris, and asked her what information she had elicited from them to pass to her German handlers. She replied that she had not sought or passed any military information to the Germans. She added that her relationships with these men were because she had a great love of officers and liked to have sex with them.[31]

This interrogation was the main turning point in the case against Mata Hari. She had admitted to having been recruited by the Germans, receiving at least two, if not three, payments from them, and having approached Kalle for help. In addition, her ex-lover Hallaure cast doubt on any illness, the very reason for her trip to Vittel, the implication being that she had wanted to go to the spa town to gather information for the Germans. Finally, she admitted her love of officers and sex. She thought this showed how she was innocent of gathering information from the Germans; all it did was provide further proof to Bouchardon of her depravity. It had all come together for 'the grand inquisitor'. Mata Hari was a depraved woman, and thus the type to be a spy and to tell lies easily. She admitted to having been recruited and paid by the Germans. Her ex-lover cast doubt on her reasons for travel, and the telegrams from Berlin further identified her as an agent.

There was no evidence of what information Mata Hari had passed to the Germans, but within cases of espionage that was seldom available. Identification as an agent and a confession of recruitment and payment from the accused were, within the French military tribunal system, adequate grounds to take a prisoner to trial. What Mata Hari did not know when she spoke to Bouchardon on 21 May was that in the previous fortnight, when she had been left alone in her cell, the examining magistrate had interviewed many of her previous lovers, in addition to Hallaure.

Denvignes had been interviewed on 4 May. He told Bouchardon that Mata Hari had said to Denvignes that she was a French spy and had told him some confusing information. Denvignes described how he advised her to visit Kalle again for clarification of the information. Denvignes then described how Ladoux had dismissed the information as being 'already known'.[32] He finished his statement thus:

> My absolute conviction is that MacLeod was in the service of German intelligence. Because of the surveillance of which she was the subject in Madrid, she could not hide her visits to Kalle from Captain Ladoux ... She had to pretend that she was going to the German military attaché for us. Otherwise, she needed to give us the illusion of great zeal in order to avoid arrest when she returned to France.[33]

On 22 May, Bouchardon interrogated Mata Hari again. He started by concentrating on the information he had received the day before:

> We have recorded your conversation yesterday, but you can hardly expect us to believe that Kroemer gave you 20,000 francs point-blank, without demanding any proofs from you. The Germans give nothing for nothing, and the sums that Germany gives to its agents for travelling expenses are very far from that much.[34]

Mata Hari replied quite simply, 'You cannot simply send a woman like me, who has a house and lovers in the Netherlands, without giving her anything.'[35]

This answer did not help Mata Hari. If she had a house and lovers, why did she need money? If her entire goal was the acquisition of money, then this merely rendered her alleged service to France up for sale.

Before Mata Hari could elucidate further, Bouchardon surprised her by bringing Ladoux into the interrogation. Without the aid of a lawyer, Mata Hari was now faced with Bouchardon, to whom she had admitted being recruited and paid by Kroemer, and Ladoux, who, by her own admission, had accused her of being a German agent when they had met for the first time. The interrogation developed into a series of statements and counter-statements between Ladoux and Mata Hari.

Ladoux started by denying that Mata Hari had been 'engaged' by him. She had not been given any money, had not been allocated an agent number and no protocol for communication had been established.[36]

Mata Hari responded, 'Captain Ladoux promised me, if I succeeded, one million as payment.'

Ladoux stated that he had made no such promise, but had said that if she had penetrated German Headquarters and had brought back information of Germany's military operations, then that information would be worth a million francs.[37]

Mata Hari countered this by saying, 'The Captain was more affirmative than that.'[38]

She restated that she had only worked as a spy for France. Ladoux replied that from the start he had suspected her of being a German agent and could, therefore, never have engaged her to work for France. Moreover, he had told Mata Hari that he suspected her of being a German agent, which indeed she was, having been employed by Kroemer. If she was so innocent, why had she not mentioned this at their meeting?[39]

She replied that she 'didn't dare', before adding, 'Besides, I never considered myself a German agent with a number, because I never did anything for them.'[40]

Ladoux then said, 'One cannot give a mission to an agent unless one is certain of him. MacLeod was always suspect to me.'[41]

The claim by Mata Hari that she had worked as a spy for the French was then challenged when Ladoux said that despite repeated requests on his part, she had failed to deliver any information about German intelligence. Mata Hari answered, 'I said nothing to you because you didn't want to pay me and because I didn't feel obliged to give you my great secret [of being engaged by Kroemer].'[42]

Bouchardon concluded the interrogation by warning Mata Hari, 'We must make clear that, from our point of view, maintaining contact with the enemy is considered legally to be a crime equivalent to actually furnishing information to the enemy.'[43]

The interrogation of 22 May reinforced the evidence brought out in the previous day's questioning. Mata Hari's assertion that she had been recruited, and Ladoux's denial, shed little new light on the matter. However, Ladoux's revelation that she had not been paid or allocated a number, which was true, did support his statement that he had always considered her an enemy agent. The minutes of their earliest meeting were evidence of this belief on Ladoux's part, as was the telegram he had sent to British intelligence in November 1916.

Mata Hari's statement that she had not told Ladoux her 'great secret' about Kroemer because Ladoux had not paid her may have made sense to her, but led to a deadlock. If she would not give information until Ladoux paid her, and Ladoux would not pay her until she produced information, then the spy and handler relationship descended into farce. Equally, this insistence on payment served to corroborate the belief that Mata Hari was a mercenary, rather than a patriotic spy. Enemy agents were considered the lowest form of life within the intelligence services. Sneaking and spying, listening into secrets and stealing plans, although an essential part of war, were considered dishonourable activities. Those who spied out of patriotism were generally disliked, but those who spied for merely financial gain were loathed and despised. A patriotic spy was unlikely to change sides, but a mercenary one would run to whoever paid the most. Comparisons between mercenary spies and prostitution were frequently made. Mata Hari's statements that she took the money from the Germans but did not spy for them did not help prove her innocence, but damned her as a mercenary prostitute who had not even shown basic loyalty to her German paymaster. As Bouchardon said, he did not need to prove whether or not actual information had been passed: he merely needed to show sufficient contact for the case to continue to trial. This legal point had never been properly explained to Mata Hari, or indeed Clunet, and as the interrogation entered its final stages, time was running out for Mata Hari to explain her actions in such a way that did not serve to further incriminate her.

In addition, by failing to reveal to Ladoux her connection with Kroemer, Mata Hari merely added to her apparent guilt. If she had told

Ladoux at their first meeting that she had been employed by Kroemer, it might have strengthened her credibility with him and even have prompted him to pay her some money in advance. By not revealing the 'secret' until under interrogation, Mata Hari had been hiding the reality of her connection with Kroemer.

The following day, 23 May, Bouchardon interrogated her again. He told her about Denvignes' statement, including his conviction that she was a German agent. Mata Hari replied:

> A man of Colonel Denvignes' rank should not throw stones at a woman in trouble. All the more so since he asked me to become his mistress, to which I responded that my heart was taken by a Russian captain who wanted to marry me. Nonetheless, he invited me to dine with him in Paris, gave me his address at the Hotel d'Orsay (so I could visit him). On the subject of his suppositions that I was part of German intelligence, I respond thus: it is completely ridiculous, if he had believed this idea, he would never have displayed himself in public with me in Madrid as he did. He kept a bouquet of violets and a ribbon of mine [as souvenirs].[44]

The revelations in Denvignes' statement had upset Mata Hari. She wrote to Bouchardon and accused Denvignes of having betrayed her. She wrote that he must have spoken against her to Masloff's commander. She reiterated her version of the events in Spain: Denvignes had pursued her and encouraged her to revisit Kalle. Mata Hari stressed his behaviour in Paris, when Denvignes had deliberately avoided her.[45]

On 30 May, Bouchardon interrogated her again. She repeated her accusations against Denvignes. Bouchardon then revealed to her that he had also interviewed Masloff. He showed Mata Hari Masloff's deposition, in which the Russian denied being in love with her. Their relationship, according to Masloff, had merely been a casual affair. She replied, 'I have nothing to say.'

She followed that with the statement, 'I am not guilty of the death of even one of our soldiers.'[46]

After that short meeting, Mata Hari was taken to her cell, before being brought back to meet Ladoux. This meeting was equally short, and concluded when her told her that unless she revealed the names of her accomplices, she would be shot as a spy.

On 31 May, she wrote to Bouchardon:

> Captain Ladoux … understands nothing of my character. Me, because of my travels, my foreign acquaintances, my manner of living, I see grand events and grand methods. For him, it is the opposite. He sees everything as petty and small … He did not know how to use me. It was his fault, not mine … Today, all around me, everything is collapsing, everyone renounces me, even he for whom I would have gone through fire. Never would I have believed in such human cowardice. I will defend myself and if I fall, it will be with a smile of profound contempt.[47]

The interrogation, the revelation about Masloff's denial of love for her and Ladoux's threat that she would be shot must have shaken Mata Hari. She wrote Bouchardon a second letter, asking again for her freedom and promising that she would deliver secrets about German military intelligence within a month. In response to Ladoux's demand that she name her accomplices, she answered, 'I cannot tell you what I do not know.'[48]

It was a sign of just how desperate she had become that Mata Hari thought that Bouchardon would consider such a ridiculous request. Abandoned by Masloff and threatened by Ladoux, she may have known subconsciously that such a request at that stage in the proceedings was laughable, but in desperation still made the attempt. Bouchardon did not bother to reply. Clunet also wrote to Bouchardon on 3 June to ask once more for her to be granted provisional liberty. The request was denied. He wrote again on 8 June and was yet again denied.

On 5 June, Mata Hari wrote another letter to Bouchardon:

> There is still something which I beg you to take into consideration, it is that Mata Hari and Madame Zelle MacLeod are two completely different women. Today, because of the war, I am obliged to live under the name of Zelle, and sign

it, but this is a woman unknown to most people. As for me, I consider myself to be Mata Hari. For twelve years, I have lived under this name. I am known in all the countries and I have friends everywhere. That which is permitted to Mata Hari – dancer – is certainly not permitted to Madame Zelle MacLeod. That which happens to Mata Hari, these are events which do not happen to Madame Zelle. Those who address one do not address the other. In actions and their manner of living Mata Hari and Madame Zelle cannot be the same. For this reason, my Captain, do not be astonished at that which had befallen me … Mata Hari is obliged to defend herself. I learned this to my downfall. Everywhere that I dance, I am celebrated, I love my jewels, furs. I am everywhere pursued by vendors who work at the theatres. The lawsuits are numerous, the seizures are immediate, and to avoid this, it is I or a lover who 'pays' or else I leave my coveted possessions in the hands of others. I know that there is nothing to do about it. It is the life of the famous, of all women of the theatre. These are things of which one does not speak. But, one makes up the loss when the occasion presents itself. And that is what happened to me, with my furs in Berlin when the war broke out. I assure you, my captain, at eight o'clock in the morning, when the Berlin police went to every hotel, knocked on every door to see who lived there, that morning of the declaration of war, the bank seized the deposits and valuables of foreigners. All the vendors presented their notes and since no one could pay, they seized the trunks, the stored furs. That is what happened to me, and happened to others. And since they pretended that I had lived more than ten years in France, and that I had lost my Dutch nationality, I was treated very harshly … And so, when Mata Hari had the occasion to take a little reimbursement [from the Germans] she did it. All this letter is to point out to you that everything has happened to Mata Hari – and not to Madame Zelle. It was Mata Hari that was obliged to go to Paris to protect her interests. Madame Zelle had nothing to do there. I beg you, my captain, take this into consideration and do not be so hard on me. Realise that I have lived all my adult life as Mata Hari, that I think and I act as her. I have lost the notion of travel, of distances, of dangers, nothing exists for me now. Even the difference between races [has disappeared]. Everywhere, I encounter rascals and brave people. I lose – I win – I defend myself when I am attacked – I take – sometimes I am taken. But I beg you to believe me that I never did a single act of espionage against France. Never, never. And I beg you, my captain, I have suffered enough.

Let me leave Saint-Lazare. It is not just to keep me locked up. I have never carried out any espionage.[49]

On 10 March, Dr Socquet had described Mata Hari as being 'in a very extreme state of nervousness and never stopped crying'.[50] By the latter half of May, she was describing herself as 'completely mad',[51] and on 24 May, Socquet found she had 'an extremely nervous temperament'.[52] This letter, written on 5 June, saw her mental state deteriorate still further. The explanation that she had accepted payment from the Germans in lieu of the seizure of her furs was the consistent argument that Mata Hari put forward throughout her interrogation. Unfortunately, that argument, and the further information about the social realities of women in the theatre who had to maintain a certain appearance, was lost within the bizarre irrationalities of the rest of the letter. Within the theatrical profession, adopting a stage persona that became a reality through long usage was not unknown. However, the tone of her letter appeared to be that of an individual who thought of herself as two distinct people.

The fantasy of being Mata Hari had begun when she had become a dancer. However, what had been harmless fantasy, in which everyone had participated, of being an Eastern dancer had become a reality that was now falling apart. Her life had been a series of fantasies. M'greet had been her father's little princess; Madame MacLeod had been the proud colonial soldier's wife; Mata Hari had been the Eastern dancer. In each case the fantasy had disappeared, leaving the brutal reality: Zelle's bankruptcy and the abandoned family's desperate times in a poor tenement; a brutal unloving husband; the death of her son; divorce and the loss of her daughter; and then changing into an Eastern dancer who could not bear comparison with trained dancers. By the time that Mata Hari had adopted her persona of the great courtesan, she had spent her entire adult life divorced from reality. Imprisonment beside other prostitutes had been the final, humiliating, brutal reality.

Arrest and imprisonment is stressful, even for those guilty of an alleged offence. But Mata Hari had been arrested for espionage during wartime and Ladoux had already threatened her with the firing squad. This would have tested the most robust of constitutions. She had spent years creating her public persona, but it was a fragile edifice that could not stand up to the rigours of her situation. It is possible that during her time in Saint-Lazare, she suffered a nervous breakdown.

Her letters to Bouchardon became even more confused when she wrote of how she had lost 'the notions of travel, of distances, of dangers'. Then she wrote about the disappearance of the 'differences between races'. This may have been an attempt by her to explain how she was feeling after so many months in Saint-Lazare and the intense interrogation from Bouchardon. However, the meaning is far from clear, and is indicative of her deteriorating mental state. If she was an active German agent, she must have realised how dangerous her situation was. If she was not a German agent, not only was she in danger – as both Bouchardon and Ladoux seemed convinced of her guilt – but the confiscation of her letters had led to uncertainty and anxiety. This mental strain was compounded by the revelation that her great love, Masloff, had abandoned her to her fate.

On 21 June, Bouchardon interrogated Mata Hari for the last time. As that was her final interview, Clunet was allowed to be present. Bouchardon informed her that as far as he was concerned, her arrest was 'a case of *en flagrant délit*'.[53] Mata Hari answered with a long and rambling reply in which she stated that she still intended to marry Masloff, and in order to do so would undertake a great espionage mission for France. She had intended in November 1916 to meet with her former lover, the Duke of Cumberland. The duke had renounced the throne of Hanover, but she had intended to persuade him to reclaim his rightful inheritance. This scheme had been thwarted by her arrest by the English, but on her return to Spain she had tried to find out great secrets for Ladoux. She had given these secrets to Denvignes, who had betrayed her. Mata Hari finished this bizarre recitation by stating her opinion of Denvignes, 'He gets all the honour, and I am in prison.'[54]

Her statement was duly recorded and Mata Hari was sent back to her cell to await the outcome of Bouchardon's investigations.

Bouchardon took three days to complete his final report. He had to collate the details of the physical evidence, the results of the financial inquiries he had set in motion, the interviews with her various lovers and the records of the interrogations that had been undertaken. He had, obviously, to abide by the law, but as in all cases of espionage, the level of physical proof he had to work with was minimal. The vast majority of the material Bouchardon had comprised was multiple statements from different individuals, all of whom could have lied to a greater or lesser degree. He also had to take into consideration the political wishes of his superiors, which may only have been transmitted to him by vague suggestions and comments. In the end, to make sense of all of this and produce a coherent report and recommendation, he had to use his own judgement.

Criticism has been laid at Bouchardon's door for his attitude towards Mata Hari and her sexual activities. To modern eyes, this coloured his judgement. However, every age has its social norms and prejudices which inform opinion. He was no more critical of her than any other individual in his place and era. His judgements on her behaviour were not overly harsh or particular to him, but represented the attitudes of the vast majority of individuals across Europe at that time. Indeed, the stresses brought about by the Great War served to heighten those social attitudes that placed such restrictions on women, and men, especially over their sexual encounters. In short, Bouchardon's attitudes were, in 1917 Paris, perfectly reasonable.

14

TRIAL AND PUNISHMENT

On 24 July 1917, Bouchardon completed his report on Mata Hari and sent it to General Dubail. The report was long and thorough. Bouchardon stated that he agreed with his colleague Ladoux's assertion that she was a German agent whom Ladoux had 'employed' in order to entrap her. Bouchardon's evidence consisted of the payment from Kroemer, the intercepted telegrams and the receipt of monies through the Dutch Consul. Moreover, this evidence was based on the foundation of Mata Hari's behaviour. Decent women did not behave like her, therefore she was indecent; indecent women were immoral, and those without morals were the sort of people who became spies.

Bouchardon completed his report with a damning pen portrait of Mata Hari, reinforcing society's view of women as dangerous and untrustworthy. He wrote:

One can see that a woman such as Mata Hari, with her successive liaisons, could play a useful role in obtaining the half-secrets that fit together. It is in vain that her partners tried to keep up their guard. In the battle of the sexes, men, so skilled in other things that they are usually the victors, are always defeated. This dangerous creature is even more so because her primary education permitted her, when she wished, to speak and hold herself correctly in order to create an illusion. Speaking several languages, having lovers in all the capitals of Europe, spread across all the world, there finding discreet collaborations, she flatters herself that she is, in her own words, an 'international woman'.[1]

Bouchardon's final recommendation was that Mata Hari should be remanded for trial to the military tribunal on eight charges:

1. Entered the entrenched camp (war zone) of Paris in December of 1915, in any case within the statute of limitations, in order to obtain documents or information in the interest of Germany, an enemy power;
2. In Holland ... notably during the first half of 1916, procured for Germany, an enemy power, notably in the person of Consul Kroemer, documents or information susceptible to damaging the operations of the army or of compromising the security of places, posts, or other military establishments;
3. In Holland, in May 1916 ... maintained contact with Germany, an enemy power, in the person of the aforementioned Kroemer, in order to facilitate the enterprises of the enemy;
4. Entered the entrenched camp of war in Paris in June 1916 ... in order to secure there documents or information in the interests of Germany;
5. In Paris, since May 1916 ... maintained contact with Germany, with the aim of assisting the enterprises of the aforementioned enemy;
6. In Madrid, in December 1916 ... maintained contact with Germany ... in the person of military attaché Kalle, with the aim of assisting the enterprises of the enemy;
7. In the same circumstances of time and place ... delivered to Germany ... in the person of military attaché Kalle, documents susceptible to damaging the operations of the army or of endangering the security of places, posts, or other military establishments, said documents or information dealing in particular with interior politics, the spring offensive, the discovery by the French of the secret German invisible ink, and the disclosure of the name of an agent in England;
8. In Paris, in January 1917 ... maintained contact with Germany ... with the aim of assisting the enterprises of the aforementioned enemy.[2]

The set format and lack of detail within the charges was a normal security procedure in cases of espionage, especially in times of war. Listing the detail, and thus success, of what a spy had achieved would have damaged morale and could, potentially, have provided valuable military information.

Dubail agreed with Bouchardon's findings and recommendations, and forwarded the report to the Third Council of War with his own recommendation that they proceed to trial. Lieutenant André Mornet was appointed as prosecutor. Clunet and Mata Hari were informed that she was to face trial.

With Bouchardon no longer in control, Mata Hari started to write to Mornet. She asked for a photograph of Masloff, for clean linen and to be allowed to write to friends. Mornet refused all her requests. She then wrote to ask for copies of documents to be sent to her lawyer. She wanted to ask for more funds to be sent to her from the Netherlands to allow her to pay for a copyist for Clunet.[3] This too was denied. There was no reason why any documentation was kept from Clunet at this point in the proceedings, and this may have been a mistake on her part. She may have imagined that Morner was refusing to hand over documents, although there are no records of any request for extra documents from Clunet. The payment for a copyist is another curious request. The law allowed for defence lawyers to see and copy prosecution documents. Clunet as a lawyer would have known this and for the need to use copyists for this purpose. Most legal offices employed their own copyists for just such work, or occasionally employed a copyist for a single case, recouping the costs at the end of the trial. Clunet at that point in his life had no real legal practice to speak of, and so would have needed to employ a copyist. Was he also so short of funds that he was unable to bear the cost of a copyist himself until the trial was over?

Despite the Dutch Consul in Paris having been aware of Mata Hari's arrest and imprisonment on charges of suspected espionage, it was 30 June before the Dutch government expressed any interest in the case. The lack of official interest in her situation by the Dutch government may well have been due to the country's neutral status in the war. The

Netherlands was not a large country, and was not militarily strong. To protest to the French about her treatment would have brought them into conflict with the Allies. Equally, to completely abandon Mata Hari to her fate might signal to Germany a movement towards favouring the Allies. When she was originally arrested, the matter had been relatively secret and the Dutch government had been able to remain detached from the situation. However, as the weeks had dragged on, press speculation had started as to Mata Hari's whereabouts, and the government in The Hague began to feel under pressure.[4] Curiously John Louden, the Minister of Foreign Affairs, wrote via his secretary to Clunet and asked to be kept informed of the case. Louden had been involved when she was arrested and questioned by the British. Despite his official position of neutrality, Louden was known to be actively pro-French.

The records show Clunet asking the commissioner of the Dutch government for help in releasing some of Mata Hari's clothing, but not for any legal assistance. No records exist detailing any requests from him for help in obtaining documents from the prosecution, or help with the services of a copyist. If Clunet was encountering difficulties in obtaining the paperwork he needed to conduct her defence, he failed to ask for any assistance from the Dutch government.

On 20 July, Mata Hari was transferred from her cell at Saint-Lazare to one at the prison of Conciergerie to await the trial. The proceedings began on 24 July at the Palace de Justice. Despite having been told the date of the trial on 20 July, Clunet only informed the Dutch government about the situation on the morning of 24 July. The trial was that of a military tribunal, and as such Mata Hari was faced with seven military judges: Lieutenant Colonel Albert-Ernest Semprou, president of the tribunal; Major Ferdinand Joubert, judge; Captain Lionel de Cayla, judge; Captain Jean Chatin, judge; Lieutenant Henri Deguesseau, judge; Second Lieutenant Joseph de Mercier de Malval, judge; and Sergeant Major Berthommé, judge. The clerk to the tribunal was Sergeant Major Rivière.

News of the trial had leaked out, and the public gallery was full of spectators and a large number of reporters. When Mata Hari arrived in the courtroom, she was wearing a military style tri-corned hat, matching military skirt and jacket and a somewhat low-cut blouse. She had had little choice in the clothes she wore, but the outfit made a somewhat unfortunate impression. Semprou started by asking Mata Hari her full name, date and place of birth, civil status, profession and address. Once these details were established, the tribunal was officially convened at 1 p.m.

Mornet started proceedings by requesting that the public gallery be cleared of spectators for reason of state security, and that the publication of the trial record be prohibited. After a brief discussion by the judges, both motions were granted. The guards cleared the courtroom of all spectators, and it was noted that publication of the trial record was to be prohibited. The detail of the proceedings of the trial, therefore, comes from the official judgment, a letter about the trial written by Chatin and two eyewitness accounts of court officials. The formal court record remains restricted.

Mornet started the prosecution case against Mata Hari by presenting to the court Bouchardon's report and its conclusion and recommendations. He then called six witnesses to give evidence. Police Inspector Monier, who had followed Mata Hari with his colleague Tarlet, gave evidence first. He testified about her lovers and extravagant behaviour. He offered no proof of espionage, but his testimony laid the foundation of her as a depraved and immoral woman capable of being a spy, the foundation upon which Ladoux and Bouchardon had built their case against her. Police Commissioner Priolet then testified as to the circumstances of her arrest and detailed the belongings seized. He offered no proof of espionage. Then Captain Ladoux gave evidence.

He detailed his initial meeting with Mata Hari, his impression of her and what she had and had not told him about her involvement with Kroemer. Ladoux testified that he had never employed her as an agent for France, but had merely pretended to do so in order to entrap her. He also stressed the fact that Mata Hari had said she had told Kalle she only pretended to work for the French. Ladoux's superior, Colonel Goubet, was the next to give evidence. His testimony, mostly based on what he had been told by Ladoux and the content of the telegrams, merely supported what Ladoux had stated. He repeated his statement to Bouchardon that he believed that Mata Hari was 'one of the most dangerous that counter-espionage ever encountered'.[5] Goubet never elaborated on the statement or explained on what it was based.

Mornet's last two witnesses did not attend the trial to give evidence. One was Masloff, whose whereabouts were unknown at that time, and the other was Hallaure. It is not clear why Lieutenant Hallaure did not attend the tribunal. The statements both had given to Bouchardon were read to the tribunal. Mornet closed the prosecution case by giving a summation of the evidence presented against the accused, and the tribunal rose at 7 p.m. Mata Hari was taken back to her cell in the prison of Conciergerie.

At 8 a.m. on 25 July, the tribunal reconvened and Clunet began his defence. As the court was a military tribunal, he was not allowed to cross-examine the prosecution witnesses. He was further constrained by being barred from directly questioning his own witnesses. The tribunal system allowed witnesses to make statements about the case and the accused, but did not allow for these statements to be directly challenged, either by the defence or the prosecution. Clunet called several witnesses to give testimony on Mata Hari's behalf; not all attended. Paul Cambon gave evidence that she had never asked him about either military or diplomatic matters. Henri de Marguérie testified that she had not asked him about military matters. Alfred Messimy was called but did not attend. Messimy had been the Minister of War at the outbreak of the Great War. His wife, Andreé Messimy neé Bonaparte, wrote to Semprou, informing him that her husband had never met Mati Hari and was too ill with rheumatism to attend the tribunal. Messimy and Mata Hari had actually had a brief liaison in the summer of 1914. Semprou accepted the letter and Messimy was excused from attending the tribunal, and was not named in the court record but merely referred to as 'Monsieur M, a cabinet minister'.

In addition to his witnesses, Clunet methodically worked through the charges laid against Mata Hari and the lack of proof of her having passed any information to the Germans. What he could do little about, although he tried, was her confession that she had accepted payment from German intelligence, the fact that the head of French intelligence stated that she had never been employed by them and the intercepted telegrams. The acceptance of money from Kroemer to pay for her furs made sense to Mata Hari, but pointed to her guilt as far as the tribunal was concerned. The story of the furs did not explain the other payments from the Germans. On the point of her employment by French intelligence, the tribunal could not believe her, as this would have meant calling Ladoux a liar. In addition to which, the intercepted telegrams from Berlin 'proved' Ladoux had been correct in his assumption of her guilt.

The three sets of telegrams are confusing, but were not so for the tribunal, as they were not aware that multiple copies existed. As Clunet was also unaware that there were three sets, he could not query their provenance. The use of the broken German code raises problems. Were the Germans using the broken code to send misinformation about an innocent woman or an agent of little worth? The problem also did not arise for the tribunal, however, because they did not know the telegrams were sent via the broken code. Similarly, Clunet could not argue the veracity of the content of the telegrams as he was never told of the broken codes.

Taking all of the evidence presented to them as correct, the tribunal had a decision to make. If Mata Hari was innocent, then Ladoux, the head of the *Deuxiéme Bureau*, was either an incompetent fool or a dangerous liar, who had possibly forged telegrams to support his case. In addition, France's main ally, the British, were also wrong in their assumptions about Mata Hari, as were the rumours circulating in the Russian Army. Alternatively, if she was a German agent, then Ladoux, and the British, had been correct all along. The lack of physical evidence did not prove her innocence, but showed either how poor a spy she had been, passing no information to the Germans, or how good a spy she had been in being able to hide her activities.

At 7 p.m., the judges rose to consider their verdict.

The judges considered each of the eight charges against Mata Hari in turn. Under the law at that time, guilt was determined by a majority vote. On the first charge of having entered the entrenched camp of Paris in December 1916, she was found guilty unanimously. No evidence had been produced to show she had done so to procure documents for the Germans. On the second charge, that she had given documents to Kroemer in the first half of 1916, she was found guilty by a majority vote of six to one. No evidence had been produced to show she had given Kroemer any documents. On the third charge of having maintained contact with Kroemer in May 1916, she was found guilty unanimously. Maintaining contact did not require her to have met Kroemer, but merely to have met with someone who had intimate knowledge of him, e.g. his housemaid. The next charge was more complicated as it had two parts. Had Mata Hari, firstly, entered the entrenched camp of Paris in June 1916 and, secondly, had she done so in order to obtain information for the Germans? She was unanimously found guilty of this charge. There was evidence of her presence in Paris, which she did not deny, but there was no evidence of her intent to obtain information for the enemy. She was found guilty by a majority vote of the fifth charge of maintaining contact with Germany with the aim of assisting them. One judge found her not guilty of this charge. No evidence had been produced to show she had maintained contact. She was found guilty by unanimous vote of the sixth charge. She had been in Madrid and in contact with Kalle, although Mata Hari insisted this was to get information from him for France, not give information to Kalle about France. The seventh charge was another complex one. Had she given documents to Kalle that contained military information and revealed the name of an enemy agent? As in charge four, innocence of one part of this charge could not be detached from guilt in another. Mata Hari had confessed to Bouchardon that she had told an unnamed Allied agent and Kalle about the Belgian couple on board the SS *Hollandia*. She was found guilty by majority vote, with one judge finding her innocent. She was found unanimously guilty of the final charge, that she had maintained contact with the enemy in January 1917.

On all the charges, the only physical evidence brought before the court were the financial transactions through her bank and the telegrams from Berlin. No evidence was produced to show what documents or information she had passed to Germany. However, as was common in espionage trials at the time, lack of evidence of spying activity was not considered evidence of a lack of spying activity, but, if supported by other statements and proofs, was indicative of a clever spy who had hidden their tracks well.

After Mata Hari had been found guilty of all charges, Semprou recommended that she be shot and the other six judges agreed. They returned to the courtroom to render their judgement:

IN THE NAME OF THE PEOPLE OF FRANCE,

The Third Permanent Council of War of the military government of Paris had rendered the following judgement:

Today, the twenty-fifth of July 1917, the Third Permanent Council of War in Paris, heard by the Commissioner of the Government in the requisitions and conclusion, had declared the named ZELLE, Marguerite, Getrude, called Mata-Hari, divorcée of Mr MacLeod, guilty of espionage and intelligence with the enemy with the end of assisting his enterprises.

In consequence, the aforementioned Council condemns her to pain of death, by applications of articles 205 paragraph 2, 206 paragraphs 1 and 2, 64, 69, 269, 139, 187 of the Code of Military Justice and 7 of the Criminal Code. And, by the articles 139 of the code of Military Justice and 9 of the Law of 22 July 1867, the Council condemns the aforesaid ZELLE to reimburse, by the gifts of her property and by sale, to the Public Treasury, the costs of the trial.[6]

After the verdict and sentence were delivered, Mata Hari, who had shown little reaction, was taken back to Conciergerie prison and the following morning was then returned to Saint-Lazare, where she was placed in the condemned cell, number 12. Clunet started work on her appeal.

Clunet was barred from visiting Mata Hari, but was allowed to write to her about her appeal and what she might do to help herself. He started by lodging a basic appeal on technical grounds. This was a wide-ranging appeal that was usually lodged after most convictions, and required the appeal judges to satisfy themselves that the trial had been conducted correctly. At the same time, Clunet wrote to de Stuers, the Dutch ambassador in Paris, requesting his Excellency to attempt to have her sentence commuted to life imprisonment if the appeal was unsuccessful. Mata Hari spent the following days in her cell awaiting developments. On 7 August, she turned 41. On 17 August, her appeal was heard. Five judges, three of them from the military, reviewed the trial and were satisfied that her trial had been carried out correctly.[7]

Clunet then approached the Supreme Court of Appeals and lodged an appeal against her conviction. At the same time, Mata Hari wrote to Consul Bunge asking what the Dutch government was doing to help her.[8] His reply is not recorded. Did she also write to Bunge as a 'German agent', as he was suspected of being? Was this a final desperate plea for help from Germany?

On 12 September, a Dutch publisher, A.J. Kooji, wrote to Mata Hari to ask for the publishing rights to her memoirs.[9] The letter was forwarded to the Military Governor, Dubail, on 29 September. She did not reply to Kooji, and may never have seen his letter. However, she had written a memoir and had asked a military clerk to make four copies for her. She had to request the 5.50 francs from her account to pay the clerk. The request for the release of funds was denied, however, as the chief of the Bureau of Military Justice found it 'repugnant' that any soldier should receive payment from the convicted spy Mata Hari.[10] The memoir was destroyed.

The Supreme Court of Appeals refused to overturn her conviction. On 22 September, she wrote to Stuers asking him to request a presidential pardon.[11] Stuers and Clunet met to discuss the matter, and as a matter of protocol Clunet wrote the formal letter to the Dutch government. A request for clemency from the Dutch government in The Hague was sent to President Raymond Poincaré. On 13 October, Clunet received Poincaré's reply; there was to be no request for a presidential pardon. Clunet made a final attempt to save Mata Hari's life. On 14 October, he wrote to Semprou:

In the theatre world, where everyone is naturally interested in the fate of Mata Hari, the rumour is that she is pregnant. If this is so, and if the pardon is rejected, the execution by the Third Council of War will naturally be suspended. My concern is to beg you to order that a medical expert be consulted to determine the physiological state of the condemned?[12]

As Mata Hari had been in prison for some eight months and had met no men other than Clunet, the two prison doctors, Bouchardon and Ladoux, it was extremely unlikely that she could have become pregnant, although not impossible. But Clunet had made a second offer in his letter of 14 October:

My compatriot and friend, the eminent General Merchand, reported as missing in a recent combat, was not killed but imprisoned by the Germans. Why not impose on our enemies the restitution of this general, in exchange for Mata Hari, deprived by us of all value, and the capital punishment commuted to exile?[13]

This second manoeuvre by Clunet was a slightly more intelligent one than that of a fake pregnancy. General Jean-Baptiste Marchand was a well-respected military officer and African explorer. He had commanded the French Expeditionary Forces during the Fashoda Incident in 1898. In 1900, he had fought with the French Expeditionary Forces in the Boxer Rebellion. He had been promoted to the rank of general in 1915. He had been wounded in 1915 at the Battle of Champagne and again in 1916 in the Battle of the Somme. By the summer of 1917, he had been posted missing presumed dead. The news in the autumn of 1917 that he was not dead but was merely a prisoner of the Germans was welcomed in the press, and pressure was placed on Poincaré and Paul Painlevé, the Minister of War, to secure his release. Had Clunet made this suggestion earlier, it might have been considered as it would have allowed France to regain a much-respected and needed general and eliminate a spy, while at the same time showing clemency to a woman. However, at the same time as Clunet was sending his last letter of appeal, Mata Hari's order of execution was signed.[14]

Clunet had received Poincaré's refusal of a presidential appeal on Saturday, 13 October. The Dutch Consulate was closed for the weekend and Clunet had not thought it proper to disturb the Dutch envoy with this matter at his private home. Subsequently, the appeal decision was not delivered until the morning of 15 October, by which time Mata Hari was already dead. It is possible that Clunet had not realised that the moment the final appeal was refused, the order for execution would be signed. With his lack of experience in espionage trials, he may not have realised how quickly events moved and still thought that he had a few more days left in which to try to save her life.

The execution order detailed that Mata Hari was to be taken to the place of execution at Vincennes to be executed at 6.15 a.m. on 15 October. Lieutenant Colonel Semprou, Captain Thibaut, chief scribe for the Third Council of War, Lieutenant Choulot, Pastor Arboux, Sister Léonide and Sister Marie were to be present. Also to be in attendance were Dr Robillard, the military physician, who would pronounce Mata Hari dead, and Clunet, her only permitted witness. The firing squad comprised twelve men of the 4th Regiment Zouaves, under the command of Sergeant Major Petoy of the 23rd Regiment of the Dragoons. Petoy was to deliver the *coup de grâce*.

Mata Hari was wakened just before 5 a.m. on 15 October by Bouchardon, Bizard, Jean Estachy, the prison director, Captain Émile Massard, the chief of Military Staff in Paris, and Clunet. She was told she was to be shot, and then the men left the room, except Bizard, while she dressed. She wore an elegant outfit trimmed with fur.[15] The report of this in the first early edition of *Le Petit Parisien* was subsequently censored by the authorities. After she dressed, she wrote three letters: to Non, Masloff and de Marguérie. She handed them over to Father Arboux with a request that they be sent on to their respective recipients. Bouchardon took the letters from Arboux and they subsequently disappeared.

When Mata Hari was ready, she left her cell and was escorted out to a waiting car. Five identical black cars with their blinds drawn were parked inside the prison courtyard. News of the execution had leaked out and several journalists and onlookers were waiting as the cars left the prison and drove to the execution ground at Caponnière, the barracks of the old fort of Caserne de Vincennes. She stepped out of the car and was taken out to the parade ground, where the twelve Zouaves and Sergeant Major Petoy were waiting. Two guards escorted her to the wooden stake that stood in front of the back wall.

Father Arboux spoke a few final words to Mata Hari. She declined to wear the blindfold or be tied to the stake. She stood simply and quietly in front of the stake. Thibaut read out the official sentence of the court, 'By the order of the Third Council of War the woman Zelle has been condemned to death for espionage.'[16]

Petoy gave an order and the soldiers came to attention. After a second order, 'en joue', they brought their rifles smartly into position at their shoulders. Petoy waited a few seconds, then raised his sword and brought it quickly down while shouting 'tirez'.

Henry Wales, a British reporter, witnessed the execution:

At the report Mata Hari fell. She did not die as actors and moving picture stars would have us believe that people die when they are shot. She did not throw up her hands nor did she plunge straight forward or straight back. Instead she seemed to collapse. Slowly, inertly, she settled to her knees, her head up always, and without the slightest change of expression on her face. For the fraction of a second it seemed she tottered there, on her knees, gazing directly at those who had taken her life. Then she fell backward, bending at the waist, with her legs doubled up beneath her. She lay prone, motionless, with her face turned towards the sky. A non-commissioned officer, who accompanied a lieutenant, drew his revolver from the big, black holster strapped about his waist. Bending over, he placed the muzzle of the revolver almost – but not quite – against the left temple of the spy. He pulled the trigger, and the bullet tore into the brain of the woman. Mata Hari was surely dead.[17]

Dr Robillard walked over to the body and pronounced Mata Hari dead. Robillard, Choulet and Thibaut then signed the execution order, verifying that it had been carried out according to due procedure. Thibaut then asked if anyone claimed the body. Clunet, who was her only representative, did not answer. It is not clear why he had failed to make any arrangements about the body. With no formal claim on the body, Thibaut ordered the gun carriage bearing a coffin, which had been standing by for this eventuality, to be brought forward. Mata Hari's body was placed in the coffin, loaded onto the gun carriage and driven away with an escort. The carriage drove to a nearby graveyard, where the body was committed to the ground and Father Arboux said a few words. Then the coffin was removed and reloaded onto the gun carriage, and driven off to the faculty of medicine at the Sorbonne.

In October 1917, France was still in the grip of spy fever and the press reports of Mata Hari's execution reflected that paranoia. Most followed the facts quoted in the official press statement:[18]

> Woman dancer shot by French as spy. Mlle. Mata-Hari suffers penalty for betraying secret of 'Tanks' to Germans.[19]
>
> The Spy Mata Hari paid yesterday for her crimes.[20]
>
> Lovely spy shot. Mata Hari executed by the French at Vincennes. Romantic career of infamy.[21]

The authorities censored any press stories that deviated from the official statement or criticised Mata Hari's interrogation, trial, sentence or execution.[22] Few, if any, offered any direct opposition to her conviction, but many softened their tone with regards to her execution. The tragic and romantic death of a woman who had been fêted by the press gave rise to several stories with a sympathetic tone. These stories were quickly withdrawn. In contrast to Mata Hari, the press lauded Bouchardon as the hero of the hour.[23]

15

THE DENOUEMENT

Throughout her life, Mata Hari created fantasies about her origins: she was variously Lady MacLeod, a Javanese princess, the daughter of a Hindu priest and a trained dancer. Her year of birth varied between 1880 and 1884; her place of birth from Java to Malay and the banks of the Ganges River. All of which was untrue. However, it must be remembered that it was common practice for entertainers, especially female entertainers, to invent a persona for themselves as part of their act. Audiences were well aware of this and accepted the fantasy, so long as it was not taken too far. For any entertainer to appear to believe the fiction and, more importantly, to expect the audience to do so, was skirting dangerously close to delusion on the part of the individual while underestimating the intelligence of the audience. A harmless mutual fantasy was one thing; living a lie was quite another. In her case, however, she seems to have transcended the usual rules and lived a life of lies, half-lies and complete fantasy; a life in which the public, the press and her various lovers colluded until the Great War shattered the fantasy.

In trying to understand Mata Hari's life, as in all historical research, it is important to remember the following: not all records are complete; some of what is recorded may not be accurate due to error, misinterpretation, bias or malicious intent; the memory of most human beings is not perfect; and people lie. This last point is especially true in cases of espionage, where information and misinformation are deliberately told, denied, repeated and retold. Mata Hari was herself a consummate liar. One of her biggest mistakes was in failing to understand that the harmless lies of a dancer and courtesan before the war could prove fatal after war was declared.

So was she a spy? Mata Hari certainly took money from the German intelligence service, but does not appear to have given them any real information in return. Had they employed her as a 'tension traveller' rather than a more active agent? She appears to have been used by the Germans to deflect interest from other agents such as Clara Benedix. Was this part of the original German plan, and was it with her knowledge? She accepted money from Kalle in Madrid; a gift or a payment? She received a payment from Bunge; a further payment from the Germans or another gift from her lover Capellan? She gave the French intelligence service some slight information, but received no money in return. She was suspected of being a German spy by the French, who treated her accordingly. Although suspected, the French were unable to find proof of any information, other than generally known gossip, that she passed to the Germans.

Was she mercenary? Her jewels, furs and money had been taken by Schultz, the manager of the Metropol theatre at the beginning of the war. She felt her payment by the intelligence services was merely compensation for that loss. Mata Hari wanted to marry her Russian lover, and treated her work for France as a means to make money to enable the marriage to go ahead.

Was she promiscuous? By the standards of the day, she was considered depraved. Her sexual appetite and openness about sexual matters shocked. The criminologists and sociologists of the early twentieth century were adamant that sexually active women were criminal types. Mata Hari's sexual behaviour, and lack of shame regarding it, condemned her as the sort of woman who would be a spy.

Was she conspired against by the intelligence services? The British seemed convinced she was an enemy agent, but no 'proof' of any espionage activities exist in their files. The rivalry and politicking between the India Office, Scotland Yard and MI5 probably added to the suspicions against her. The French were convinced she was an enemy agent, but although they found out about her payments from Kroemer and Kalle, still no proof of the passing of any actual information is to be found in the *Deuxiéme Bureau* files. The relationship between Wallinger of the British India Office and Ladoux seems to have been close, opaque and unofficial. Did the French and British, each genuinely believing Mata Hari was the promiscuous type of woman who would be a spy, encourage each other in that belief until it reached an unstoppable momentum? Or did they need her to be a spy, albeit without proof, who could be executed to aid morale after Verdun?

Did the Germans 'help' in her arrest and conviction by conveniently leaking information to Allied agents, most notably the telegrams about H21? That cannot be known for definite, but the French and British intelligence services certainly acquired the information about the payments Mata Hari received with extraordinary ease. In addition, the original telegrams were conveniently sent in the code known to have been broken. The original telegrams are missing from the French archives, which hides exactly what they contained. Did Ladoux tamper with the telegrams in order to trap an innocent woman and cover up his incompetence? Or did Ladoux 'interpret' the telegrams as best he could, based on the firm belief that Mata Hari was guilty? Or was this a sign of something even more extraordinary?

On 19 October 1917, four days after Mata Hari's execution, Ladoux was arrested and charged with being a German spy. He was suspended from the Deuxiéme Bureau and placed under house arrest. The case against him was dismissed on 1 January 1918, but he was then rearrested on 2 January. He was held in the Cherche-Midi prison for four months. Ladoux was acquitted of all charges on 8 May 1919 but his reputation was permanently tarnished. The files pertaining to Ladoux's arrest remain sealed, so the nature of the charges and evidence against him remain unknown. He could, of course, have been completely innocent and merely a victim of 'spy mania' that gripped France. But it remains astonishing that the man who was instrumental in Mata Hari's arrest was himself arrested.

Was Mata Hari stupid? If she is to be believed, then she never had any intention of working for the Germans. If she had taken money from the German intelligence services and not done any work for them in peacetime, it is likely that public opinion would smile at her audacity. In wartime, even the kindest of opinion would see such an action as rank stupidity.

Mata Hari treated her work as a spy as a method by which to earn money. She had danced in front of men for money; she had had sex with men for money; she tried to spy for men for money. She had been successful as a dancer, despite having no training; she had been successful as a courtesan, despite being older than most. The war had stopped her dancing and had taken away many of the officers who were her lovers. She had no financial security and was getting older. Mata Hari was too old to dance, was becoming too old to be a successful courtesan and needed to marry for her long-term security. To marry Masloff, she had to overcome his family's objections, and she believed that money would allow her to do so. Mata Hari was always an opportunist, and the war presented her with a new opportunity as a spy.

So was Mata Hari a German spy? Well, she took the money, so probably yes. Initially perhaps as a 'tension traveller', and when she supplied no real information, as an unwitting decoy for other German agents. Was she an opportunistic, if somewhat naive, mercenary? Probably. Was she condemned, in part, because of her sexual nature? Certainly. She had plied the oldest profession in the world, and gained a reputation for being depraved along the way. She had spent all of her adult life spinning a web of fantasies to survive as best she could. At another time, she might just have been seen as the 'scandalous Mata Hari'. The coming of the new science of criminology hardened society's view of women, sexual excess and criminals, giving a scientific basis for the double standards at work in society. Women who titillated men with their dancing and sexuality were no longer to be dismissed as merely lower-class creatures; they were now a criminal element to be feared. The outbreak of the Great War heightened that fear. By the time Mata Hari realised, in her cell at Saint-Lazare, the reality of her situation, the web around her was so dense and the prevailing belief in her depravity so strong that nothing could save her.

As with most societies, during happy, peaceful times, what is new, daring and exotic is exciting and interesting. However, when put under stress, societies retreat to what is familiar and certain, no matter how bourgeois, old fashioned or prescriptive. Part of Mata Hari's misfortune was to fail to recognise that change. The exotic dancing and sexual behaviour that had delighted and excited Europe in 1910 became a matter of suspicion by 1914.

The French, who had adored Mata Hari in 1910, were a very different nation when the Great War broke out, and by the time of her arrest they were almost a broken people. With the horrors of Verdun fresh in their minds, and the legacy of Dreyfus still haunting their intelligence services, the French needed to catch a spy. Mata Hari fitted the bill perfectly. Did the French accept her guilt too easily and overlook the ease with which the incriminating telegrams had been intercepted? Did they allow their belief in depraved women as criminals to overcome the lack of hard evidence? Was the trail of suspicion started by the British because she was a 'bold' type of woman and because of interdepartmental rivalries between MI5, Scotland Yard and the India Office? Had the Germans decided to sacrifice her to save another more important spy? If so, did they merely 'give' evidence to the British and French intelligence services, or did they have agents working in the *Deuxiéme Bureau*?

Mata Hari's behaviour may, in part, be forgiven as she was operating as a woman in a man's world. She may also be afforded some sympathy for having suffered abandonment by her father and the indifference of her family in early life. Her abusive husband, the death of her son, a brutal divorce and the loss of her daughter were also times in her life when history can be kind to her. However, her spoilt and petulant nature led her to make some poor, and incredibly stupid, choices. She wasted opportunities, such as that presented when Kiepert gave her the gift of 300,000 marks in 1907. Had she taken the money and travelled to somewhere like New York, she could easily have built a new life for herself. Equally, had she accepted the role of docile mistress to Capellan, she could have seen out the war in the safety of her house in The Hague. Unfortunately, either option called for a degree of sense which she either lacked, or refused to adopt. When she had first attempted to make a living as an exotic dancer, she had taken a great risk. Unfortunately, she was instantly successful. Within a year of starting to dance, she was rich, famous and fêted wherever she went. When she started to become a great courtesan, she was equally successful, capturing rich bankers and army officers who lavished her with gifts and compliments. During all of this time, her adoring public and besotted lovers allowed her to continue with her fantasies, lies and half-truths. By the time the war came along, Mata Hari was starting to think she could do no wrong. Money was there for the taking, fantasies were harmless fun and men would always allow her to behave outrageously.

When Mata Hari met Masloff, it does appear that she finally looked to the future and what it might hold, but even in that the fantasies continued; she would marry Masloff and become a respectable member of the Russian aristocracy. Was this in any way realistic? She was a 39-year-old divorcée; she had been a notorious 'naked dancer' and was a courtesan with a poor reputation. Masloff was 21 years old, a member of an aristocratic Russian family and a junior officer in the Russian Imperial Army with an impeccable reputation. He had been warned against marrying Mata Hari, and it seems hard to believe that all family opposition to the 'old adventuress' would have dissolved simply by the application of some money. Even if she had acquired a large sum of money from her work with Ladoux, which was in itself something of a fantasy, would she necessarily have married Masloff? Given her life of fantasy, she may have imagined she loved Masloff – indeed that love may have been genuine – but would it have survived her becoming independently wealthy?

It could be argued that Mata Hari's fantasies hurt only herself, and admittedly there is little evidence that she passed any information to the German intelligence service that cost the life of a single Allied soldier. Did she cause the intelligence services to waste time in surveillance that could have been put to better use? Ladoux certainly sent Tarlet amd Monier to follow her around Paris, gathering information that proved her promiscuity but little else. Such is the nature of much intelligence work. Most of Mata Hari's ex-lovers survived their association with her unscathed.

Did her behaviour upset her daughter? It is difficult to say, as Non left no diary and no personal papers. However, Non grew up as a young adolescent girl in a nice respectable town, the daughter of one of the most notorious women in Europe. Most newspapers carried Mata Hari stories, of her exploits on the stage, apparently naked, and her love affairs with multiple married men. For Non, it may have been hard to deal with the gossip and disapproval of those who knew whose daughter she was. In addition, Non would have had to contend with her own feelings towards her mother, who apparently preferred a life of gaiety in Paris to motherhood in the Netherlands.

Mata Hari remains a maddening, frustrating enigma, a spoilt fantasist who was also alluring and enchanting. It is noticeable that she is now remembered for the fantasy name she adopted and not as Margaretha Geertruida Zelle from Leeuwarden. Perhaps that is how she would have wanted it to be.

❖ ❖ ❖

In 1929, Major Gempp, head of German intelligence, stated in a Cologne newspaper that Mata Hari 'never did anything for German intelligence'.[1]

It was a startling statement. But was he telling the truth or was he defaming the French by inferring they had executed an innocent woman? In 1929, the Germans were involved in negotiations desperately trying to obtain a reduction in the payments due under the Versailles Treaty. These discussions had been undertaken sporadically since the initial signing of the treaty in 1919, as Germany, whose economy had been shattered by the war, tried to have the payments reduced. The French, under Poincaré, were adamant that the cost of rebuilding France should be borne by the aggressors. The British and the Americans had initially been aware of the burden the reparations would place on Germany, urging restraint on the part of the Allies. By 1921, however, the British were concentrating on their own affairs, with various issues such as the situation in Ireland being the main focus. America, too, had quickly lost interest in European affairs. As a result, the French were relatively unopposed in their demands for the payment of reparations to the fullest extent.

In January 1929, fresh discussions about the payments began in Paris, under the leadership of American diplomat Owen D. Young. The French again demanded that the Germans, as the aggressors in the war, pay the full amount, as had been agreed in 1919. The Germans reiterated their three-fold position: the German economy was not in any fit state to make the payments called for; they had not been the main aggressors in the war; and the French were being deliberately provocative, knowing the state of the German economy. Many in the German press ran anti-French stories, claiming that the French were deliberately trying to bankrupt Germany. Stories of French atrocities committed during their occupation of the Ruhr and at the end of the war were commonplace. Gempp's statement about Mata Hari was used as an example of French intransigence; the execution of a woman, even a spy, was still considered shocking. The statement about her was repeated by Gempp in a further newspaper article later that same year. Its veracity may, therefore, be argued.

In 1930, *Geschichte des Weltkrieges und Nachkriegsspionage* (History of World War and Post-war Espionage) was published in Germany. The book was widely acclaimed for the accuracy of the information it contained. In the chapter on Germany's female spies, Frau Doktor Schragmüller, head of the Intelligence Bureau IIIC in Antwerp, stated, 'All H21's information for Germany was false. She was never one of ours.'[2]

It is unclear if Schragmüller meant that Mata Hari was never one of Germany's spies, or never one of the spies working from the Antwerp bureau.

❖   ❖   ❖

MATA HARI

Mata Hari's body remained unclaimed by her family and was therefore, according to normal practice of the time, used for medical study. Her body was given to the Museum of Anatomy in the faculty of medicine at the Sorbonne in Paris. After dissection, the body was disposed of but the head was embalmed and kept in the museum as an example of a 'criminal type'. In 2000, it was discovered that the head was missing. After some internal inquiries, it became clear that the loss may have occurred as early as 1954, at a time when the museum had been relocated and its artefacts boxed up for removal to new premises.

BENEDIX

Little is known of Clara Benedix, although it is thought that at the end of the war she left Spain and returned to Germany. There are no extant records about her within the German archives. The photograph of Benedix is missing from the Metropolitan police files, and there is no photograph of her within the French files. Her true identity has never been discovered.

BOUCHARDON

After Mata Hari's execution, Bouchardon continued his career in the law. He was appointed President of the Paris Court of Appeal in 1924. He served as President of the Commission investigating abuses during the Vichy régime and ended his career as a counsellor of the Court of Cassation. He wrote some thirty books on major criminal cases of the nineteenth and twentieth centuries, many of which were used for instruction within the legal profession.

BUNGE

Despite the unresolved questions surrounding the Dutch Consul's involvement in the Mata Hari case and the situation regarding Denvignes and Ladoux, no investigation was held into Otto Bunge's conduct. He continued in his position as Dutch Consul in Paris until 1919, when he retired to the Dutch countryside with his family on a full pension.

CAPELLAN

Capellan remained somewhat reclusive after Mata Hari's trial. He stopped paying for the house in The Hague and focussed on his military career. He retired from the army in 1923 with the rank of major general, and lived out the rest of his life in relative obscurity.

CLUNET

Mata Hari's old lawyer disappeared very quickly after her trial. He had been extremely upset at her execution, possibly blaming himself for the outcome of the trial. Given the centralised nature of French records, it is somewhat curious that even after the war ended, no definitive record of Clunet can be found in the archives. It is of course possible that he left France, but even that event does not appear to be recorded anywhere.

DENVIGNES

In January 1918, Denvignes was arrested for treason. He was held in jail for four months and interrogated. In April 1918, he was acquitted on all charges. Possibly another victim of the 'spy mania', his arrest barely three months after Mata Hari's execution is striking. Despite the acquittal, he was demoted, and due to the subsequent rumours about his alleged treasonous activities, his military career was all but over.

HALLAURE

Despite being seriously wounded in the autumn of 1917, Hallaure survived the Great War. He met a young American woman and settled in the village of Sainte-Marine in Brittany. He died in 1960.

HOEDEMAKER

Hoedemaker claimed to have been instrumental in Mata Hari's final arrest due to his denouncement of her in 1916. He continued to publicly make these claims until 1921, when he committed suicide. The reason for his suicide was not established.

KALLE

Kalle remained in post in Madrid until the end of the war, when he returned to Berlin. He was a loyal German officer and fought for the government during the turbulent early years of the Weimar Republic. He became a *ministerialdirektor* in the government in 1928. He retired in 1933 and lived relatively quietly, dying in 1952.

KROEMER

After the war, Kroemer spent a few brief months closing up his offices in the Netherlands before returning to Germany in 1919. He wrote no memoirs and left no papers about his life. He died in 1938.

LADOUX

Despite his acquittal on 8 May 1919 of all charges against him, Ladoux's reputation was permanently tarnished. Moved to a job in the army records department, in 1923 he was promoted to the rank of major before retiring from the service. He wrote memoirs in which he reiterated his belief that Mata Hari was a German agent but mentioned his own arrest and imprisonment only briefly, stressing his acquittal on all charges. The fact that the files pertaining to Ladoux's arrest and acquittal remain sealed is both curious and frustrating. Was he completely innocent, a victim of the 'spy mania' that gripped France, or was he a German agent? As in much of Mata Hari's story, there is no definitive answer. It remains astonishing that the man who was instrumental in Mata Hari's arrest and had been convinced of her guilt as a German agent was himself arrested.

LINTJENS

Mata Hari's maid helped to close up the house in The Hague and then retired to the Dutch countryside in Limburg. She fell ill in 1931 and, believing herself to be near death, burnt all of Mata Hari's papers. In fact she survived until 1935.

MACLEOD

On hearing of Mata Hari's death, MacLeod approached the Dutch legation in Paris to ascertain what money she had left Non in her will. He discovered that Mata Hari had left no will, had a large amount of unpaid debt and that the French prison authorities were still holding many of her possessions. On 30 January 1918, Mata Hari's possessions were auctioned off in Paris by the prison authorities. They fetched 14,251 francs. The outstanding debts were then settled, although the French authorities never released the remaining money to Non. In 1924, a further auction was held in Paris of several items, including jewellery, belonging to Mata Hari. The items were put up for auction by the clerk of prisons and the clerk of the Council of War. No explanation was ever given as to why these items had not been produced at the 1918 auction, what authority these two clerks had to auction the items and who received the proceeds. MacLeod's second marriage, in 1907, to Elizabeth van der Mast had ended in separation in 1912 and divorce in 1917. Elizabeth had taken their daughter, Norma, born in 1909, with her. He was married for a third time, in 1917, to 25-year-old Griejte Meijer. They had a daughter in 1921, whom they called Non. MacLeod died in 1928 in Velp in the Netherlands.

MARCHAND

Marchard, the general whom Clunet had suggested be swapped for Mata Hari, was released by the Germans at the end of the war. He retired from the military in 1919, and in 1920 was awarded the Grand Cross of the Legion of Honour. He died in 1934, aged 71.

MARGUÉRIE

Mata Hari's lover Marguérie, who had testified on her behalf at the trial and to whom she had written on her last morning, saw out the war at his office at the Quai d'Orsay. He entered politics in 1918 and was elected as a senator for the Moselle in 1920. Marguérie seldom spoke publicly of Mata Hari. He never married, and died in 1963 at the age of 95.

MASLOFF

Masloff did not attend Mata Hari's trial. After the abdication of Tsar Nicholas II on 15 March 1917 (2 March in the Julian calendar), there was a great deal of confusion in the Russian Army. In April, Masloff had been wounded whilst fighting in the Aisme valley, part of the attack on the Chemin des Dames. It was one of the last engagements in which his regiment, the 1st Regiment of the 1st Brigade, participated. By July 1917, Masloff's regiment had rioted. The ordinary soldiers refused to follow their officers' orders and demanded to return home to Russia. There were armed demonstrations in Petrograd, encouraged by the Bolsheviks, demanding 'all power to the Soviets'. On 14 September, Russia was declared a republic. On 7 November (25 October in the Julian calendar), the October Revolution began and Masloff disappeared into its chaos. He reappeared briefly at the beginning of 1919, when he married a French Russian woman, Olga Tardieu, in Paris. He and his wife then returned to Russia and disappeared from the records.

NON

Mata Hari's daughter trained as a kindergarten teacher. In 1919, she decided to travel to work in the Dutch East Indies. After passing the general medical required to obtain a permit for such work, Non booked passage for 10 August 1919, but she died in her sleep on the night of 9 August from a cerebral haemorrhage, a common effect of congenital syphilis. She was buried in the graveyard at Worth-Rheden. Her gravestone was simply marked 'Our Non', with her birth and death dates. This was done by MacLeod, presumably, to detract from any unwanted attention her grave might otherwise receive.

THOMSON

In 1919, Thomson was appointed Knight Commander of the Order of the Bath (KCB). At the same time, while remaining as Assistant Chief Commissioner for the Metropolitan Police (Crime), he was appointed Director of Intelligence at the Home Office. This role saw him in overall charge of all of the intelligence agencies in Great Britain. However, in 1921, he was involved in some sort of disagreement with Lloyd George, the Prime Minister, and was asked to resign. The reasons for the disagreement remain unknown. In 1922, Thomson wrote a memoir of his time in the police, *Queer People*, in which he referred to Mata Hari's case. In December 1925, Thomson was arrested in London's Hyde Park, and charged with 'committing an act in violation of public decency' with a young woman. Thomson denied the charges, claiming that he was undertaking research for a book on vice in the city of London, and had approached the lady, Miss Thelma de Lava, to interview her. Thomson tried to half bluff and half bribe his way out of the arrest, but to no avail. He was found guilty of public indecency and fined £5, the average weekly wage of a police constable in 1925.

WALLINGER

Wallinger continued with the Indian intelligence missions across Europe. He personally recruited and trained several agents, most notably Somerset Maugham, the playwright and novelist. He died in 1931.

NOTES

CHAPTER 2

1 Dossier Zelle, Centraal Bureau voor Genealogie

CHAPTER 3

1 Bossenbroek, *Volk voor Indië. De werving van Europese militairen voor de Nederlandse koloniale dienst*, 1814–1909, Amsterdam, pp.357–8
2 *Nieuws van de Dag*, 1895
3 Heymans, *La Vraie*, p.15
4 Waagenaar, *Mata Hari*, p.18

CHAPTER 4

1 Zelle, *De Roman van Mata Hari*, p.62
2 Heymans, *La Vraie Mata Hari*, p.18
3 Priem, *De naakte Waarheid*, p.56
4 Zelle, *De Roman van Mata Hari*, p.81
5 Waagenaar, *Mata Hari as a Human Being*, pp.9–10
6 Waagenaar, *Mata Hari as a Human Being*, p.10
7 Heymans, *La Vraie Mata Hari*, pp.38–9

CHAPTER 5

1 Heymans, *La Vraie Mata Hari*, p.42

2 Heymans, *La Vraie Mata Hari*, p.48

3 Heymans, *La Vraie Mata Hari*, p.51

4 Kolonial Verslag, app. A. 1899 Principal Illnesses

5 Zelle, *De Roman van Mata Hari*, pp.122–6

6 Zelle, *De Roman van Mata Hari*, pp.122–6

7 Death certificate, Jeanne Louise MacLeod, 1919

8 Zelle, *De Roman van Mata Hari*, p.62

9 Stamboeken Officieren, item 405, p.110

10 Zelle, *De Roman van Mata Hari*, pp.110–12

11 Zelle, *De Roman van Mata Hari*, pp.110–12

12 Heymans, *La Vraie Mata Hari*, pp.53–5

13 Waagenaar, *Mata Hari*, p.29

14 Waagenaar, *Mata Hari*, pp.12–13

15 Waagenaar, *Mata Hari*, p.32

16 Waagenaar, *Mata Hari as a Human Being*, p.16

17 Zelle, *De Roman van Mata Hari*, pp.110–12

18 Zelle, *De Roman van Mata Hari*, pp.12–126

19 Zelle, *De Roman van Mata Hari*, p.115

20 Zelle, *De Roman van Mata Hari*, pp.116–17

21 Zelle, *De Roman van Mata Hari*, pp.116–17

22 Heymans, *La Vraie Mata Hari*, p.61

23 Zelle, *De Roman van Mata Hari*, pp.116–17

24 Zelle, *De Roman van Mata Hari*, pp.151–4

25 Zelle, *De Roman van Mata Hari*, p.155

26 *Nieuws van de Dag*, 27 August 1902

27 Ritman, *Ik kende Mata Hari*, p.7

28 Zelle, *De Roman van Mata Hari*, pp.168–9

29 Zelle, *De Roman van Mata Hari*, pp.172–5

CHAPTER 6

1 Zelle, *De Roman van Mata Hari*, p.188; Heymans, *La Vraie Mata Hari*, p.80

2 *The King*, 4 February 1905

3 *La Vie Parisienne*, 14 March 1905

4 *Le Gaulois*, 17 March 1905

5 *Éclair*, 15 March 1905

6 *La Presse*, 16 March 1905

7 *La Presse*, August 1905

8 *Le Journal*, August 1905

9 Boxer, *Women in Industrial Homework*, pp.401–23

10 Zelle, *De Roman van Mata Hari*, pp.196–88
11 Zelle, *De Roman van Mata Hari*, pp.196–88
12 Shirman, *Mata Hari*, p. 21
13 Waagenaar, *Mata Hari*, p.67
14 *Nieuws van de Dag*, 17 April 1905
15 *Nieuw Rotterdamsche Dagblad*, 31 May 1905
16 Records van de Amsterdamse rechtbank, 1906
17 Records van de Amsterdamse rechtbank, 1906
18 *The Era*, 3 October 1908
19 *The Era*, 3 October 1908
20 *Neues Wiener Journal*, 1908

CHAPTER 7

1   Priem, *De naakte Waarheid*, pp.22–4
2   Priem, *De naakte Waarheid*, p.44
3   Priem, *De naakte Waarheid*, p.32
4   Priem, *De naakte Waarheid*, p.56
5   Priem, *De naakte Waarheid*, pp.44–5
6   SHAT, pièce 363, 15 February 1917
7   *Le Temps*, 21 March 1907
8   *Le Temps*, 21 March 1907
9   Waagenaar, *Mata Hari*, pp.85–8
10 Waagenaar, *Mata Hari*, p.89
11 SHAT, pièce 363, 15 February 1917
12 Waagenaar, *Mata Hari*, p.94
13 Waagenaar, *Mata Hari*, p.97
14 Waagenaar, *Mata Hari*, pp.98–9
15 Heymans, *La Vraie*, p.257
16 Waagennar, *Mata Hari*, pp.91–2
17 The Mata Hari Museum/Fries Museum
18 SHAT, pièce 149–51, 9 May 1917
19 *Tatler* magazine, No 639, pp.376–7
20 *The Era*, 3 October 1908
21 Bizard, *Souvenirs d'un médecin de Saint-Lazare*, p.45
22 SHAT, pièce 363, 15 February 1917
23 SHAT, pièce 363, 15 February 1917
24 SHAT, pièce 363, 15 February 1917

CHAPTER 8

1 SHAT, pièce 363, 15 February 1917
2 SHAT, pièce 363, 15 February 1917
3 *Mata Hari scrapbook*, Mata Hari Foundation

CHAPTER 9

1 Kroemer's name was variously spelt Craemer, Cremer, Kremer and Kramer
2 SHAT, pièce 404, 21 May 1917
3 Gempp report, vol. 8, Fribourg, 50
4 SHAT, pièce 404, 21 May 1917
5 KV 2/1, 85, 4 December 1915
6 MEPO 3/2444, 22, 9 December 1915
7 KV 2/1, 85, 4 December 1915
8 MEPO 3/2444, 22, 9 December 1915
9 http://www.legislation.gov.uk/ukpga/Geo5/4-5/17/enacted
10 KV 2/1, 81, 3 February 1916
11 KV 2/1, 81, 3 February 1916
12 KV 2/1, 78, 16 February 1916
13 MEPO 3/2444, 5, 22 February 1916
14 Telegram, John Louden to *Nederlandse Gezantshap*, 27 April 1916
15 Telegram, Reneke de Marees van Swinderen, to *Nederlandse Gezantshap*, 4 May 1916
16 SHAT, pièce 366, 4 November 1916
17 Correspondence, *Ambassade de la République Français*, to Van Royen, 17 June 1916
18 SHAT, pièce 9, 21 June 1917
19 SHAT, pièce 27, 21 July 1916 & 31, 25 July 1916
20 SHAT, pièce 149/151, 9 May 1917
21 SHAT, pièce 149, 9 May 1917
22 SHAT, pièce 149, 9 May 1917
23 SHAT, pièce 149, 9 May 1917
24 SHAT, pièce 35, 19 July 1916

CHAPTER 10

1 Ladoux, G., *Les Chasseurs d'espions*, pp.188–9, Correspondence to Alexandre Millerand and Louis Malvy
2 KV 2/1, 85, 4 December 1915
3 MEPO 3/2444, 5, 22 February 1916

NOTES

4   Falkenhayn, E., *Die Oberste Heeresleitung 1914–1916*, pp.219–18

5   Morel, B.A., *Traité des dégénérescences physiques, intellectuelles et morales de l'espèce humaine et des causes qui produisent ces variétés maladives: atlas de xii planches*

6   Ladoux, G., *Les Chasseurs d'espions*, p.231

7   SHAT, pièce 366, 21 February 1917

8   SHAT, pièce 366, 21 February 1917

9   SHAT, pièce 366, 21 February 1917

10 Ladoux, G., *Les Chasseurs d'espions*, pp.231–32

11 Ladoux, G., *Les Chasseurs d'espions*, pp.233–35

12 Ladoux, G., *Les Chasseurs d'espions*, pp.233–35

13 KV 2/1, 81, 2 February 1916

14 KV 2/1, 81, 2 February 1916

15 Mss Eur C500, 8 August 1917

16 Plowman, M. *Irish Republicans and the Indo-German Conspiracy of World War I*, pp.81–105

17 Correspondence, Wallinger, 22 September 1911

18 Report Home Department B, June 1910, 26 February 1910 and report Home Department B, August 1910, 3 May 1910

19 Correspondence, Cleveland, 21 August 1915

20 Correspondence, Cleveland, 20 January 1915

21 SHAT, pièce 41, 3 August 1916

22 SHAT, pièce 41, 3 August 1916

23 SHAT, pièce 43, 4 August 1916

24 SHAT, pièce 57, 18 August 1916

25 SHAT, pièce 58, 19 August 1916

26 SHAT, pièce 367, 23 February 1917

27 SHAT, pièce 63, 24 August 1916

28 SHAT, pièce 68, 29 August 1916

29 SHAT, pièce 71, 2 September 1916

30 Ladoux, G., *Les Chasseurs d'espions*, pp.233–35

31 SHAT, pièce 367, 23 February 1917

32 SHAT, pièce 367, 23 February 1917

33 SHAT, pièce 69, 30 August 1916

34 SHAT, pièce 77, 8 September 1916

35 SHAT, pièce 173, 29 May 1917

36 SHAT, pièce 174, 30 May 1917

37 SHAT, pièce 367, 23 February 1917

38 Ladoux, G., *Les Chasseurs d'espions*, pp.237–40

39 Ladoux, G., *Les Chasseurs d'espions*, pp.237–40

40 Ladoux, G., *Les Chasseurs d'espions*, pp.237–40
41 Ladoux, G., *Les Chasseurs d'espions*, pp.241–4
42 SHAT, pièce 367, 23 February 1917
43 SHAT, pièce 368, 24 February 1917
44 SHAT, pièce 367, 23 February 1917
45 SHAT, pièce 367, 23 February 1917
46 SHAT, pièce 367, 23 February 1917
47 Correspondence, Mata Hari to Dutch Consul, 13 October 1916
48 SHAT, pièce 84, 14 October 1916
49 SHAT, pièce 88, 18 October 1916
50 SHAT, pièce 87, 17 October 1918; pièce 89, 19 October 1916
51 SHAT, pièce 96, 26 October 1916
52 SHAT, pièce 98, 28 October 1916
53 SHAT, pièce 105, 4 November 1916
54 SHAT, pièce 106, 5 November 1916

CHAPTER 11

1 SHAT, pièce 251, 31 May 1917
2 SHAT, pièce 368, 24 February 1917
3 KV 2/1, 85, 4 December 1915
4 KV 2/1, 69, 14 November 1916
5 KV 2/1, 69, 14 November 1916
6 MEPO 3/2444, 22, 14 November 1916
7 Correspondence, Mata Hari, to Reneke de Marees van Swinderen, 14 November 1916
8 Waagenaar, *Mata Hari*, p.157
9 SHAT, pièce 368, 24 February 1917
10 MEPO 3/2444, 39–41, 16 November 1916
11 MEPO 3/2444, 42–43, 16 November 1916
12 MEPO 3/2444, 42–43, 16 November 1916
13 MEPO 3/2444, 43–44, 16 November 1916
14 MEPO 3/2444, 44, 16 November 1916
15 MEPO 3/2444, 9, 15 November 1916
16 MEPO 3/2444, 10, 15 November 1916; 11, 15 November 1916
17 MEPO 3/2444, 11, 15 November 1916
18 Correspondence, Thomson, to Reneke de Marees van Swinderen, 16a, 16 November 1916
19 Correspondence, Thomson, to Reneke de Marees van Swinderen, 16b, 16 November 1916
20 KV 2/1, 43, 18 November 1916

21 KV 2/1, 46, 17 November 1916
22 MEPO 3/2444, 7, 18 November 1916
23 MEPO 3/2444, 28, 23 November 1916
24 Correspondence, van Swinderen, to Van Royen, 1 December 1916
25 SHAT, pièce 368, 24 February 1917
26 Waagenaar, *Mata Hari*, pp.201–2
27 Ladoux, Les Chasseurs d'espions, p.246
28 SHAT, pièce 369, 28 February 1917
29 SHAT, pièce 369, 28 February 1917
30 SHAT, pièce 369, 28 February 1917
31 SHAT, pièce 369, 28 February 1917
32 SHAT, pièce 369, 28 February 1917
33 SHAT, pièce 369, 28 February 1917
34 SHAT, pièce 369, 28 February 1917
35 SHAT, pièce 369, 28 February 1917
36 SHAT, pièce 369, 28 February 1917
37 SHAT, pièce 369, 28 February 1917
38 SHAT, pièce 404, 21 May 1917
39 SHAT, pièce 237, 13 December 1916
40 SHAT, pièce 240, 20 December 1916
41 SHAT, pièce 242, 25 December 1916
42 SHAT, pièce 243, 26 December 1916
43 SHAT, pièce 246, 28 December 1916
44 SHAT, pièce 370, 1 March 1917
45 SHAT, pièce 107, 3 January 1917
46 SHAT, pièce 370, 1 March 1917
47 SHAT, pièce 370, 1 March 1917
48 SHAT, pièce 370, 1 March 1917
49 SHAT, pièce 370, 1 March 1917
50 Locard, *Mata Hari*, pp.142–4
51 SHAT, pièce 108, 4 January 1917
52 SHAT, pièce 111, 7 January 1917
53 SHAT, pièce 110, 6 January 1917; pièce 111, 7 January 1917; pièce 112,
    8 January 1917
54 SHAT, pièce 116, 12 January 1917
55 SHAT, pièce 117, 13 January 1917
56 SHAT, pièce 118, 14 January 1917
57 SHAT, pièce 370, 1 March 1917
58 SHAT, pièce 370, 1 March 1917
59 SHAT, pièce 231, 25–31 January 1917
60 Shirman, *Mata Hari*, pp.135–6

61 SHAT, pièce 329, 9 April 1917
62 SHAT, pièce 148, 7 May 1917
63 SHAT, pièce 306, 24 May 1917
64 SHAT, pièce 1, 10 February 1917
65 SHAT, pièce 176, 12 February 1917

CHAPTER TWELVE

1 SHAT, pièce 177, 13 February 1917
2 Collas, *Mata Hari*, p.284
3 SHAT, pièce 362, 13 February 1917
4 Bouchardon, *Souvenirs*, pp.305–6
5 Article 9, *Déclaration des droits de l'homme et du citoyen*, 1789
6 SHAT, pièce 422, 24 June 1917
7 Bentley & Bernard, 'The French Army Mutinies of 1917', pp.26–9
8 Bizard, *Souvenirs*, p.45
9 SHAT, pièce 422, 24 June 1917
10 SHAT, pièce 363, 15 February 1917
11 SHAT, pièce 363, 15 February 1917
12 SHAT, pièce 125, 15 February 1917
13 SHAT, pièce 366, 21 February 1917
14 SHAT, pièce SDR 14, 5 May 1917
15 SHAT, pièce 366, 21 February 1917
16 SHAT, pièce 422, 24 June 1917
17 SHAT, pièce R 8, no date
18 SHAT, pièce R 7, 1 March 1917
19 SHAT, pièce 127, 10 April 1919
20 SHAT, pièce 128, 10 April 1917
21 SHAT, pièce 368, 24 February 1917
22 KV 2/1, 43, 18 November 1916
23 SHAT, pièce 135, 26 February 1917
24 SHAT, pièce 182, 23 February 1917
25 SHAT, pièce 182, 23 February 1917
26 SHAT, pièce 130, 10 March 1917
27 SHAT, pièce 373, 12 March 1917
28 SHAT, pièce 275, 16 March 1917
29 SHAT, R 4, no date
30 SHAT, pièce 276, 16 March 1917
31 SHAT, pièce 131, 26 March 1917
32 SHAT, pièce 233, 2 April 1917
33 SHAT, pièce 233, 2 April 1917

34 SHAT, pièce 233, 2 April 1917
35 SHAT, pièce SDR 12, 4 April 1917; pièce SDR 9, 11 April 1917
36 SHAT, pièce 284, 6 April 1917
37 Telegrams, Louden and Bunge, 23 April 1917
38 SHAT, pièce 399, 12 April 1917
39 SHAT, pièce 399, 12 April 1917
40 SHAT, pièce R 6, no date
41 SHAT, pièce 278, 13 April 1917
42 SHAT, pièce 289, 23 April 1917
43 SHAT, pièce 249, no date

CHAPTER THIRTEEN

1 SHAT, pièce, 235, 31 December 1916
2 SHAT, pièce 237, 13 December 1916
3 SHAT, pièce 240, 20 December 1916
4 SHAT, pièce 242, 25 December 1916
5 Trumpener, 'War premeditated?', p.66
6 SHAT, pièce 243, 26 December 1916
7 SHAT, pièce 244, 28 December 1916
8 SHAT, pièce 236, 31 December 1916; pièce 235, appendix 1, 31
   December 1916
9 SHAT, pièce 231, 25–31 January 1917
10 SHAT, pièce 403, 1 May 1917
11 SHAT, pièce 251, 31 May 1917
12 SHAT, pièce 404, 21 May 1917
13 SHAT, pièce 169, 24 May 1917
14 SHAT, pièce 169, 24 May 1917
15 SHAT, pièce SDR 13, 4 May 1917
16 SHAT, pièce SDR 13, 4 May 1917
17 SHAT, pièce SDR 14, 5 May 1917
18 SHAT, pièce SDR 14, 5 May 1917
19 SHAT, pièce 297, no date
20 SHAT, pièce 299, 10 May 1917
21 SHAT, pièce 302, 15 May 1917
22 SHAT, pièce 302, 15 May 1917
23 SHAT, pièce 304, 15 May 1917
24 SHAT, pièce 133, 24 May 1917
25 SHAT, pièce 130, 10 March 1917
26 SHAT, pièce 404, 21 May 1917
27 SHAT, pièce 404, 21 May 1917

28 SHAT, pièce 404, 21 May 1917
29 SHAT, pièce 404, 21 May 1917
30 SHAT, pièce 149, 9 May 1917
31 SHAT, pièce 159, 9 May 1917
32 SHAT, pièce 404, 21 May 1917
33 SHAT, pièce 146, 4 May 1917
34 SHAT, pièce 146, 4 May 1917
35 SHAT, pièce 405, 22 May 1917
36 SHAT, pièce 405, 22 May 1917
37 SHAT, pièce 405, 22 May 1917
38 SHAT, pièce 405, 22 May 1917
39 SHAT, pièce 405, 22 May 1917
40 SHAT, pièce 405, 22 May 1917
41 SHAT, pièce 405, 22 May 1917
42 SHAT, pièce 405, 22 May 1917
43 SHAT, pièce 405, 22 May 1917
44 SHAT, pièce 405, 22 May 1917
45 SHAT, pièce 406, 23 May 1917
46 SHAT, pièce 306, 24 May 1917; pièce 307, 24 May 1917
47 SHAT, pièce 407, 30 May 1917
48 SHAT, pièce 267, 31 May 1917
49 SHAT, pièce 269, 31 May 1917
50 SHAT, pièce 312, 5 June 1917
51 SHAT, pièce 130, 10 March 1917
52 SHAT, pièce 133, no date
53 SHAT, pièce 130, 10 March 1917
54 Bouchardon, *Souvenirs*, p.311
55 SHAT, pièce 414, 21 June 1917

CHAPTER FOURTEEN

1 SHAT, pièce 422, 24 June 1917
2 SHAT, pièce 422, 24 June 1917
3 SHAT, pièce R 9, no date
4 Telegram, Ministry of Foreign Affairs, to Edouard Clunet,
   30 June 1917
5 SHAT, pièce 169, 24 May 1917
6 SHAT, pièce not numbered, *No. 2793 d'Ordre de Judgement (article 151
   du code du Justice militaire), Judgement Exécutiore de Condamnation*, 24 July
   1917
7 SHAT, *Décision du Conseil Permanent de Révision du Paris*,
   17 August 1917

NOTES

8 SHAT, pièce R 31, 10 September 1917
9 SHAT, pièce SDR 39, 11 October 1917
10 SHAT, pièce SDR 40, 15 October 1917
11 Correspondence, Mata Hari to Ridder van Steurs, 22 September 1917
12 SHAT, pièce R 45, 14 October 1917
13 SHAT, pièce R 45, 14 October 1917
14 SHAT, pièce SDR 45, 14 October 1917
15 *Le Petit Parisien*, 16 October 1917
16 SHAT, pièce SDR 45, 14 October 1917
17 *International News Service*, 19 October 1917
18 SHAT, pièce 5N 403, 15 October 1917
19 *Daily Mail*, 16 October 1917
20 *L'Excelsior*, 16 October 1917
21 *Daily Express*, 16 October 1917
22 SHAT, folder 5N 510, 16–21 October 1917
23 *The Times*, 1–31 October 1917

CHAPTER FIFTEEN

1 *Kölnische Zeitung*, 31 January 1929
2 Henning and Grote, *Geschichte des Weltkriegs und Nachkriegssionage*, p.73

BIBLIOGRAPHY

Bentley, Gilbert B., & Bernard, Paul, P., 'The French Army Mutinies of 1917', *Historian* (1959) Vol. 22, No.1, pp.24–41.

Bizard, Léon, *Souvenirs d'un médecin de Saint-Lazare* (Paris: Albin Michel, 1923).

Bossenbroek, Martin, *Volk voor Indië. De werving van Europese militairen voor de Nederlandse koloniale dienst, 1814–1909* (Amsterdam), pp.357–8.

Bouchardon, Pierre, *Journal Excelsior*, 2 August 1919.

Bouchardon, Pierre, *Souvenirs* (Paris: Albin Michel, 1954).

Boxer, Marilyn J., 'Women in Industrial Homework: The Flowermakers of Paris in the Belle Époque', *French Historical Studies*, Vol. 12, No.3 (Spring, 1982), pp.401–23.

Collas, Philippe, *Mata Hari, sa véritable Histoire* (Paris: Plon, 2008).

Coulson, Thomas, *Mata Hari, Courtesan and Spy* (London: Harpers, 1920).

Editorial, *Daily Express*, 'Lovely Spy Shot', 16 October 1917.

Editorial, *Deli Courant*, 28 June 1899.

Editorial, *Le Parisian*, March 1905.

Editorial, *La Vie Parisienne*, 14 March 1905.

Falkenhayn, E., *Die Oberste Heeresleitung 1914–1916 in ihren wichtigsten Entschliessungen* (Berlin: Mittler & Sohn, 1919).

Feature article, 'Cocquelin and charity', *The Era*, 3 October 1908.

Feature article, *Kölnische Zeitung*, 31 January 1929.

Feature article, *Le Galouis*, 17 March 1905.

Feature article, 'A Story', *Le Petit Parisien*, 16 October 1917.

Feature article, *Tatler Magazine*, No.639, pp.376–7, 24 September 1913.

Feature article, 'Commerce and Intelligence with the Enemy', *The Times*, 1–31 October 1917.

Ferrare, Henri, *La Press*, 16 March 1905.

Henning, Hans, & Grote, Baron, *Geschichte des Weltkriegs und*

BIBLIOGRAPHY

Nachkriegssionage (Berlin, 1930).

Heymans, Charles S., *La Vraie Mata Hari: Courtisane et Espionne* (Paris: Étoile, 1935).

Howe, Russell Warren, *Mata Hari, the True Story* (London: Dodd Mead, 1986).

Huisman, Marijke, *Mata Hari (1876–1917): de levende legende* (Hilversum: Verloren, 1998).

Keay, Julia, *The Spy Who Never Was: Life and Loves of Mata Hari* (London: Michael Joseph Ltd, 1987).

Keyzer, Francis, 'The Parisians of Paris', *The King*, 4 February 1905.

Kupferman, F., *1917 Mata Hari* (Bruxelles: Editions Complexe, 1982).

Ladoux, G., *Les Chasseurs d'espions: Comment j'ai fait arrêter Mata Hari* (Paris: Librairie des Champs-Elysées, 1932).

Lepage, Edward, *Éclair*, 15 March 1905.

Locard, E., *Mata Hari* (Paris: Flammé D'Or, 1954).

Morel, Benedict Augustus, *Traité des dégénérescences physiques, intellectuelles et morales de l'espèce humaine et des causes qui produisent ces variétés maladives: atlas de xii planches* (Paris, 1857).

Newman, Bernard, *Inquest on Mata Hari* (London: Robert Hale, 1956).

Neues Wiener Journal, 1908.

Nieuw Rotterdamsche Dagblad, 31 May 1905.

Nieuws van de Dag, 1895.

Nieuws van de Dag, 28 August 1902.

Nieuws van de Dag, 17 April 1905.

Paux, René, 'De Paris à Khartum', *Le Temps*, 21 March 1907.

Plowman, Matthew, 'Irish Republicans and the Indo-German Conspiracy of World War I', *New Hibernia Review* 7.3 (2003), pp.81–105.

Popplewell, R.J., *Intelligence and Imperial Defence* (London: Frank Cass Ltd, 1995).

Ross, Tomas, *De tranen van Mata Hari* (Amsterdam: De Bezige Bij, 2007).

Shipman, Pat, *Femme Fatale: Love, Lies, and the Unknown Life of Mata Hari* (London: Weidenfeld & Nicolson/New York: William Morrow, 2007).

Shirman, Léon, *Mata Hari: Autopsie d'une machination* (Paris: Éditiones Italiques, 2001).

Skinner, Richard, *The Red Dancer: The Life and Times of Mata Hari* (London: Harper Collins, 2003).

Trumpener, Ulrich, 'War premeditated? German intelligence operations 1914', *Central European History* Vol. 9, 1976, pp.67–70.

Waagenaar, Sam, *Mata Hari* (New York: Appleton-Century, 1965).

Wales, Harry, *International News Service*, 19 October 1917.

West, Nigel, *Historical Dictionary of World War I Intelligence* (Plymouth:

Rowman and Littlefield, 2013).

Wheelwright, Julie, *The Fatal Lover: Mata Hari and the Myth of Women in Espionage* (London: Collins and Brown, 1992).

Zelle, Ardum, *De Roman van Mata Hari, Mevrouw M.G. MacLeod Zelle: De Levensgeschiedenis Mijner Dochter en Mijne Grieven tegen Haar Vroegeren Echtgenoot* (Amsterdam: C.L.G. Veldt, 1906).

References

PAPERS FROM THE ALGEMEEN RIJKSARCHIEF, THE HAGUE, NETHERLANDS

Correspondence, Mata Hari to Reneke de Marees van Swinderen, 13 November 1916 (the letter was incorrectly dated, the actual date was 14 November 1916)

Correspondence, Basil Thomson to Reneke de Marees van Swinderen, a, 16 November 1916

Correspondence, Basil Thomson to Reneke de Marees van Swinderen, b, 16 November 1916

Correspondence, Reneke de Marees van Swinderen to Van Royen, Dutch legation Madrid, 1 December 1916

Telegram, John Loudon to *Nederlandse Gezantshap in Groot-Brittanie*, 1813– 1932, no.849, 27 April 1916

Telegram, Reneke de Marees van Swinderen to *Nederlandse Gezantshap in Groot-Brittanie*, 1813–1932, no.849, 4 May 1916

Correspondence, *Ambassade de la République Français* to Van Royen, Dutch legation, Madrid, 17 June 1916

Telegrams, John Louden to Dutch Legation, Paris, and Dutch Legation to Louden, *Ministrie von Buitenlandse Zaken*, Archives of the Embassy at Paris, 1866–1940, no.1306, 23 April 1917

Telegram, Ministry of Foreign Affairs to Edouard Clunet, *Ministerie von Buitenlandse Zaken*, Archives of the Embassy at Paris, 1866– 1940, no.1306, 30 June 1917

Correspondence, Mata Hari to Ridder van Steurs, *Ministerie von Buitenlandse Zaken*, Archives of the Embassy at Paris, 1866–1940, no.1306, 22 September 1917

Verbaal, Kolonial Verslag, app. A. (1899), Principal Illnesses, 1899

PAPERS FROM THE ARCHIVES DE PARIS, PARIS, FRANCE

Gempp report, *Archives Militaires Allemande*, Vol. 8, Fribourg, 50

PAPERS FROM THE BRITISH LIBRARY, LONDON, UNITED KINGDOM

Mss Eur C500

PAPERS FROM THE CENTRAAL BUREAU VOOR GENEALOGIE, THE HAGUE, NETHERLANDS

Dossier Zelle

PAPERS FROM THE FRIES MUSEUM, LEEUWARDEN, NETHERLANDS

Waagenaar, Sam., *Mata Hari as a Human Being* mss., 1927
Mata Hari scrapbooks, Mata Hari Foundation

PAPERS FROM THE HOUGHTON LIBRARY, HARVARD UNIVERSITY, USA

Correspondence, Mata Hari to Dutch Consul, bMS 1553M, 13 October 1916

PAPERS FROM THE NATIONAAL ARCHIEF, THE HAGUE, NETHERLANDS

Stamboeken Officieren (Register of officers) 1814–1929, Inv. Nr. 624, item 405, p.110
Stamboeken Officieren 1814–1929, Inv. Nr. 624, item 624, p.198
Records van de Amsterdamse rechtbank, April 1906

PAPERS FROM THE NATIONAL ARCHIVES, KEW, UNITED KINGDOM

KV 2/1
KV 2/2
MEPO 3/2444
Report, Home Department B: June, 1910, nos.1–8, 26 February 1910

REFERENCES

Report, Home Department B: Aug, 1910, nos.1–9, 3 May 1910

Correspondence, Wallinger, *Extension of the Deputation of Mr Wallinger in England*, Home Department A. Nov 1911, no.87, 22 September 1911

Correspondence, Cleveland, *Extension of the Deputation of Mr Wallinger in Europe for One Year from 1 April 1915*, Home Department A: Mar 1915, nos.14–16, 20 January 1915

Correspondence, Cleveland, *Spread of the Ghadr Movement in the Far East*, Home Department B: Oct 1915, nos.369074, 21 August 1915

India Office and Records Department, IOLR IOR.POS.9840

India Office and Records Department, IOLR IOR.POS.8965

India Office and Records Department, IOLR IOR.POS.6048

India Office and Records Department, IOLR IOR.POS.7151

PAPERS FROM THE SERVICE HISTORIQUE DE L'ARMÉE DE TERRE (SHAT), FRANCE

Dossier Mata Hari

INDEX

INDEX

INDEX